SHADOWS ON THE SAND

Shadows on the Sand

The Memoirs of Sir Gawain Bell

Sweet to ride forth at evening from the wells
When shadows pass gigantic on the sand. . . .
James Elroy Flecker, 'Hassan'

C. HURST & COMPANY, LONDON

ST. MARTIN'S PRESS, NEW YORK

Published in the United Kingdom by
C. Hurst & Co. (Publishers) Ltd.,
38 King Street, London WC2E 8JT,
and in the United States of America by
St Martin's Press, Inc.,
175 Fifth Avenue, New York, NY 10010

ISBNs
Hurst: 0-905838-92-0
St Martins: 0-312-71418-1

Library of Congress Cataloging in Publication Data

Bell, Gawain, Sir.
Shadows on the sand.

Includes index.
1. Bell, Gawain, Sir. 2. Colonial administrators--Great Britain--Biography. 3. Colonial administrators--Near East--Biography. 4. Near East--Biography. 5. British--Near East--Biography. I. Title.
DS61.52.B44A37 1984 956'.04'0924 83-40286
ISBN 0-312-71418-1

Printed in Great Britain

For Martin Parr

PREFACE

Between 1931, when at the age of twenty-two I first went to serve in the Sudan, and the end of 1944, when I had a short spell of war-time home leave and got married, I wrote over a thousand letters to my parents. These they preserved. From the spring of 1945 until the present I have kept a diary. I have in my possession a great number of pertinent photographs. These and other records, reinforced by a memory — at least for the years up to the age of fifty — which is still tolerably reliable, have provided me with a fund of material from which I have been able to draw and thus reconstruct something of the past.

It has been my lot to experience a colourful and immensely interesting Service life. I have also been extraordinarily fortunate, because the opportunities offered two generations ago to young men with a taste for the sort of career I followed were many and varied. These opportunities no longer exist and I suppose they never will again. As time passes the events we witnessed and the affairs we helped to shape will seem increasingly remote and strange to those who come after us.

Unimportant as my own story is in isolation, it did form a fragment of that vast pattern of events, namely the afternoon and twilight of the British imperial age. It chanced that in most of the countries in which I served, the period of my service coincided with the end of an epoch.

In the perspective of sixty years how far can I be expected to see all these happenings in their correct proportion and in their true colours? I know well that memory, even when helped by contemporary documents, is an unreliable instrument and that it selects and rejects — almost, it would seem, at random. All I can say is that the pictures I have drawn are as accurate as I have been able to make them. I have tried not to be too egotistical, and to be as objective as is possible when writing principally about oneself.

For fifteen years I was an administrative officer in remote and lonely districts in the Sudan and Palestine. For two and a half years of the war I served in the Arab Legion under Glubb Pasha. Between 1949 and 1951, as Deputy to the Sudan Government Agent in Egypt, I saw the end of the *Wafd* and of the monarchy. I was closely involved in the negotiations and events which led to self-government in the Sudan, and after self-government, I was the last British Permanent Secretary to the Ministry of the Interior. I was one of the last members of the Sudan Political Service to leave the country under the terms of the Anglo-Egyptian Agreement of 1952. I was Political Agent in Kuwait at the time of Suez, and shortly afterwards Kuwait became formally independent. My departure from Kuwait is the point at which the present book ends. I was the last British Governor of Northern Nigeria. I helped to draft, during the winter of 1965/6, a constitution for what was then called the Federation of South Arabia, a constitution that was intended, but failed, to give that unhappy corner of Arabia Felix a stable framework in which to develop when British control ended. From 1967 to 1970 I was the last European Secretary-General of the South Pacific Commission. Since then I have been called upon three or four times to advise on situations which have arisen in various parts of the Arabian Peninsula.

On the face of it I might well exemplify almost everything that in the eyes of many Arab and African politicians was misguided and obtuse, if not downright wicked and oppressive. I shall try and show that those of us who were engaged in the tasks of colonial administration and all that it implied were neither as foolish nor as Machiavellian as we are still sometimes represented as having been; I shall endeavour to tell something of what we were trying to do and of how we did it; and of the joys and sorrows, triumphs and disappointments that accompanied our work. We naturally made mistakes, but I doubt whether others could have done better, and our successors have not always shown that their intentions or methods are much wiser, or for that matter any more humane.

The years immediately after the end of the war saw a sharp and sudden decline in Britain's authority throughout the Middle East. Soon the same thing happened in our African and other possessions. The Indian sub-continent became independent. There was much unhappy and unfortunate misunderstanding between ourselves and the United States on the best ways of solving these problems. Under the pressure of these events we became increasingly sensitive to the criticism of others. Our self-confidence was bruised. Knowing that we could no longer rely on the use of power we became obliged to depend mainly on such prestige as we had inherited from an earlier period. But in spite of these almost unavoidable developments, we handled the difficult task of surrendering our imperial responsibilities with, I believe, a fair measure of skill and wisdom. It is for history to judge how far the misfortunes and tragedies that have often followed the surrender of our responsibilities were basically our fault, the fault of those who succeeded us, or the fault of third parties.

Three principal elements control the lives and careers of those in particular who enter public service: natural ability, energy and sheer luck. Each plays an approximately equal part, but a shortfall in any one can easily nullify a full measure of both the other two. I was fortunate in having a very full share of luck.

I owe gratitude to many, particularly to the Sudanese and to others in the Arab World who gave me their friendship. They have provided the background to most of this narrative. A few were distinguished, but the majority were not. Many are now dead. More specifically, there are some who either helped me directly or put me in the way of help. Of these the first are my family and a few friends who encouraged me to set about writing. I am indebted to Tony Kirk-Greene of St Antony's College, Oxford, who read the text and sent it to Christopher Hurst. To Christopher Hurst I am grateful for much wise advice and the reduction of an over-long text. In reminding myself of the factual background to some parts of the narrative I owe a debt to J.S.R. Duncan's *The Sudan* and *The Sudan's Path to Independence*, to Sir James Robertson's *Transition in Africa* and to G.N. Sanderson's Introduction to Volume 2 of *The Memoirs of Babikr Bedri*. Brigadier Keith Dunn has been kind enough to let me read his papers on the part played by the 5th Cavalry Brigade in Syria in 1941.

I am grateful to my son-in-law, Toby Buchan, for drawing the maps. And finally I wish to thank Mrs Margaret Currall and Mrs Elizabeth Orpwood for typing what was often an appallingly indecipherable handwritten text.

Hidcote Bartrim,
Gloucestershire,
May 1983

G.W.B.

CONTENTS

PLATES

(between pages 162 and 163)

EGYPT & THE ANGLO-EGYPTIAN SUDAN, 1951
Boundaries: international
provincial
Railways
0
miles
400
MEDITERRANEAN
Alexandria
Port Said
Canal
CAIRO
Suez
Aqaba
Sinai
LIBYA
EGYPT
ARABIA
Aswan
Nile
RED SEA
Wadi Halfa
Jidda
Kassala
Northern
SUDAN
Abu Hamed
Port Sudan
Suakin
Sinkat
Merowe
Atbara
Ed Damer
Haiya Junc.
Khartoum
Shendi
Atbara
Keren
Massawa
Omdurman
KHARTOUM
Khashm el Girba
Kassala
Asmara
ERITREA
Darfur
Kordofan
Sodiri
Wad Medani
Geneina
El Fasher
Bara
Rahad
Setit
Jebel Marra
El Obeid
Sennar
Gedaref
En Nahud
Er Rahad
Umm Ruwaba
Kosti
Singa
Gallabat
El Odaiya
Dilling
Delami
Rashad
Blue
L. Tana
Nuba
Heiban
Er Roseires
El Muglad
Kadugli
Mts
Nile
Nile
Bahr el Arab
Talodi
Kaka
Kurmuk
White
Blue Nile
FRENCH
Tonga
Malakal
Bahr el Ghazal
Upper
ADDIS ABABA
EQUATORIAL
Wau
Bahr el Jebel
Nile
ETHIOPIA
AFRICA
Equatorial
Juba
L. Rudolf
BELGIAN CONGO
UGANDA
KENYA

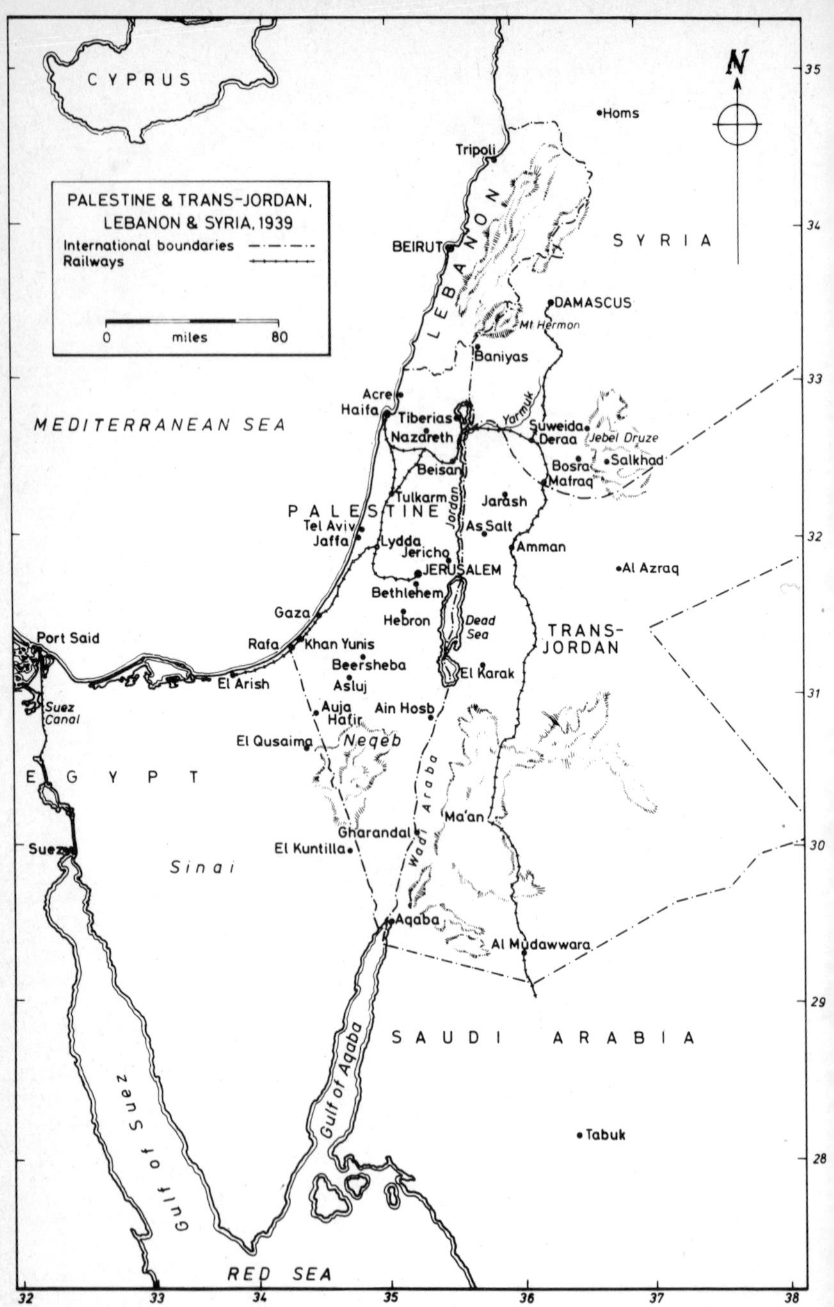
PALESTINE & TRANS-JORDAN, LEBANON & SYRIA, 1939
International boundaries
Railways
0 miles 80
CYPRUS
MEDITERRANEAN SEA
LEBANON
SYRIA
PALESTINE
TRANS-JORDAN
EGYPT
SAUDI ARABIA
Sinai
Neqeb
RED SEA
Gulf of Suez
Gulf of Aqaba
Wadi Araba
Jordan
Yarmuk
Dead Sea
Jebel Druze
Mt Hermon
Suez Canal
Homs
Tripoli
BEIRUT
DAMASCUS
Baniyas
Acre
Haifa
Tiberias
Nazareth
Beisan
Suweida
Deraa
Bosra
Salkhad
Mafraq
Jarash
Tulkarm
Tel Aviv
Jaffa
Lydda
Jericho
As Salt
Amman
JERUSALEM
Al Azraq
Bethlehem
Hebron
Gaza
Port Said
Rafa
Khan Yunis
Beersheba
Asluj
El Arish
El Karak
Auja Hafir
Ain Hosb
El Qusaima
Ma'an
Gharandal
El Kuntilla
Suez
Aqaba
Al Mudawwara
Tabuk
N
32
33
34
35
36
37
38
28
29
30
31

Part I
'SWEET TO RIDE FORTH'

1
EARLY YEARS
(1909–1931)

Family

My ancestors, the Bells, were of hill sheep-farming stock and from the early seventeenth century they owned land at Latterhead in Cumberland. Such people were known locally as 'statesmen'. Latterhead is still farmed by Richard Bell with whom I share an ancestor five generations back, John Bell. Late in the eighteenth century a part of the Bell family moved to the coast, to Whitehaven and Workington, where they pursued various activities connected with shipping. A William Bell was master of two brigs, and his son Tiffin Bell had a sailmaking business. But Tiffin's son, William Henry Bell, my grandfather, became a commercial chemist, and in 1868 married Jane Westray, daughter of Thomas Westray of Whitehaven. Jane's brother, James Brown Westray, became in due course the founder of J.B. Westray & Co., shipbrokers, and subsequently in 1872 of the New Zealand Shipping Company. At no time until the First World War do any of the Bells or the Westrays appear to have entered the civil or armed services or the professions.

My paternal grandparents had six children, three sons and three daughters, and my father, William Westray Bell, was the eldest son. Both parents died while the children were still of school age or younger. The commercial chemist venture appears to have failed and the Westrays had to come to the rescue. When my father left school J.B. Westray took him into the New Zealand Shipping Company, and after serving an apprenticeship as a clerk in Leadenhall Street he was sent to Basrah to gain overseas experience. Basrah in 1898 and 1899 no doubt provided my father with useful experience, and certainly with wonderful snipe and duck shooting, but it also plagued him with malaria and dysentery. After two years in the Gulf he was invalided home, and in 1901 he went to South Africa as the agent of the New Zealand Shipping Company. Meanwhile his younger brother Gawain had won a mathematical scholarship to Cambridge, and James the youngest had gone to the Royal Agricultural College at Cirencester. The three girls, Winifred, Mary and Gertrude were all, thanks to the Westrays, sent to good schools. Mary and Gertrude subsequently taught at the Ladies College, Cheltenham, Mary later becoming a lecturer in physics at the Royal College of Science. Only Winifred, who was musical, married.

My mother came from a family of mixed English and Austrian stock named Kisch, and her father, who had the unusual Christian name of Tiberias, and whose ancestry appeared to be unknown, was a mining engineer in South Africa in the 1870s. He was evidently something of an irresponsible rolling stone for he abandoned his wife and three children in the Cape shortly after my mother's birth in 1880, disappeared into the Transvaal and, as far as his family were concerned, was never heard of again. My parents met in Cape Town and were married there in 1907. I was born two years later. And in South Africa I grew up until, in 1919, my father left the New Zealand Shipping Company and we came to live in England.

I was an only child. This had its advantages and disadvantages, but I tend to think that I gained more from my parents' sole attention and self-sacrifice than I lost by missing the companionship of brothers and sisters. Certainly if there had been other children my parents' resources would never have stretched to my being sent to Winchester and Oxford, and in that case I would never have gone to the Sudan. We lived unpretentiously and economically, as neither of my parents had means beyond my father's salary.

My father was gentle, courteous, patient and self-effacing, and quite unambitious in matters affecting money and position. But he had a quick kindly sense of humour and he was warm-hearted and sentimental. He was a countryman and a very fair shot. Among the many lessons I learnt from him was the importance, particularly from the point of view of consideration towards others, of punctuality. He used to tell me how the Prince Imperial lost his life at the hands of the Zulus in 1879 because of his incurable habit of declaring that there was no need to hurry. He was essentially conservative both in manner and thought. 'I cannot understand', he said to me in 1935, 'this modern sex nonsense.' As a young man he had joined the London Scottish and worn the hodden grey kilt, and during the 1914–18 war he served as a Company Commander with a South African Defence Unit in Cape Town. I cannot remember a time when he did not suffer, and with great patience, from poor health, perhaps a legacy of the dysentery and malaria he contracted in Basrah.

Gawain, the second son, was more ambitious and enterprising and dynamic. Having been Senior Wrangler of his year at Cambridge, boxed as a heavyweight for the University and rowed for his college, Trinity, he went to Winchester as an assistant master in 1908 and in due course became a housemaster. In addition to his academic achievements — he wrote several books on mathematics — he believed passionately in the merits of physical fitness and kept himself in hard training. In the school holidays he went mountain climbing, and trout fishing and swimming, usually with a party of boys, and was an early enthusiast for ski-ing. He joined the Hampshire Regiment in 1914, won the DSO and was fatally wounded near Ypres in July 1917. Having been the first member of the school staff to volunteer for active service, he was also the only Winchester master to be killed. Gawain Murdoch Bell was frequently held up to me, when I was a child, as a man on whom I should endeavour to model myself. Although my direct contact with him was limited to a fortnight spent in his House at Winchester in 1914 and my recollection of him is nebulous, the legendary figure had an effect on me. He possessed many of the attributes of a hero and I have always been a hero-worshipper.

James Foyster Bell, the youngest of the family, was a very different type from his two elder brothers. After Cirencester he went to South Africa, bought a farm near Standerton in the Transvaal and won prizes for his pedigree cattle. He joined the South African Horse as a trooper in 1914 and although he saw a great deal of action in South West Africa, East Africa and France, where he was wounded, he remained a private soldier until he was demobilised. Once in 1916 he was persuaded by his Company Commander to accept promotion to the rank of Corporal, but a few weeks later asked to be relieved of the responsibility. After the war he left South Africa and bought a farm at Shilton near Burford in Oxfordshire where I spent many holidays with him shooting and riding, and learning something of farming. On the Shilton farm I learnt to shoot rabbits and pigeons. My holidays there and with my aunt Mary at her cottage at Kencot nearby made me the countryman I like to think I am.

Despite the very great affection I had for my father my attitude towards him varied according to our respective ages, as is the case between all fathers and sons. A French commentary on this subject under the title of *Ce que les enfants pensent du Père* sums the matter up with charm and accuracy: ‘Six ans: notre Papa sait tout. Dix ans: notre Papa sait beaucoup. Quinze ans: nous savons autant que Papa. Vingt ans: décidément Papa ne sait pas grand chose. Trente ans: nous pouvions tout de même demander l’avis de Papa. Quarante ans: Papa sait quand même quelque chose. Cinquante ans: Père sait tout. Soixante ans: Ah! si nous pouvions encore le demander à Père.’

Whereas my father was on the whole content with his lot, my

mother was ambitious. She was observant, cautious, extremely methodical in thought and practice, shrewd, and very neat and trim. She was an excellent bridge player. In 1963, when she was just over eighty, she had a stroke and was partly paralysed, and although she displayed immense courage and good humour in fighting her way back she did not make a great deal of progress, and at the end of two or three months we all wondered whether she would ever be able to lead a normal life again. Then one morning she heard that she had won £1,000 on a Premium Bond. From that moment she never looked back, and within a few weeks she was out of hospital. She preserved all her faculties and all her intense interest in people and affairs until the day of her death in 1971 aged nearly 91. The end came with merciful suddenness while she was buying a hat in Bond Street.

My father loved the country; my mother adored London. He shot and rode and fished whenever opportunity offered, which was seldom; she had few if any sporting tastes and strongly distrusted horses and cows. Both had great reserves of resistance and courage and I owe them both an immense debt. They guided me with devoted but self-effacing skill. I was rather closer to my father in sympathy for we shared very similar tastes and interests, but it was my mother who tended to exert the stronger influence on my attitudes and judgements.

As I have said I was born in South Africa and at the age of eight I went, as a day-boy, to my first preparatory school near Wynburg in the Cape. This was a fairly tough sort of establishment, run by a terrifying man called Stansbury, a great believer in corporal punishment for small boys. Half the boys were of English stock and the other half were Afrikaners, and while we were taught in English we learnt Afrikaans. We lived a rough and tumble sort of life, and there was a fair amount of bullying. When I went to a preparatory school in England, I felt rather blasé that I had known a place where life was less gentle and kindly; and I was proud of my South African accent which I thought was tough and virile compared with the plummy style of speech affected by English boys.

With my uncle as a Housemaster at Winchester it had always been assumed that I would go to school there. Because he was a bachelor his sister Mary kept house for him, and it was she who, after his death, urged my parents early in 1920 to bring me back to England from South Africa so that the standard of my Latin, which she rightly suspected to be poor, should not disappoint the Winchester examiners. My parents wisely accepted her advice and in that autumn I was sent to the Dragon School at Oxford. I achieved little distinction there in work or games. I was a member of no team, and took part in none of the school plays; I was small and insignificant.

Towards the end of my time two episodes brought me momentarily into the limelight. Every year the whole school took an open examination in mathematics, for which I had a certain gift, and the boy with the highest marks received a special prize. By a lucky chance all but one of the questions happened to suit me. While the invigilator was out of the room for a brief moment I asked my neighbour, a boy called Vinicomb, how this remaining question ought to be tackled and generously he told me. Some days later the results were announced and certainly to my surprise, and no doubt even more to the astonishment of the staff, I had gained full marks. I don't think it ever occurred to me to do other than accept my unexpected good fortune, and Vinicomb naturally said nothing. This was the only academic prize I ever received. My second mark of distinction was to win, in my last term, the open obstacle race. This was solely because I was very small for my age and thus able to squeeze through and negotiate the obstacles with greater agility and speed than the other runners. But in the same term, to my great disappointment, I failed by a single mark to win the rifle shooting cup I had long coveted. Being cheerful and extrovert, I was sorry to leave the Dragon School.

Winchester

I took the Winchester examination, which was more difficult than the normal Public Schools entrance, in the early summer of 1922. Despite all the special coaching to which I had unenthusiastically submitted, my papers disappointed the examiners, as did my appalling inability to spell. I failed dismally in Latin, and in common with St Augustine all the angles described in my answers to the geometry examination appeared as angels. I have never been able to spell, and I suspect I was mildly dyslectic. Nevertheless because of the prestige of my uncle's name and memory I was provisionally accepted as a special case — a fine instance of nepotism — and to Winchester I went the following September. My parents, following the normal practice with new boys, took me down by train from Waterloo at the beginning of my first term. I wore the darker of the two clerical grey tweed suits which was the weekday garb laid down for Junior boys. In my trunk lay the other, the marginally lighter suit, together with the black jacket and striped trousers which, with top hat and Eton collar, I would wear on Sundays until three years later I would be promoted to a tail coat. I had also brought a regulation pattern wooden 'tuck box' containing a currant cake, six pots of jam and three of Shippams fish paste, together with a few personal possessions.

At the beginning of that first term I found myself placed in the lowest form, 5th Book, Junior Part II, and was very conscious that even here I might well find the standard of many of the subjects above me. Rustication I knew would follow failure to keep up, for I had been accepted on that understanding. It was necessary for me to get out of Junior Part II in one term if possible, certainly in two. This realisation acted as a spur. I worked hard. At the end of term I was third out of a form of seventeen. To the relief of us all I was promoted into Junior Part I. There was no longer any immediate danger.

I was happy throughout my five years at Winchester and was conscious within a short time of my arrival of the all-embracing traditional grace of the school. It would be difficult not to be deeply influenced by an atmosphere in which there prevailed the beauty of ancient stone and sun-warmed brick, giant plane trees and the sound of rooks, the wide sweep of turf, still watermeadows and windswept downs. Day after day we absorbed this tranquil beauty and with it, by contact with those who taught us and those with whom we lived in such close and barrack-like proximity, an awareness of those virtues which are not, I think, taught or absorbed under any other system or in any other country. The ghosts of past generations were never far away. In the year after my arrival the five hundred Wykehamists who had died in the First World War were commemorated in the calm beauty and solemnity of Sir Herbert Baker's Memorial Cloister. We walked through it half a dozen times a day on our way to and from our classrooms and the names and the regimental badges (my uncle's among them) caught our eyes as we passed. There were memorials too, and lists of names of those who had fought and died in the South African war and in the Crimea. In the Chantry Cloister, around which we strolled on Sunday mornings before Chapel, stood the memorial plaques of old Wykehamists who had achieved distinction in other spheres, not necessarily in war. Among them was a gateway dedicated to my uncle, known to this day as 'Bell Gate'.

In all this close proximity with both the living and the dead we learnt — we could hardly have done otherwise — a measure of humility without which no one can rightly exercise power. We learnt to appreciate the value and virtue of tolerance and to differentiate between conceit and pride, between authority and arrogance, between obedience and submissiveness. We learnt to put our thoughts on paper clearly and grammatically, to choose words for their proper meaning as well as for their sound. We read and learnt a great deal of the Bible. We went to Chapel every morning and twice on Saturdays and Sundays. We had House prayers daily and were expected to say our own personal prayers before going to bed. Few of us were particularly devout, but we accepted this as the normal background to our day-to-day lives. Our monastic existence effectively ensured freedom from the complications of romantic entanglements with girls and I have to say that I believe we were the better and also the happier for being thus protected. Alternative complications were rare and ephemeral. We were conscious of being an élite but we were equally, if only dimly, conscious that in time much would be required of us and that we were accumulating a debt we would have to repay — and repay, like the Just Steward, with interest.

Our life was fairly spartan by present standards. Every morning, summer and winter, a cold plunge. We went to morning school before breakfast, in the autumn and summer terms starting at 7.30. On six out of the seven days of the week we had to take some form of physical exercise. Until we had been in the school for three years we were obliged to submit in writing on Saturday evenings the details of our exercise during the week, be it football, cross-country running, fives or some equivalent. A good deal of corporal punishment was meted out and I doubt if it did us any harm. For the first two years we served the prefects. We kept, pressed and folded their clothes, cleaned their shoes, kept their football boots dubbined and their cricket boots whitened. We were sent by the prefects on frequent errands, and on Sundays we prepared their tea, their hot buttered toast and crumpets. In our turn we came to enjoy similar services from those junior to us — and responsibilities towards them. No one should be in a position to give orders and exercise authority without learning first to serve and obey. We learnt to be disciplined and generally to accept the established order of things without complaining. Should we have been more critical, and questioned more vigorously or even rejected the standards that earlier generations had set for us? This is what our children and grandchildren have done. But they have done it at their peril, for we inherited a framework in which to grow up, and it is a mistake to think that the young can develop happily or successfully without a framework.

The Headmaster for the first half of my time at Winchester was Montague John Rendall. His vision of education was aristocratic; he placed his confidence in an élite of race and training. He was also an imperialist. The highly educated élite were to be dedicated to the public service; they were obliged to repay their debt by going forth to serve mankind over the widest possible field; be it at home or abroad, whether in the armed and Civil Services or in the Church and the professions. The money-making, the flamboyant, the aggressive view of life was quite excluded from his view of the things that were right. From him and from others we absorbed the virtues of understatement, reticence, modesty and apparent detachment. We came to feel instinctively that in the long run it is not ingenuity but conduct and principle that decide events. 'It is the privilege of a gentleman', the father of Flora Shaw (Lady Lugard) used to tell her, 'to get the worst of a bargain.' I think we would have accepted that as only a slight exaggeration of what we felt. Gentleness and courtesy must walk hand in hand with privilege and power, a principle I heard expressed many years later in the Gilbert and Ellice Island proverb, 'Small is the voice of a chief'.

I owe much of my Winchester debt to the influence of two masters in particular: my housemaster Frederick Paul David and John Willoughby Parr, who taught me for a year after I had worked my way at the age of fourteen out of Junior Part II.

David was one of the school chaplains. He was also an enthusiastic territorial officer and had at one time commanded the Officer Training Corps (OTC) and coached the School Shooting VIII. Not everyone in his house found him sympathetic; he was a classicist who had little time or sympathy for modern subjects of learning — he once thundered at a boy who had incurred his displeasure for some reason 'Since you took up science your whole character has deteriorated' — and he was more than suspicious of the activities of the Roman Catholic Church. He had been a close friend of my Uncle Gawain and my Aunt Mary, and thus welcomed me to his house despite my poor showing in the entrance examination. I was worried that scholastically I was below standard and very much on trial, and although I was not withdrawn or unfriendly, I was unusually short and young looking for my age. I feared too that no one would take me seriously. Frederick Paul David took me seriously and with a warmth and good humour that immediately did me good. At the end of each week in my first term he would ask me how things were going; he encouraged me where he thought encouragement was needed, and was relieved as with each week's form results it began to look as if I was holding my own. As I moved up the school he remained friendly and encouraging. I never ceased to find him somewhat intimidating but I valued his approval and therefore strove to avoid disappointing him.

I was never anything of a games player — not that I objected to making the attempt, but I never managed to hit or propel a ball with any effective force or accuracy. I got out of cricket after my second summer by taking up rifle shooting, but continued to play compulsory winter games with limited enjoyment, although again I preferred the alternative exercise of long runs through the water-meadows around St Cross and over the downs about St Catherine's Hill. Apart from rifle shooting I never represented my house in any contest except singing. I was dragooned into that in my second term while still a treble and was much embarrassed because each verse of the song set for the competition ended with the appalling words 'but I *adore* [on a series of rising notes] my bonny belle.' My leg was pulled in consequence. Although therefore I brought little credit to my House in these activities, David approved my early interest and success in rifle shooting and enthusiasm for the OTC.

James Willoughby Parr — Jack Parr — was a Wykehamist and the son of a Wykehamist. He had won a classical scholarship to New College, and had distinguished himself and been wounded five times in the First World War. He was a bachelor, debonair and well-dressed, amusing and witty. I greatly admired him from the moment I became his pupil, and throughout my time at Winchester. The excellence of his scholarship would have qualified him to take any form at the top of the school, but no one else among the masters had the same extraordinary gift and capacity for inspiring fourteen-year-olds and making them work. Because of this gift he continued to teach the one-but-junior form in the school for an unbroken period of no less than a hundred terms. In my last two years I saw as much of him as when I had sat at his feet, for he commanded a Company in the OTC in which as a Sergeant I was Second-in-Command of my House platoon, and he was responsible for training the Shooting VIII of which in my last year I became captain. That was in 1927. Eighteen years later, shortly before the end of the war, I married his young cousin, and he was my best man. My affection for him remained unimpaired up till his death in 1981.

I acquired a collapsible .22 rifle and poached pheasants at Chilcomb on the edge of the Downs. I became interested in ancient firearms, particularly pistols, and cast lead shot for these in the House stoke hole. In my last year I became a House Prefect and in my last term, to my surprise, a School Prefect. As such I was entitled to wear on Sundays a grey double-breasted waistcoat with my tail coat, striped trousers and top hat, and to carry my umbrella rolled. In general I was law-abiding, adaptable, moderately conscientious and conventional. I was a late developer. I had my friends and I enjoyed life. Winchester gave me a great deal, but less intellectually than I might have gained had I been more aware and less immature.

The problem of a career began to exercise both my father and me during my fourth year at school. I had few positive ideas. I was fond of the countryside and country pursuits and so considered farming, but for all its attractions it seemed a little too unenterprising. There was always the possibility of joining my father on the Stock Exchange, but a City life did not attract me. The more I considered it the more I inclined towards the army, but my father in his wisdom, and at the cost of further financial sacrifice, proposed that I should first go to Oxford. I could always join the army from the University if after a couple of years I still felt that way. I willingly accepted this suggestion and it was agreed that I should aim for a modest college where the fees would be lower and the temptations to a more extravagant way of living less. I was accepted into Hertford after taking an entrance examination and attending an interview, and went up in the autumn of 1927.

Oxford

I have a feeling that the end of the 1920s was a somewhat barren period in the life of the University. It produced no giants. The immediate post-war years, in which many of the undergraduates were men who had endured the fighting and who in consequence were that much more mature, had passed. The General Strike of 1926 had been forgotten, and the financial crisis of the early 1930s, the threat of German expansion and the likelihood of another world conflict were still to come. The circles in which I moved during my four years at Oxford were neither highbrow nor entirely philistine — and, I believe, were thus representative of a large proportion of the undergraduates. We talked a great deal, but our thoughts were seldom of religon or philosophy, or of our less fortunate countrymen, or of world affairs. Active interest in politics was mainly limited to members of the Oxford Union and the few who belonged to the political clubs. We suffered, I daresay, from a certain measure of snobbishness but we were surely not consciously arrogant, although we took a lot unthinkingly for granted. But whether we came from the public and grammar schools or — in smaller numbers — from state schools, we were all working towards finding places in the same professions or the same industries, or in the Civil Service.

I worked moderately hard and I thoroughly enjoyed myself. For my first two years I had a bedroom and a sitting room in College, and for the last two years lived in lodgings, looked after by a landlady who provided breakfast and made my bed. I played College games but without distinction. Twice a week, during the winter terms, I followed the Magdalen and New College Beagles. Oxford and its immediate surroundings were far more rural then than they are today. In 1930, on a winter afternoon, I shot a snipe within the city boundaries, and in the same year I was able to ride my horse down the High Street, hacking to a meet, without too much worry about the traffic.

I joined the Artillery Section of the Officers Training Corps and became an enthusiastic amateur gunner, attending the weekly parades, lectures and riding school regularly, and soon being promoted to Bombadier. We were trained on 18-pounders, which were drawn by a team of six horses. This meant learning to ride as a mounted member of the gun team and to drive and manoeuvre the gun and its limber. I passed an efficiency test known as Certificate B, and in my second year the Colonel invited me to take a Territorial

Commission. I agreed readily and enjoyed the subsequent fortnightly summer camps at Larkhill where we got a great deal of riding and fired off our guns. I became Captain of the University Shooting VIII and spent a fortnight each year under canvas at Bisley.

I had first gone to Bisley in 1926, and thereafter my shooting activities, which embraced service rifle, match rifle and revolver, continued, apart from unavoidable intervals when I was abroad, until 1954, the year when the Sudan team won all the international matches open to it.

I rode, and in my last two years I hunted, for my father gave me a horse as a twenty-first birthday present. 'Don't give your son money,' Winston Churchill wrote a year later in *My Early Life*. 'As far as you can afford it, give him horses.' The riding of horses has remained a continuing delight to me up to the present time, although I can no longer afford to keep one.

One of the broad divisions that marked Oxford and Cambridge undergraduates was that between the 'horsey' and the 'non-horsey'. By the late 1920s the horsey were a declining minority but they formed nonetheless an easily distinguishable caste, and that mainly by their dress. The majority of undergraduates wore flannels and tweed jackets, and in cold weather they wrapped a woollen scarf of team or College colours around their necks. Above all they went hatless. The horsey men likewise wore flannels but their tweed jackets were long in the skirt with a single vent, and the pockets were cut at an angle. And for them it was essential that they should wear a flat tweed cap on all occasions. I counted myself among those who were horsey and so I wore a long brown jacket made for me by Hall Brothers in the High Street which I only finally abandoned three years ago. And those were the days of 'Oxford Bags', light grey in colour or even, if their possessors were very dashing, lavender. Their essential feature was the great width of the lower end, but the horsey men cared little for the extravagances of this fashion and their trousers were narrow.

By the standards of even half a generation later our roots were surprisingly deep in the past. We were perhaps the last of the Edwardians. A friend and I spent a fortnight or so in the spring of 1928 in Italy. We travelled inexpensively and stayed in modest hotels. But while we wore informal clothes for sight-seeing and walking, it would never have occurred to us not to take our dinner jackets with us; and into these we changed every evening as a matter of course. Antony Maitland, a close friend with whom I lodged in Oriel Street, was in love with a girl, the daughter of a Brigadier. She came at his invitation to a number of lunch parties, to Eights week and to the Summer College Ball. At the end of a year of advances along these conventional and essentially proper lines, he summoned up sufficient courage to say to her, 'Miss Markham, may I call you Edith?' To this she consented.

There was little at Oxford in the way of confrontation with authority. And I am sure we were happier and gained more from the friendships we enjoyed with our tutors and lecturers than has ever been derived from the 'sit-ins' and 'demos' of later times. Not that we were uninterested in university or national politics, a number of us were, but we did not believe that injustices are best righted by breaking up things or shouting down those with whom we disagreed. In some ways we were less mature than the undergraduates of today, but I cannot help believing that in others we were better balanced. A clue to this may lie in the fact that most of our tutors were unmarried men, and women played only a marginal part in the lives of most of us. And then too, we had been brought up in an age in which authority stood for something and was generally held in respect. At heart we all want people to look up to, and it is a sad and frightening feature of our present age that so many people think that in some way it is weak or wrong to do so. Our lives were pretty virginal, and we tended to look down on those few who regularly indulged in what was strangely called 'poodlefaking'. I don't suppose that we can claim any particular credit for our general celibacy, which arose from the spirit of the time, but I do believe that we were fortunate not to be exposed to all the distractions that the present age so liberally affords.

I do not think that I was especially influenced by any one individual, either don or contemporary, during my four years at Oxford. I had many friends among both, and all no doubt helped in one way and another towards my growing up. And I was influenced of course by the whole intangible atmosphere and beauty of Oxford and its surrounding countryside. Of the dons I came to know well it was T.S.R. Boase to whom I owe the greatest debt. Tom Boase was a history don, a medievalist, a lover of art and beauty, a stimulating and witty conversationalist, and it seemed to us surprising, in view of his gentle charm, that he had served with distinction and gallantry in the 1914–18 war. He was Dean of Hertford and my tutor in medieval history and I saw a lot of him both as his pupil and socially. He was a bachelor, lived in College and had an enormously wide acquaintance and influence over a host of undergraduates. Once a week for three years I submitted my essays to him, and once a week in a group of three or four we met for an hour in his attractive book-lined study to discuss with him what we had written. I read medieval and modern history under Tom Boase and C.R.M.F. Cruttwell, and military history as a special subject under General Sir Ernest Swinton (who as

Lt.-Col. E.D. Swinton, RE, had been in 1915–16 the principal originator of the tank) and C.T. Atkinson. Our particular area of study was the Peninsular War. Without too much difficulty I got a good Second in the Final Schools. I was never within hope or likelihood of a First.

I have endless bright pictures in my mind of those intensely happy years. Sitting on winter evenings before the fire in some friend's rooms, four or five of us, engaged in easy talk with a huge pot of tea and a plate of anchovy toast standing together on the trivet. Walking down 'the High' with Antony Maitland — soon to die serving with his regiment on the North West Frontier — and laughing aloud for no reason other than that life was so good. Trudging back from a long grey afternoon's beagling near Challow in the Vale of the White Horse, dead tired and icy cold, knowing that the pub at which tea had already been ordered was less than a mile away. Dressing in the winter before dawn to be in time for the weekly OTC mounted parade at the riding school or to catch a bus to Burford for a day with the Heythrop. Beer on a summer's evening at the White Hart at Wytham. Sitting in Paul Foster's rooms in Hertford listening to a record of Schubert's 'Trout' Quintet. Standing on Magdalen Bridge at dawn on May Morning with the choir singing at the top of the tower. Dinner and talk with Tom Boase and others. Reading in the calm of the Codrington Library at All Souls. How fortunate we were.

In my last year at Winchester I had met Martin Parr, Jack Parr's brother.* Martin was a member of the Sudan Political Service and at the time of our meeting and for some years thereafter was Private Secretary to the Governor-General, Sir John Maffey.† Despite a glass eye, the result of a war wound, he was a noted international rifle shot, and each summer he too came to Bisley. At the end of my first year at Oxford I had already decided that the Colonial Service rather than the Army would give me more the sort of life and career I wanted. Martin Parr suggested the Sudan as an alternative. In the autumn of 1929 therefore, I submitted my name as a candidate for the Sudan Political Service. I did not rate my chances of selection very high, and applied at the same time for the Colonial Service giving Tanganyika, Uganda and Nigeria as my order of preference.

* M.W. Parr, CBE, *b.* 1892. War service 1914–18. Sudan Political Service 1919–42. Alderman LCC 1954–61.

† Sir John Loder Maffey, GCMG, KCB, KCVO, CSI, CIE, created 1st Baron Rugby 1935, *b.* 1877, *d.* 1969. Indian Civil Service 1899–24; Governor General Sudan 1926–33; Permanent Under Secretary of State for the Colonies 1933–7. UK Representative in Eire 1939–49.

My parents, to their great credit and despite what must have been regret and anxiety over my wish thus to exile myself, put no difficulties in my way.

I think it is generally accepted that the Sudan Political Service ranked highest among the overseas administrative services with the possible exception of the Indian Civil Service. The only way of entry was by interview. There was a brief preliminary interview conducted by the University Appointments Committee to weed out those considered markedly unsuitable. Then there was a more prolonged one at Oxford or Cambridge, or possibly elsewhere if there happened to be candidates from any other university, which was rare. This second interview was far more searching and was attended by two or three senior members of the Political Service who were on leave. A short list of thirty or so candidates thus emerged and a final selection board then sat in London presided over by the Civil Secretary of the Sudan Government and attended by five or six Provincial Governors or their deputies. But before the sitting of the final board the selectors consulted Headmasters and Tutors and Deans and the Masters of Colleges; they took up references; they paid attention to the sort of degree a candidate was expected to get, and to his spare-time and vacation activities. A known tendency to 'poodlefaking' would certainly rule a candidate out. In 1930 the Sudan Government had introduced a regulation which banned a Political Service officer from bringing his wife out until he had either completed five years' service or reached the age of twenty-eight. Although this led to a few cases of hardship it did not act as a deterrent towards recruitment, and I have no doubt it was a good regulation. It is difficult to imagine such a rule being acceptable today in any service.

Lord Cromer had laid down the criteria required of candidates for the Sudan Political Service many years before: 'active young men, endowed with good health, high character and fair abilities . . . the flower of those who are turned out of our schools and colleges'. A Blue was an advantage but not a necessity. A Second in the Final School or at least a good Third was essential. Active habits, an indication of enterprise, and an adventurous turn of mind counted in a man's favour. That a candidate had been to one of the well-known Public Schools helped. And of course at the final interview there was always a certain element of luck. Some years later while still an Assistant District Commissioner and happening to be on leave, I was called on to serve as Secretary to the Final Selection Board. My job was to usher the candidates in and out, to reassure those who appeared nervous, to give the Board my own impression of each man and to report any fact or incident I thought might be relevant to the Board's deliberations. Among the score or so who appeared that year was one of fine athletic achievement and sterling character but with a dangerously poor degree. He arrived half an hour or more early for his interview and as the candidate who preceded him went in to face the Board, this man opened his *Times*, took out a pencil and addressed himself in a detached sort of way to the crossword puzzle. Three quarters of an hour later when the previous candidate emerged he had already put away his pencil. I opened the door and showed him in. The *Times* lay where he had been sitting and I glanced at his solution. It was evident that it was both complete and correct. When he in his turn emerged I informed the Board. They were impressed as well they might be. He was a tight borderline case but the crossword just swung the selectors in his favour. He proved to be an excellent choice.

After my retirement I served for some years as a part-time chairman of Civil Service Selection Boards, and although the present methods of selection are very much more detailed and rigorous than those which were used in choosing men for the Sudan Political Service, basically the principles are the same: namely a whole view of the candidate, his achievements and his potential. When in 1954 the Sudan Political Service ceased to exist, twelve of the younger members were taken into the Diplomatic Service, and in due course seven of them became ambassadors.

I remember little of my own final interview apart from the long mahogany table at the head of which sat H.A. MacMichael,* then Civil Secretary and as such Head of the Service, flanked by half a dozen bronzed, lean men. I sat alone at the far end and faced this formidable group. The room was blue and fragrant with pipe smoke. I wore a dark suit, a stiff collar and a black and white spotted tie. I had been carefully briefed by Martin Parr who had sponsored my candidature. I was asked whether, as I had neither brothers nor sisters, my parents would willingly see me go to the Sudan. I said they would. My Territorial Commission and Captainship of the Oxford Shooting VIII were a help. Tom Boase had told the selection board even before I took the examination for my final schools that he would guarantee my getting a Second. He took a risk for which I am eternally grateful, for his assurance must have materially strengthened my candidature. In one of my university vacations I had spent some weeks working in Liechtenstein as a labourer for a voluntary service organisation known as the 'Fellowship of Reconciliation'. I

* Sir H.A. MacMichael, GCMG, DSO, *b.* 1882, *d.* 1969. Sudan Political Service 1905–34. Governor Tanganyika 1934–8. High Commissioner Palestine and Trans-Jordan 1938–44. Special Representative HMG Malaya 1945. Constitutional Commissioner Malta 1946.

had recorded this modest venture in my application form and was asked to describe what it had involved. This small indication of enterprise also probably worked in my favour.

The interview over I went home and waited for the result. A week later, to my great delight and amazement, the Sudan accepted me together with seven others. One was a London University man, one was from Cambridge and the remaining five of us were from Oxford. One had a First, three had Seconds and four had Third class degrees in their final schools. Four of the eight of us had a Blue or a Half Blue. Two were to die in the Sudan within the first three years of their service. One dropped out.

The practice that had prevailed hitherto was that newly selected members of the Political Service did a three months' course in Arabic at the School of Oriental and African Studies before leaving for the Sudan. However, in 1930 and subsequent years, those aged less than twenty-two were sent back to the University for a full year's attendance at the Tropical African Services Course. This course included, apart from five Sudan men, sixty or seventy others who had been selected by the Colonial Office for the administrative services of various other British possessions overseas. We of the Sudan looked upon the men chosen for Nigeria as the nearest to ourselves in excellence and good fortune, but I cannot recall that the sixty or so Colonial Service men shared our opinion of our own superiority in any way. There was not a single black or brown man among us. In 1938 when I attended, during my last leave before the war, a short refresher course at Lady Margaret Hall, organised by Margery Perham,* there was a handful of Africans among the fifty or more of us. Twenty-five years later, when I presided over a week's introductory Summer School at Oxford for members of a 'Devonshire Course', only two out of the seventy students were white. The 1930 Course involved the study of Criminal and Civil Law, Tropical Agriculture and Forestry, Tropical Hygiene, Colonial History and Anthropology. We were also taught First Aid and were encouraged to attend operations at the Radcliffe Infirmary to accustom ourselves to the sight of blood and severed limbs. I went somewhat unwillingly, and on the first two or three visits was overcome by nausea as soon as the knives got to work and obliged to lie on the floor of the operating theatre to recover. I soon became used to these sights.

We attended lectures by distinguished visitors, among them Lord Lugard who had retired from the Governor-Generalship of Nigeria

* Dame Margery Perham, DCMG, CBE, *b.* 1895, *d.* 1982. Author of the definitive biography of Lugard.

in 1919. At the end of his talk we lined up and shook hands with him. To me at the time he seemed extremely old — he was in fact seventy-two — and extraordinarily small and frail. How, I wondered, had one so apparently insignificant in appearance and physique achieved such momentous things? I still judged much by superficialities. Lady Lugard had died the year before and he lived in Abinger where he used regularly to be visited by a little girl of twelve who took tea with him, and wondered at the museum-like collection of spears and shields and masks and other Africana in his house. The same girl became my wife fourteen years later. As Sir Frederick Lugard, he had been the first British Governor (with the title 'High Commissioner') of Northern Nigeria. In time I was to be the thirteenth and the last.

One of our visiting lecturers, who had served for many years in Africa, made an observation which impressed me strongly. 'You will be of little use in your job until you have mastered the language of your area sufficiently well to be able, as you walk through a village market, to set the merchants and bystanders guffawing with merriment.' By far the most important of all the subjects which we were taught during that year was the language of the country where we were destined to serve. For us it was Arabic and in our introduction to the study of that elusive and fascinating language we sat at the feet of Lawrence Dewhurst. He was an irascible man, unprepossessing, grubby and untidy, but he taught us with a tireless vehemence and a gift for transmitting his enthusiasm. I enjoyed those first lessons, worked hard and passed the final exam.

As the time for our departure for the Sudan approached it became necessary to buy the required kit, and for this purpose Messrs Griffiths McAlister of Warwick Street, Piccadilly, was one of the firms recommended by the Sudan Government. Armed with a list provided by the Sudan Agent in London I called on Griffiths McAlister one morning in the early summer of 1931. The ground floor entrance was by the way of a narrow corridor along one side of which were stacked wooden crates. On these were stencilled names and destinations well calculated to impress and indeed overawe a modest and diffident overseas Civil Service cadet such as myself: '*Captain J.W.F. Horton-Gardiner, Accra*', '*Mr B.J. Bryanston, CMG, The Residency, Zanzibar*'. I was back to my first term at Winchester, eyeing the trunks and tuckboxes on the platform at Waterloo. I felt suddenly inadequate and forlorn and wondered whether I had the resource and was sufficiently robust for all this. At the end of the corridor was a steep stairway leading up to the show-room on the first floor. Lining the walls of the stairway were framed photographs of many distinguished and presumably satisfied clients of Griffiths McAlister. Some were in uniform, and all had large and virile moustaches. Their eyes were steady, their mouths firm. It was abundantly clear that without exception these paragons possessed in the fullest possible measure the qualities essential to a successful colonial administrator: resolution, fortitude, fair dealing, integrity and supreme self-confidence.

I stood irresolute and glanced diffidently through the doorway of the showroom. In the centre was a camp bed realistically made up with scarlet blanket and green mosquito net. Beside it stood a number of folding chairs of various kinds draped with bush shirts, spine pads and other items of tropical clothing. There were saddles, and canvas basins and baths and buckets. There were safari tables on which stood an assortment of all kinds of impressive articles: hurricane lamps, sparklet soda syphons, solar topees, cartridge belts and hunting knives. From the walls peered down the stuffed heads of Kudu, Bush Buck and Impala. A man dressed in morning coat and striped trousers, who looked superbly incongruous in that contrived tropical scene, came forward. 'May I help you?' he said, a little patronisingly I thought. I put myself doubtingly into his presumably competent hands. Within three quarters of an hour I had ordered much of the contents of the showroom, including, as a protection against the sun, a red flannel spine pad which in fact I never wore. When I emerged, my self-confidence was slightly restored. In a week or so the corridor would be filled with crates marked '*Mr G. W. Bell, Khartoum via Port Sudan*'. The moment of near-panic had passed.

Two years later, during my first leave, I returned to Griffiths McAlister to replenish my tropical wardrobe and to order stores and supplies for my next tour. I was received by the same impressive assistant and with the same courtesy, but this time there was added to it something more. I was no longer a cadet. I knew what I wanted. I had had fever and lost a stone in weight. My new status was clear. I was addressed constantly as 'Sir'. Although it was not yet eleven o'clock in the morning I was offered a whisky and soda.

2
FIRST STEPS
(The Eastern Sudan, 1931–1933)

Four out of the seven of us who had been selected for the Sudan in the previous year, and had attended the Oxford course, left Victoria Station for Marseilles and Port Sudan in September 1931. One had failed his examinations and had gone elsewhere. We were all aged twenty-two. It was a hard moment for my parents but they accepted it with brave resignation. Three subalterns of the Manchester Regiment on their way back from leave to rejoin their battalion in Khartoum shared a table with us in the dining saloon. They also were twenty-two, but to me at any rate they seemed eminently men of the world. They had already served in India as well as in the Sudan.

The 6,000-ton SS *Chindwin* of the Henderson Line carried us comfortably through the Mediterranean. We docked for twelve hours at Port Said to refuel. This operation consisted of an endless stream of Egyptians coming aboard, each carrying a basket of coal on his back which he tipped into the bunkers, to the accompaniment of a cheerful but monotonous chant. We had now entered 'the tropics', and therefore went ashore to provide ourselves with solar topees. These, by tradition, were bought from Simon Artz's emporium, which stood square and solid facing the canal quays. It symbolised in appearance and atmosphere something of the position held by the West at their gateway to the East. Here the traveller could buy anything he might require for life in the tropics, and a good deal more besides. The shop, on several floors and equipped with a tea terrace, looked eastwards to Sinai across the northern entrance to the Canal. (Half a mile away, at the point where the Canal joined the Mediterranean, stood the statue of de Lesseps, pitched into the sea by an Egyptian crowd in 1956.) In the street opposite Simon Artz a line of a dozen dingy and flyblown horse cabs waited for customers who might wish to take a drive around Port Said and see the 'Native Quarter'. The drivers waved their whips and shouted encouragement. Their thin horses stood head down, patient and dejected. People of every nationality and every colour walked the streets or sat at open-air cafés. Groups of pimps, touts, boys and beggars hung around the gates of the dock, watched lethargically by two or three down-at-heel policemen armed with canes. A few of the more presentable of the Port Said peddlers and traffickers in local crafts were allowed on board the ship, where they set out their wares along the deck; leather pouffes, baskets and fly whisks. Surreptitiously they also offered aphrodisiacs and pornography. And around the ship clustered the bum boats and boys who swam and dived like porpoises shouting to the passengers to throw them coins.

Over the whole of Port Said there hung a particularly pungent smell which once experienced is never forgotten. Approaching the town one could discern it from many miles out at sea. It was compounded of dust, humanity, decaying vegetable matter, horse manure and human urine. The sky was cloudless. It was a fly-blown, sleazy place. We sailed at midnight, and the *Chindwin* edged her way slowly past the arc lights, pushing her bow wave along the stone revetted banks of the Canal.

Twenty-four hours later, with Suez behind us, the ship throbbed and hummed her way slowly past the scarred and sunsmitten mountains of Sinai. As we entered the damp heat of the Red Sea, I began to wonder once again why exactly I had chosen this sort of career, and the Sudan in particular, and what I hoped to gain from it. I am sure I never saw myself as likely to play a part of any significance in the development of the Empire. The Empire — and the word was in everyday use — was stable, and as we saw it, unlikely to be subject to a great deal of change in our time. Article 22 of the League of Nations Covenant had, as we knew, applied the principle that 'the well-being and development of peoples not yet able to stand by themselves under the strenuous conditions of the modern world' formed a 'sacred trust for civilisation'. The Article concerned Mandates, but was clearly in spirit applicable to the Condominium of the Sudan as well as to our colonies. In so far as we were able to envisage what all this might involve in practical terms, we certainly accepted it without question. But as for self-government and more remotely independence, why, these were goals, yes, but surely far distant. The Empire had passed its high noon a generation earlier and yet even now, in 1931, it had not reached its final limit in extent and population; that was to come two years later with its extension into the Hadramaut eastwards from Aden. None of us could have imagined for a moment that the Sudan would be independent before we reached our retiring age of fifty. And yet of course by the very nature of the work we were about to undertake — keeping the peace, developing local government, encouraging the spread of education, fostering economic development and a dozen other similar activities — we were taking part without fully realising it in a movement that was to create with ever-increasing momentum the circumstances that would bring about the end of the regime of which we formed an integral part. The better and more zealously we carried out our tasks, the sooner the Sudanese would wish to see us go.

We knew that we would certainly not make our fortunes in the Sudan, and that we were unlikely to receive much public recognition by way of honours or awards. There was no system whereby a man might transfer to another service and become possibly a Colonial Governor or a High Commissioner or an Ambassador. The climate we knew to be one of the hottest and unhealthiest in the world. Why therefore? We had been told by those already there that the Sudanese were a fine, brave, attractive people. We were soon to share this opinion. We saw ahead of us an open-air adventurous life, with annual leave after our initial twenty months of probation. In due time, we would be entitled to a pension that might come to as much as £800 or even £1,000 a year. We were content, as we sailed southwards towards Port Sudan, in the knowledge that we were members of a service with standards of integrity, comradeship and morale that matched and, we believed, surpassed all others. For the moment that was enough.

We reached Port Sudan four days later, shortly after dawn. Throughout the previous afternoon the distant outline of the Red Sea mountains had shown itself to the west. The port consisted of a few quays and corrugated iron warehouses, and half a dozen cranes. A long white train, its windows shuttered against the sun, stood on the railway tracks nearby. A score of dock labourers with heads of wild frizzy hair were looking up patronisingly at the ship. On the dock side there was a group of khaki-uniformed Sudanese Port and Customs officials, and three or four policemen in starched white shorts, tunics and turbans. They were impressively smart. There were few white faces to be seen. Surrounding a central square fringed with rows of young trees we could make out a dozen or so white-washed buildings. On the largest of these there flew the Union Jack and the green flag of Egypt. Beyond, in the rising heat haze, there was a town of low mud-brick houses, and behind lay a line of mountains that looked down on the narrow scrub-covered plain that fringes the Red Sea. Everything appeared remarkably ordered, and calm and silent. No Simon Artz, no dilapidated horse cabs, no touts or pimps here.

We dressed ourselves in our white tropical suits for the first time, a little self-consciously, and went ashore. It was nine o'clock and already hot and disagreeably humid. Our luggage was checked. As newly appointed officials we were entitled under the privilege accorded by *première installation* to exemption from customs dues on essential articles of kit and equipment, but I had to pay a percentage on the value of my portable gramophone and on my shot-gun for which I was given a licence. It was now eleven o'clock. Under the corrugated iron roof of the Customs shed the heat had grown stifling. W.T. Clark,* the assistant to the Commissioner of Port Sudan, presented himself to us. The heat apparently left him unmoved. He was poised, relaxed and elegant. He informed us that his chief, Major Douglas Stoker Brownlie Thomson, had invited us to luncheon, and that we would be expected at one o'clock. Places had been reserved for us in the Khartoum train which would leave during the afternoon; he would arrange for the loading of our luggage. He gave us our tickets. I was filled with admiration for this calm efficient young man who seemed to speak Arabic so fluently, and to be so very much at ease.

At a few minutes to one, Clark accompanied us to the Commissioner's Residence. Passing through a garden of zinnias, cannas, bougainvillias and petunias, we entered a cool arched hall-way. The floor was of polished black tiles, there were several fine brass-studded Kuwaiti chests, the walls were white and decorated with spears and other military trophies. The house was not unlike a service mess. Everything shone. Two white-robed and turbaned servants, bare-footed and splendid in scarlet cummerbunds, led us through to the drawing room. Major Thomson, in addition to his name, could well have been the prototype for Pierre Daninos' *Les carnets du Major Thompson.* From Shrewsbury and Trinity College, Dublin, where he had read medicine, he had joined the Egyptian Army and subsequently in 1909, the year in which I was born, he had been seconded to the Sudan Political Service. For five years he had been engaged in the repression of the slave trade. Now at just over fifty he had reached the age of retirement and would be leaving before the end of the year. He was in tropical drill uniform, and in addition to his general service ribbons he wore those of the Order of the Nile and the Star of Ethiopia. We sat around his polished table and consumed our cold consommé, our cold lamb cutlets and salad, and our caramel custard. We drank fresh lime juice. As we were soon to learn, alcoholic drinks only made their appearance after sunset. Lunch over, we returned to the drawing room for Turkish coffee and Egyptian cigarettes, and in due course we took our leave. Clark saw us on to the train and we steamed slowly out of the damp heat of Port Sudan up to the Red Sea hills and towards Khartoum. Our service had begun.

On the re-occupation of the Sudan, after the victory of Omdurman in 1898, by a joint Anglo-Egyptian expeditionary force,

* W.T. Clark, OBE, *b.* 1905. Sudan Political Service 1928–53, UNRWA, Jordan 1953–4. Adviser to Ruler of Abu Dhabi, 1954–65.

a British Governor-General, who also held the appointment of Commander-in-Chief (*Sirdar*) of the Egyptian Army, was charged with supreme military and civil command. For the first year it was Kitchener, and in December 1899 he was succeeded by General Sir Reginald Wingate who was to remain as Governor-General for the next sixteen years. It was not until 1924, with the appointment of the first civilian, that the Governor-General ceased to hold the additional assignment of *Sirdar*.

The pattern of administration as set out by Kitchener established fourteen Provinces, each under the civilian control as well as the military command of a Governor (*Mudir*), who was a British officer serving in the Egyptian Army. The Provinces were divided into Districts and these were administered by Egyptian officers, usually captains or subalterns, bearing the title of *Mamur*. An additional level in this structure was the appointment in each Province of one or two British officers with the designation of Inspector (*Mufettish*). The Inspector, by means of constant touring, supervised the work of the *Mamurs* and reported directly to the Provincial Governor, but it was soon evident that with the constant and unavoidable posting elsewhere of British officers, the continuity, and thus the stability of the administration would suffer. It was necessary therefore to establish the nucleus of a civilian administrative service. A beginning was made in 1901 when six young men from Oxford and Cambridge were selected, and in the next four years a further twenty-six took up their appointments.* At the same time a number of British Army officers were taken into the permanent cadre of the administration. Although recruitment from this source soon ceased, a few remained on into the 1930s and '40s, particularly in the Southern Provinces.

At the time of its establishment the Administrative Service of the Sudan was in fact the Civil Affairs Branch of the Egyptian Army, and it was not until 1922, with the development of closer administrative control, that the title of Inspector was changed to District Commissioner. The Arabic word '*Mufettish*', however, remained. At the same time the term 'Political Service' was introduced. This is surprising, for the change did not mean that the Service had come to act in an advisory rather than an administrative capacity, comparable to the Political Department of the Government of India; if anything the contrary was true. The Service was therefore founded on a joint military-civil basis, and the spirit and morale reflected the traditions of both. The annual rate of recruitment seldom exceeded six. In the years between 1901 and 1952, after which recruitment

* Their starting rate of pay was £E420 a year. Thirty years later it was £E480. (£E1 then equalled £1 0*s* 6*d*).

came to an end, 182 men came from Oxford, 103 from Cambridge, and 108 were drawn from the newer universities, from the British Army and from various other sources. Of all the public schools, Winchester produced more members of the Service than any other. In the fifty-five years of its existence the British membership of the Sudan Political Service totalled just under 400, and out of these thirty-one died or were killed on duty. At no time was the strength of the British membership of the Service above 150 but, as Sudanese began to be promoted, the total strength rose in the years after the Second World War to approximately 200. Between 1898 and 1956, when the Sudan became independent, the population rose from approximately 2 million to some 8 million — an indication, if any were needed, of peace and a fair measure of prosperity.

I have given these figures to show upon how light a rein the Sudan was administered. The area of the country is a million square miles, more than ten times the size of the United Kingdom and nearly three times that of Egypt. The Sudan is the largest country in Africa, and the ninth largest in the world. The deserts of the north, the dry thorny savannas of the central belt, and the swamps and forests of the south made communications both slow and difficult. The younger Sudanese sometimes forgot these simple basic facts.

In 1931 the country was administered under twelve Provinces. The three Northern Provinces lay astride the Nile from Khartoum to the Egyptian frontier at Wadi Halfa. Their resources were limited and their population, less than three quarters of a million, consisted of a few nomads and the settled peasants who farmed the narrow strip of irrigated land on either side of the Nile, getting a sparse livelihood from dates and citrus fruit and vegetables, and from herds of sheep and goats that grazed on the corn stubbles and the thorny shrubs that grow along the river banks. The rest was desert, for the annual rainfall over the whole of this area of nearly 200,000 square miles was less than two inches. The more adventurous of these riverain people, many of whom were strikingly fine-looking, followed a traditional calling of domestic service, and were to be found in the well-to-do households of almost every country in the Middle East. They were of mixed Nubian Arab stock and they spoke Arabic and Berber.

The three Southern Provinces covered an approximately similar area but by contrast theirs was a land of wide grassy or forested plains intersected by hundreds of watercourses which for more than six months in the year flooded the surrounding countryside. The people were Nilotics and Bantus. In numbers they came near to two and a half million and they spoke well over a score of different languages. They were black and primitive, and for generations before the establishment of a stable government in 1900 they had been raided by their Northern neighbours, with the connivance and sometimes the help of the Government. Their young men had been sent down to Egypt as slaves and eunuchs or forcibly enlisted into the army, their girls had been taken as servants or concubines. Between these two Northern and Southern divisions of the country lay a great belt of savanna, turning to scrub and desert in the north, and to grassy woodland in the south. Here the majority of the people of the Sudan, between four and five million, lived the lives of herdsmen and cultivators. Some were nomadic, moving north or south, following the grazing with their herds of cattle or camels and with their horses. All, or nearly all, were of Arab stock with a greater or lesser mixture of Southern blood. All save the hillmen of the Nuba mountains were Muslims, and their culture was in general Islamic. All, or nearly all, spoke Arabic.

It was customary for newly joined officers to spend ten days or a fortnight in Khartoum before being posted to their stations. During this brief period they were instructed in the general machinery and working of government. They were interviewed by the Heads of Departments and in particular by the Civil Secretary who was responsible for the administration of the Provinces. They were shown how the buckets of night-soil were transported after dark on camel-drawn carts and emptied into pits in the desert. They were made familiar with the inside and working of the Central Prison, and of the dangerous lunatics' wing. They were initiated into the cruder sights to be seen in tropical hospitals and mortuaries. They learned too something of the necessary shibboleths of social life in an overseas territory, and in this particular they were obliged to pay evening calls on senior officials. This exercise involved placing visiting cards in the little boxes designed for that purpose and located at the garden entrance to the houses of those officers. The boxes were equipped with a sliding panel which showed 'IN' or alternatively 'OUT'. One hoped to find that the owner was out, and then all one had to do was to drop one's card in the box and slip away. By day, in the office, and in the early evening, we wore tropical suits. We dined in white dinner jackets, and if the dinner was an important one, stiff shirts were usual. For a regimental guest night we wore black tails. I dined on such an occasion with the Manchester Regiment during this fortnight in Khartoum. Those were still the days when junior officers and their guests were supposed to undergo all kinds of uncomfortable and rather stupid rituals. I was obliged to drink a glass of beer standing on my head.

The years 1931 to 1934, as is well known, marked a period of severe world recession. The Sudan, like other countries that depended on the export of raw materials, suffered sharply, and economies became essential in all areas of government if the country was to avoid financial disaster. In this crisis the Sudan turned to the British Government, and H.E. Fass, a senior Treasury official, was appointed Financial Secretary. By a relevant coincidence the word *Fass* in Arabic means an axe. Mr Fass set to work. Services were cut and staff pruned. Lightly as the Sudan was administered, and small as the Civil Services were, severe retrenchments were made over those three difficult years. Out of a total of nearly 6,000 officials of all ranks in 1930, by 1932 the number had been reduced by over 1,000. Only 69 Sudanese officials were made redundant.

Those of us who had been selected in the summer of 1930 and trained in the following year were singularly fortunate. We had just slipped in before the door closed, for between 1931 and 1935 only six Political Service appointments were made. By the end of 1934 the crisis had mercifully passed.

The Governor General was Sir John Maffey. Splendidly Olympian, six foot four in height, lean and exceptionally handsome, he had his being far beyond our horizons. The Civil Secretary was Harold MacMichael. His mind was scholarly, sharp and subtle, a shade too much so to endear him greatly to the educated Sudanese who were just beginning to manifest their existence. But he was a brilliant Civil Secretary, and much respected, and in all that I had to do with him in the Sudan and later in Palestine, I found him kind and sensitive and humorous. He was thin and austere in appearance, and a great stickler in the matter of dress. Woe betide any member of his staff who entered his office without a jacket, as one imprudently did. However hot the weather, and Khartoum in the summer could be a furnace, MacMichael always wore a tussore silk suit with a waistcoat and a watch-chain. Incongruously, as it seemed to me, he smoked a corn-cob pipe. He used to buy them in London, a dozen at a time, and each one lasted him a month. He had joined the Sudan Political Service in 1905, with a First in Classics at Cambridge.

In those days the sun south of the tropic of cancer was still regarded as deadly. We wore topees at all times until an hour before sunset. These topees were of two kinds. There was the 'Bombay Bowler', light and comparatively small, khaki in colour, not uncomfortable, and made in India of pulped old newspapers. Under heavy rain it would rapidly sag and wilt and eventually disintegrate. And termites could easily destroy a Bombay Bowler in a single night. The larger type of helmet, the 'Wolseley', which we wore with uniform — we wore uniform at all times when on duty away from Khartoum — was intolerably heavy and uncomfortable. It was shaped like a coal scuttle and the rear part of the brim projected far over the nape of the neck. It was made of reinforced and inflexible cork and it could stand a great deal of hard treatment. As an extra defence against the sun's rays the inside of the 'Wolseley' was lined with silver paper. There was also a third type of sun helmet but many considered it sartorially unacceptable. Halfway in shape between the Bowler and the Wolseley, and white, it was worn by Greek and Syrian merchants and by missionaries. During that first fortnight in Khartoum we lodged at the Sudan Club. One morning after breakfast I walked bareheaded from the wide shady verandah to the line of eight bucket latrines which were discreetly located under the trees beyond the lawn. The distance was thirty yards. On my return I was addressed by a leathery 'old-timer'. 'Young man,' he said kindly but in all solemnity, 'if you want to survive in this country you'll have to be more careful about going into the sun without a helmet.' It took the North African campaign ten years later to convince us, and others, that this veteran who had voiced an opinion which had remained unquestioned for generations had been talking through his hat.

I bought a pony and a light sporting rifle, took a daily lesson in colloquial Arabic, and engaged a cook and a butler each at a salary of £E3 a month. I was eager to get away from Khartoum and hoped that it would be to a province in which Arabic was spoken and polo was played. In this I was not to be disappointed, and within three weeks of arrival in Khartoum I was posted to Kassala, the easternmost province of the Sudan, with Egypt to its north and the shores of the Red Sea marking its eastern verge. To the south and south-east lay Abyssinia and what was then the Italian colony of Eritrea. Gedaref was to be my district. My function there would be to act as 'Supernumerary' Assistant District Commissioner.

Kassala Province covered 130,000 square miles of desert, mountain and plain, and its population was estimated at three quarters of a million people. These varied greatly in race, history, origin and culture. In the north, sometimes crossing into Egypt in the course of their migrations, were the Hadendowa, the Amarar, the Bisherin and the Beni Amer: racially Hamitic, camel-owning, an attractive and romantic people, Kipling's 'Fuzzy-Wuzzies'. Around Kassala and Gedaref a number of tribes had congregated and settled in the previous fifty years including many West Africans, the flotsam and jetsam of their 2,000-mile pilgrimage to and from Mecca. In the flat central plain, the Butana, which stretches from the river Atbara to the Nile, lived the Shukria, a camel-owning semi-nomadic Arab tribe. There was much variety of scenery too, ranging from the grey jagged peaks of the Red Sea mountains and the palms and sandy river beds around Kassala, to the open featureless plains about Gedaref, and the thick bush and broken country of the Abyssinian frontier.

My arrival in Kassala around midnight early in October gave me a first taste of the difficulties of communications in the Sudan and of one of the ingenious but simple means employed to overcome them. Between Kassala railway station and Kassala town lay the river Gash. In the winter it consisted of no more than a wide sandy depression, in which shallow wells were sunk and where cattle and goats were watered. But between July and October the rain falling in the mountains of Eritrea turned this shallow river bed into a brown swirling torrent six feet deep and more in places. It carried a rich silt and eventually spread itself in the Gash Delta, a hundred miles to the north, and provided the Beja hill tribes with a fertile area of agricultural and grazing land. There was no bridge between Kassala railway station and the town, and when the Gash was in spate — as it was that October night — the only way of getting across was seated on a wooden bedstead carried on the shoulders of four porters. The current was too swift to permit the use of a boat.

I emerged shortly after nightfall from the train which, owing to floods and washouts in the Red Sea mountains, had taken more than three days to reach Kassala from Khartoum, with no realisation that this seemingly formidable obstacle still lay between me and my final destination. I was neatly dressed in a white drill suit and a Bombay Bowler, and was the only European on the train. The Sudanese station master came to my rescue. He explained the phenomenon of the Gash flood and said that arrangements had been made for me to be carried over. With a hurricane lantern he led the way down to the river bank where a group of cheerful looking young men waited, dressed only in cotton shorts. Beside them stood a rectangular roughly hewn wooden frame, supported on four legs, and with cords closely strung back and forth across the framework. I was invited to sit cross legged in its exact centre. This was my first experience of an *angareeb* a Sudan bedstead, the equivalent of the Indian *charpoy*. For the next seventeen years in the Sudan I was to sleep on one. When provided with a cotton-filled mattress, nothing could be more comfortable provided one could ensure that the rough wooden joints were free of bedbugs.

Away on the far bank I could see lights. Four of the young men seized the legs of the *angareeb* and I was hoisted aloft. They moved carefully and slowly down the bank and into the water. It rose over their knees, it came to their waists, it drew level with their chests. It lapped against their shoulders. They went purposefully forward, exchanging a word or two, feeling their way, now with confidence now halting to test the bottom for potholes and snags. The hurricane lamp and the helpful station master had faded away behind. It was very dark and I could see little beyond the immediate swirl that marked our slow advance. The water was warm to the touch. The lights ahead seemed no nearer but there was the silhouette of palm trees against the clear sky. We were evidently approaching the middle of the river, and it was becoming deeper. These immensely powerful men extended their arms above their shoulders and raised me another six inches as the water reached their heads. It was an amazing feat of skill and strength, and knowledge of what must have been a track along the river bottom. The *angareeb* rocked but it remained securely held. And then I saw that behind us were other parties crossing the river in the same way. We were in convoy.

A quarter of an hour after we had set out the water began to fall, first to the chests, and then to the legs of my four dripping carriers. We reached the bank and I was gently lowered. There, incongruous in this setting, wearing a white dinner jacket and black evening tie, was Arthur Hankin* with the District truck. He welcomed me. The porters were paid. We drove to Hankin's house where a bed had been made up for me on the roof. I fell asleep to the sound of jackals scavenging through the sandy streets of Kassala.

The Provincial Governor, the man responsible for the peace and development of this area which was as large as Italy, was Robert (Robin) Baily.† To assist him in this task he had a deputy, four District Commissioners, and five assistants. All were British. The administrative hierarchy also included a lower rank, that of *Mamur*. The *Mamurs*, as we have seen, had originally been Egyptian officers, but were now Sudanese, and in Kassala Province there were six of them. In addition, there was a handful of medical, veterinary and other departmental officers. Baily was tall, thin and elegant, with great charm; his qualities and mannerisms were those of a kindly public school prefect. The day after my arrival in Kassala he sent for me, and spoke generally of what was expected of an administrator. As our talk drew to an end he recounted how when he had first joined the Service he had been summoned by Sir Reginald Wingate, and Wingate had impressed on him the importance, in all his dealings with the Sudanese and no matter what the circumstances, of

* A.M. Hankin, CMG, *b*. 1905, Sudan Political Service 1929–54, *d*. 1971.

† R.E.H. Baily, CBE, *b*. 1885, Sudan Political Service 1909–33, *d*. 1973. When I last saw him just before his death, a sad but amazingly alert widower in an hotel at Tewkesbury, he told me that when his contemporary batch of six probationary cadets spent their first night together on the verandah of the Sudan Club in Khartoum in 1909 each one of them, without hesitation and as a matter of course, knelt at his bedside and said his prayers. It was a practice I saw him follow on the several occasions when I was on trek with him.

courtesy. 'And I want you', Baily concluded, 'to remember that same piece of advice.' He was also full of restless energy and enthusiasm: 'Where others walked he ran, where others ran he flew,' the Hadendowa used to say of him. He had played cricket for Harrow and Cambridge, and retained a youthful delight in all games and forms of exercise. In the course of each morning a leather-bound book would be brought round the offices by a messenger boy, and we were expected to indicate against our names the particular exercise we would be taking that afternoon — squash, tennis or polo — and the games would be arranged accordingly. Failure to turn out regularly would not be favourably viewed. As a result we kept fit.

Baily was a man of idiosyncrasies. He would, for instance, entertain his guests after dinner by inviting them to sing hymns. His Sudanese butler would distribute the hymn books with the coffee, and as we sat on his lawn under the stars, Baily would select the number, give the note and lead in a rich baritone. He was a warm-hearted sympathetic man and I was fortunate to find myself in his Province for my first year in the Sudan.

During that time he sent me off, as part of my training, on two camel journeys, both of which lasted more than a month, and both of which resulted, apart from other benefits, in a marked improvement in my spoken Arabic. But while Baily as the Provincial Governor was ultimately responsible for my initial training as an administrator, my immediate tutor was to be Major E.G. Evans, the Commissioner in charge of Gedaref District.* Evans was one of those who had transferred from the Egyptian Army to the Administration. He too was a man of much restless energy; his British colleagues knew him as the *Galloping Major*, and the Sudanese, who have a great gift for producing apt nicknames, as *Abu Shabat* (a large fast-moving spider). Evans, for all that I was a civilian and must have seemed depressingly raw material, was kind to me and in my year in Gedaref I learned a great deal.

Gedaref, the headquarters of Gedaref District, was a grass-hutted town of approximately 15,000 inhabitants, more African than Arab in character and appearance. The population was a mixed lot made up of tribesmen from the surrounding area with the addition of Nigerians, Eritreans and Abyssinians. The total population of the District was about 300,000 and in area it covered, as does Scotland, 30,000 square miles. Evans's staff consisted of an Assistant District Commissioner who was British, a Sudanese *Mamur* and a Sudanese police officer. The Police Force — foot, camel and horse — totalled

* Major E.G. Evans, MC, Croix de Guerre, *b.* 1896, *d.* 1960.

about a hundred men. In the tribal areas away from Gedaref town, administration and justice rested, in accordance with tribal law and custom, mainly in the hands of the Sheikhs and their elders. In addition, Gedaref was the headquarters of the Eastern Arab Corps, one of the five battalions of the Sudan Defence Force which, together with two British regiments, were respectively responsible for the internal security and external defence of the country. The Eastern Arab Corps was mainly a camel-mounted battalion armed with rifles and a few Vickers machine-guns. In 1931 it possessed no mechanised transport. The Commanding Officers and Company Commanders were seconded from the British Army, the remaining officers and all the NCOs and men being Sudanese, the latter recruited principally from the tribes of Kassala Province. It was a smart efficient unit, discipline was good and morale was high. The battalion occupied a lightly defended hill on the edge of the town commanding the airstrip, which also served as a parade and polo ground.

Among these four or five British officers there was one who differed markedly from the rest: Orde Wingate. I got to know him, and we saw much of one another and would dine together and then sit out and talk under the stars. Stockily built, short and spare, with a large head which he carried forward on his shoulders, compelling eyes and great earnestness of manner, his appearance was more that of an untidy and absent-minded academic than of a soldier. He kept himself apart from the rest of the mess, preferring to spend as much time as he could with his troops patrolling the Abyssinian frontier, sleeping on the ground and living on dates and other local food. Here he and his men would lie in wait for and pursue the bands of ivory poachers and highwaymen who crossed the frontier from time to time. He was out of sympathy with most of his conventionally minded brother-officers, but they respected him for his dash and skill at polo, and for the fact that he had successfully completed an equitation course at Weedon. They had nicknamed him 'The Bashibazook'. He was an admirer of T.E. Lawrence, although later his loyalities became fanatically Zionist. He spoke fluent and grammatical Arabic.

Wingate was a strange moody man of refreshingly wide interests and ideas, but from what I saw of him in those days I have never been able to understand how, not many years later, he was to bewitch Winston Churchill and others. It always seemed to me that his horizons lay well beyond the bounds of reality, and that his visions were more often of alluring mirages than reliable watering places. His exploits in Palestine and Abyssinia gained him a credit that was not always endorsed by those who saw his activities at first hand. Hugh Boustead and later Field-Marshal Slim and Lord Ismay were less inclined to be carried away by the magnetism which he succeeded in exercising over others. He undoubtedly had fire in him, and a gift for dramatisation, but to many of those closest to him his subsequent reputation seemed exaggerated.

Outside Khartoum and the provincial capitals, our life was pretty austere, and I am inclined to doubt whether any European, however junior, appointed to a tropical African government today would tolerate the conditions which seemed normal to us at that time. My Gedaref house, which was built of brick and had a tin roof and a cement floor, consisted of two rooms. There was also a bathroom, but no bath and no running water. There were wooden shutters and mosquito netting in the windows, but no glass. There was no garden or verandah. A kitchen, a room for my two servants, a stable and a bucket latrine stood in different corners of the bare dusty compound. I had never had a house of my own before and was not without pride in this simple acquisition, primitive as it was. No furniture was provided in Government quarters, and so at a public auction I bought an *angareeb*, a wooden sofa, a very small dining table, a desk and two upright chairs. They cost me in all just over £E7. A carpenter made me a book-case. In the afternoons and evenings I sat in the green canvas deckchair which I had bought from Griffiths McAlister. I had neither refrigerator nor radio. Except when it rained or during the few weeks of winter, when the wind blew cold from the north, I slept, as we all did, in the open. In the summer, under one's mosquito net, a sheet was all one needed by way of covering, with a single blanket to pull up an hour or two before dawn. Not until after the war did I live in a house with electricity. In those earlier years lighting was by hurricane lamp, 'Petromax' pressure lamp or, more elegantly, by '*shamadan*'. This was a cylindrical candlestick with a spring which kept the candle gradually moving upwards as the top burnt away. The flame was protected against the wind by a glass globe, and the light was dimmed by a folding orange coloured shade, decorated with rows of small beads along the lower rim. I had bought two '*shamadans*' from Griffiths McAlister, and these lit my evening hours without going wrong or needing repair for many years.

My salary was £E40 a month, from which was deducted a pension contribution, the rent of my house and the cost of two skins of well-water which were delivered daily by an Abyssinian. I had bought a pony and was about to buy another, and so I had to buy grain and forage. My two servants, now reinforced by a groom and a kitchen lad, had to be paid and clothed. I needed a tent for touring which cost £E50, and there were various other essentials. For the first six months of my service I was in debt, but every alternate year my salary rose by £E5 a month and I was able to make ends meet. Occasionally my bank account showed a small credit, and my father persuaded me to invest in a life insurance. At no time till well after the war did I succeed in saving anything out of my salary. The fact is we were not very well paid.

Evans believed, and quite rightly, that a District Commissioner was most usefully employed away from his headquarters and among the people for whom he was responsible and that on the whole the office could look after itself. He also believed that it would be to my advantage to make an extensive tour of the district as soon as possible, and he decided that on this first occasion he would accompany me. Accordingly, and in late November, we set out for the upper reaches of the river Rahad and the Abyssinian frontier. We planned to return to Gedaref on Christmas Eve.

We had our riding camels, half a dozen beasts to carry our servants and our baggage, and we took with us an escort of three or four camel policemen. There was always the possibility of meeting armed gangs along the Abyssinian frontier. Although the weather was cool by Sudan standards and the nights were cold, we moved mostly in the early morning and the later afternoon. We aimed to pass through as many villages as possible, and the mid-day hours would thus be taken up with visiting sheikhs and other chiefs and in accepting their hospitality. This would be *abri*, a drink made of fresh limes and water to which was added pieces of unleavened bread; tea, coffee, the milk of a camel, goat or sheep, and such a generous and hospitable supply of biscuits and sweets that we were seldom able to eat our own mid-day meal. The giving and accepting of hospitality, although it seldom extended to cooked dishes which Europeans found unpalatable and difficult to digest, was a feature of our administration. It was traditional to accept the gift of a sheep or a goat if one was spending the night, and this would be slaughtered and consumed by one's followers and oneself there and then. There was much useful and friendly contact over the coffee cups and tea glasses around the fire at night.

No matter where we were, it was accepted that we always changed for dinner. Today this may seem to have been an unnecessary, even a pompous 'Imperialist' formality, but I don't think it was that. It meant that at the end of a long hot day one had a bath and put on clean clothes. Traditionally our servants did likewise if circumstances allowed. In essence it was not really very different from shaving every morning. One certainly felt better for it. Our evening clothes, particularly on trek, were simple enough: flannels or possibly white drill trousers, a white shirt, a long cummerbund to keep the stomach warm, and mosquito boots as a protection from the risk of fever. And if one wore an evening tie or even a white jacket, as we sometimes did when it was cool in winter, it was an acceptance and an indication of a standard.

The business of having a bath varied. It depended on the place. In a District or Province headquarters station you would almost certainly enjoy the convenience of a normal type of modern bath with a cold tap. The cold tap would be connected with a forty gallon drum situated somewhere against the outside wall of the bathroom. The hot water would come from two paraffin tins which would have been heated over a wood fire and then tipped into the bath by one's kitchen lad. On trek we bathed in a folding affair made of green canvas slung within a wooden frame, in which one sat crosslegged. But there were times when there was not enough water to have a bath at all.

A week after leaving Gedaref we approached the river Rahad which flows north-westwards out of Abyssinia to join the Blue Nile. In the summer flood the Rahad, like all the rivers of the Eastern Sudan, swirls and cascades between its high wooded banks, brown and rich with silt. In full and sudden spate it can be deadly. But in winter, when the Abyssinian highlands are without rain, it is reduced to a line of pools linked by a gentle trickle along the sand and rocks of the thalweg. We had slept that night at the foot of a granite outcrop and I had woken early. Before we were due to mount and move off, but with light enough to see the way, I climbed the hill. Covered with the thorn scrub which yields gum arabic, a source of income to much of the central belt of the Sudan, the brown-patterned plain stretched monotonously to the horizon. A faint line of dark green marked the serpentine course of the river. Immediately below the hill lay a village of grass huts. I sat on a boulder, glad of the warmth of a thick sweater under my khaki tunic, to watch the early morning life of these people, a scene which in the years to come was to grow so familiar. There was a group of women drawing water from the well, and I could catch faintly, and without understanding, the sound of their voices punctuated by laughter. A donkey brayed, and then another and another. A dog barked. The smoke of cooking fires lay in blue horizontal wisps like a thin still morning mist. It carried with it a sharp acrid smell, a smell that once experienced is never forgotten and which, for me, calls back memories of Africa and other distant places more distinctly than anything I know. How pleasantly the memory lingers, how sharply it returns the moment the sense identifies it anew. And each smell has its own particular memory: cooking fires in Arabia, whether of thorn scrub or camel dung; the tang of far distant rain after months of drought and the strong redolence of parched earth absorbing the first and violent downpour, which is almost more of a taste affecting the throat than a scent in the nostrils; the heavy smell of sheep and camels gathered about the wells; and the breathtakingly sweet scent of mimosa in Africa and of orange blossom in Palestine. But there are sounds too that bring back the past: sounds of animals and of men, of great herds of camels and of cattle near and distant, of violent wind at night rising suddenly and as suddenly falling; of tropical rain beating on corrugated iron and stretched canvas; of the cries of duck and geese and the croaking of frogs; the singing of a lonely herdsman; the coughing roar of a lion; the braying of donkeys at night, each taking up the cry from the other; the call of cocks an hour before dawn; and the call from the minaret.

Three men led out and mounted their donkeys, tucking up their knee-length gowns, and moved off towards the patchwork areas of farmland that lay scattered unevenly amid the thorn scrub. Their legs stuck out on either side of their diminutive beasts swinging rhythmically with the animals' pacing. Each carried a short-handled hoe balanced on his shoulder. A camel was being loaded; with open mouth, eyes half closed and head thrown back, it roared in outraged protest. These were the sights and the scenes that from now on I would come to witness daily. The soft greens and browns of the rain-washed English countryside were behind me. I wondered how far and how quickly I would come to identify myself with a completely new set of interests and affections and loyalties. I turned and looked down the hill. Our camels were being saddled and they too were protesting. Evans was talking to the Police Sergeant. I scrambled down the rocks and joined them.

In the weeks that followed I began to understand something of what was expected of a District Commissioner on tour and to learn something of what he did. At each village there would be talk of the harvest, of the need to open a motor track or construct a river crossing. Trucks were beginning to take the place of camels and donkeys as an economical means of transport. There would be demands for a new or deeper well, a dispensary, a village school or a market. There would be complaints and petitions, sometimes written but more often taking the form of a long involved protest, the speaker sitting on the ground and punctuating his story in marks and patterns on the sand with finger or camel stick. The Sudanese seldom shrank from claiming what they believed to be their rights. Sometimes they would present the case quietly, and perhaps with artfully contrived suppression of the truth or suggestion of the false, at other times with vehemently loud and passionate insistence. And sometimes a man's supporters would echo and give emphasis to his claim with cries of 'By God, what he says is true, by God he has been oppressed.' The local courts, presided over by the paramount sheikh of each area and his elders, dealt with the majority of cases, but there was always the right of appeal to the representative of the Government. We dealt with a number of such cases.

As the days passed, our party moved up the Rahad, crossed to the Dinder which lies parallel to it, and then as we drew near to the Abyssinian border we turned north-eastwards towards the frontier post at Gallabat. It was fine game country. The rivers were full of crocodiles and we caught sight of elephant and giraffe. Herds of eighty to a hundred gazelle would sweep through the tall dry grass ahead of our column. There was an occasion when a leopard sprang upon the last of the herd to pass, and then at the sudden and unexpected appearance of our leading camelmen, turned and fled, abandoning its victim. Quickly our men cut the gazelle's throat, invoking God's name, and it provided us with our dinner. As we turned away from the rivers the country changed. The heavy shady trees and the stretches of watermeadow, fed by pools along the banks, gave way first to an area of rough country with gravel underfoot and rocky outcrops, and then to forests of acacia and thorn. We came across the hurriedly abandoned camp of a party of ivory poachers. Their fires were still smouldering, and alongside them lay scores of boxes of matches, their heads removed to make a substitute for gunpowder which was hard to come by.

Our maps of this part of the country included a number of unsurveyed areas and we made a route report, sketched in with compass bearings to and from the hills along our track, and linked, when we could identify them, with the known but distant peaks that lay beyond the frontier.

We rode into Gallabat on the morning of Christmas Eve, a long straggling and rather dishevelled party, to be met by the only Englishman living there, the Commander of the Sudan Defence Force garrison. We were the first Europeans he had seen for over six weeks and he welcomed us with a gargantuan breakfast. He was to die with so many others of his regiment (the Rifle Brigade) at the defence of Dunkirk seven years later.

A fair motor track connected Gallabat with Gedaref. As the sun set we covered the last 100 miles of our 500 mile journey by car. Gedaref lies in a gentle hollow in the plain and as we came near, a golden haze of dust lay over the town. Cattle and goats were returning from their grazing grounds. As they followed their herdsmen into the sandy streets, straight and neatly lined with high grass fences surrounding each compound, every animal turned by instinct into its own familiar doorway to be milked and penned for the night. At dawn next day, the herdsman would pass on his outward way and lead them back to their grazing on the stubbles or the stony dry grass plain beyond. The smoke of cooking fires rose into the still air. There was the smell of roasting coffee beans and the resonant hollow throb as the women pounded corn for the evening meal. The *muezzin* cried his call to prayer. I thought of my friends who followed the Heythrop. They would be hacking home along wet and darkening roads from their Christmas Eve meet at Stow-on-the-Wold or Burford.

I spent the greater part of my time during the weeks that followed working in the Gedaref office, and learning something of District Headquarters routine. I sat as a spectator in the local tribal court; I was instructed in the correct way of checking the safe and the accounts; I attended police parades; I visited the prison twice a week and saw that the cells were swept and disinfected and the kitchen clean. Police animals, horses and camels, and all privately owned beasts of burden working in Gedaref town were inspected weekly, and any considered unfit were sent to the veterinary lines for treatment. The town sweepers, the public water-carriers and the horse-drawn carts were paraded for periodic inspection. And on every Saturday morning at 7 o'clock the administrative officers, the Police officer, the doctor and the chief of the sanitary men rode through the town to make sure that the sweepers were at work, that all rubbish was burnt, that the incinerators were in order, that the newly planted trees along the streets were watered and protected from goats, that the meat in the butcher's shop was properly covered with lengths of muslin and that the public latrines were washed clean with plenty of Jeyes fluid. There was much flurry and activity. For the rest of the week these things followed a quieter and less hygienic course.

Our formal office hours were from nine until two every day except Friday, the Muslim holiday. But much work was done outside the office. We rose at six and generally did an hour or two, often on horseback, before breakfast; and as a rule there was something to be seen to between sunset and dinner time. Almost all our spoken work was in Arabic. The Accounts Office and the Treasury kept their records in Arabic but much of the correspondence was in English.

A District Headquarters was normally laid out in the form of a quadrangle surrounded by a low stone wall. Within the compound were situated the Treasury, the police armoury and orderly rooms, the lock-up, the offices of the District Commissioner, the *Mamur* and the clerks, the *Qadi*'s court and the District storerooms. A sentry and a guard of five policemen were responsible for security. The Condominium flags flew over the guard room and were lowered at sunset while the bugler played the Last Post. Each morning when the District Commissioner appeared, whether at seven o'clock or thereabouts on his early morning ride or alternatively at nine when the offices opened to the public, the Police Guard turned out, again the bugler sounded the appropriate call and the Guard was inspected. It all made for a certain standard of smartness, a sense of responsibility and an air of authority.

During office hours all manner of people passed freely and continually in and out of the compound. The verandahs surrounding the various offices would be crowded with townsmen and tribesmen, and often with little parties of women and children. There would be those who had business with the *Qadi* — a divorce or a disputed will. Around the police office there was always a crowd; those involved in court cases, men volunteering for recruitment, contractors for the provision of police stores or the repair of police houses. Men of substance and position came regularly to call on the more senior officials, if only to take a cup of coffee and pass the time of day. Petitioners and complainants on a hundred and one matters would be gathered about the District Commissioner's or the *Mamur*'s office. If a criminal trial was proceeding there would be a dozen or more witnesses waiting their turn to be called, sitting around the compound in the shade of the wild fig or the neem trees. An officially stamped petition, which was often the first step in a case brought in the *Qadi*'s or the Civil Court, cost two and a half piastres or sixpence. And because few could write, there sat crosslegged on the ground, with a low wooden table before him equipped with inkpot and reed pen or steel nib, the licenced petition writer, deep in consultation with his client. Outside the Post Office there would be a letter writer. Save only on Fridays, it was a scene of great activity. Every man with a grievance, or a claim, or a curiosity to satisfy was there. It was a safety valve, a clearing house, a focus, a place where news and ideas were exchanged. It was well called *Al Merkaz* — the centre.

Social life in Gedaref was limited. From time to time there were tea parties given by the Sudanese officers of the Sudan Defence Force, or by the Sudanese civil officials at their club. At these gatherings the Eastern Arab Corps Band, preserving the balance of the Condominium, would render alternatively airs from long forgotten London musical comedies and Egyptian or Turkish military marches. And when the party ended they would play both national anthems. On Thursday nights Eric Evans and I would dine in the British officers' mess. A long whisky and one or two pink gins before dinner, with nothing to drink but water during the meal, was the rule. We seldom drank wine. On these occasions a Sudanese soldier would march round the table with considerable swagger and formality playing the bagpipes. Afterwards we sat in the open air in canvas-backed chairs until our host called for a long glass of water for each guest. This was the signal for departure.

We played tennis now and again on a cracked cement court, and polo twice a week. Most of the dozen or so polo players were Defence Force officers, British and Sudanese, but Evans and the Egyptian doctor and also, dutifully although his heart was never in it, Abdul Raziq Ibrahim the *Mamur* took part. Some of the Sudanese enjoyed the game, but some played it because in those days a confidential report which contained a reference to enthusiasm for polo could help a man's career be he British or Sudanese. I was a keen but ineffective player, hanging on the outskirts of the fray and shouting 'yours'. My two ponies were slow and hard-mouthed, nor had I quite the thrust to compete with the four or five British officers whose dash and loud and urgent cries of 'leave it' or 'ride the man' I found somewhat intimidating. I imagine most of the Sudanese players felt likewise. It was difficult for them to see polo in the same light as we did. A Sudanese officer who vied with his British Company Commander in drive and imprecation, who rode him off or shouted 'mine' and meant it, would in fact have earned much respect. But most of them in those days had been brought up in a different tradition. They had inherited a Turco-Egyptian deference to rank and position which deemed it advisable to let one's superior prevail, even in games. These attitudes led sometimes to unhappy feelings and a sense of grievance.

The first independent task that Evans gave me was to take a party of men and make a motorable road through the deeply eroded sandy cliffs that bordered both sides of the Bahr As Salam river. The Bahr As Salam rises in Abyssinia and eventually reaches the main Nile near Atbara. It was a country of thorn scrub seamed by steep ravines and dry water courses. During the rains these would be impassable in any event, but we were thinking of the dry season when all lorry traffic from Kassala to Gedaref was bound to pass through this difficult stretch. As it was, the ravines and the soft going along the river bank involved long delays while vehicles were dug out, and pushed and coaxed through the worst places with the help of sand tracks, or with the branches of trees or grass placed under the wheels. I had with me a police corporal who knew the area well, and we enlisted the willing help of the Sheikh of the neighbouring village. We took with us an adequate supply of axes and spades, and mattocks and grass baskets for carrying earth.

I had my tent and we set up a camp. We spent the first few days riding up and down the ravines, reconnoitering a trace that would follow, as far as possible, the black clay soil ('cotton soil'), and finding a route through the cliffs that would enable us to cut a serpentine motorable track which would not be too precipitous. And where soft sandy stretches were unavoidable we searched for a sufficiently solid type of gravel with which to make a foundation and a firm surface. We worked from six in the morning till mid-day, and from three in the afternoon till sunset. Most evenings the Corporal and I would go over to Sheikh Abdelrahman Ali's village for tea and coffee and a talk. He was a fine old man who had seen much adventure and violence in his early life. These evening helped to improve my still faltering Arabic.

Our mission took us a fortnight to complete, and we returned to Gedaref with the satisfactory feeling that in a small way we had achieved something. The rains when they came would demolish more than half of what we had done but I was to learn that this was a feature of much of our work not only in road building. We were continually seeing the things we sought to do destroyed and building them up again 'with worn out tools'.

During the two or three previous years the Sudan and other neighbouring countries had suffered severely from the depredations of vast swarms of locusts. They had swept over the country like an invading army consuming trees, shrubs, grazing and crops. A number of methods had been tried with greater or lesser success in attempting to defeat them; these tactics included first the identification of breeding areas, and the destruction of the eggs which were laid and hatched in the warm sand, and secondly the poisoning, and burning and burying in trenches of the young crawling locusts, the hoppers. Once they had reached the stage of being able to fly they became invincible.

In 1932 we expected and prepared for a further invasion. It came, but with less severity than in previous years. Nevertheless, even a single swarm was an awe-inspiring sight. One would first see what appeared to be an approaching dust storm. Gradually the grey-brown cloud would advance, and the sky overhead would be dark with millions of flying creatures, silent except for the soft hissing murmur of their wings. Tens of thousands would settle and start consuming whatever vegetation existed. In no time every tree and bush would be stripped, and every sign of vegetation and greenery would have disappeared. Hundreds of thousands would pass on, as if directed by some overall controlling command, to ravage whatever lay ahead. The swarms were followed by flocks of storks and other birds which gorged themselves on locusts until they could eat no more, but much as we welcomed these allies, they made no impact on the enemy. Villagers tried to keep the swarms away from their crops by banging empty petrol tins and other similar devices. Their efforts availed little. How graphically and how accurately the author of the Book of Exodus described the plague of locusts in Egypt in Moses' time: '*And they shall cover the face of the earth that one cannot be able to see the earth . . . and they shall eat every tree that groweth for you out of the field.*' More than three thousand years later in the Sudan trains were frequently brought to a stop by the thousands of locusts that met their death on the lines and in doing so prevented the engine wheels from gripping the track. At times the swarms were so dense that it was impossible to see to drive a car. Enterprising villagers collected baskets of locusts and fried and ate them. It was the only benefit that came from this plague.

Throughout 1933 and 1934 we were ready for a fresh invasion. Stores of poisoned bran which the hoppers consumed avidly were distributed and held at tactical points throughout every administrative district, together with tools to destroy the breeding areas. But although there were outbreaks and some districts were attacked, the invasion was never as extensive as it had been before.

In the years that followed, well organised anti-locust teams led by entomologists operated throughout the Middle East and gradually succeeded first in containing and finally in overcoming the menace of this recurrent plague. The desert breeding grounds were identified and the young were destroyed before they were able to come to maturity. By the end of the 1940s the locusts had been finally conquered.

I tried my first case, concerning the theft of a camel saddle, two or three months after my arrival in Gedaref. Evans had gone off for a few days and left me in charge. The case was ready, the witnesses were hanging around, and the accused was in prison awaiting trial. I felt that I ought to have a go, but I made a complete mess of it. I framed the charge incorrectly, and under the wrong clause of the Criminal Code. I failed to bring out essential points in the evidence both for the prosecution and the defence. The record of the case went off to Kassala for confirmation or revision by the Province Judge* and the Governor. They must have been dismayed at the number of legal mistakes I had managed to make. In due course the papers came back to Gedaref. 'The learned magistrate', the Province Judge minuted, 'has misdirected himself.' I was greatly impressed by this example of legal courtesy and phraseology. But I was also firmly bidden to study the Penal Code and the Code of Criminal Procedure with greater diligence, and the Governor's

* He was Eric Flemming-Sands, a man of particular charm and gentleness. He had won the VC in 1917 in France.

covering letter to Evans ordered him to instruct me more closely before permitting me again to try my hand alone.

A few weeks later a case arose in which five Abyssinians waylaid and murdered a Sudanese merchant on the road to Gallabat. They were traced, arrested, tried and found guilty. It had been a particularly brutal and callous affair and they were sentenced to death. The sentence was confirmed by the Governor-General. The condemned men were kept together in a separate cell of the prison until such time as they could be sent to Kassala for execution for there was no gallows in Gedaref. The cell had a single small barred and shuttered window, seven or eight feet from the floor, that gave on to the outside of the prison. The weather was hot, and as the window provided the only means of ventilation, the shutter was left open. The Prison Sergeant and I had examined the cell on our routine Sunday morning inspection, and had tested the bars. But the condemned men had compatriots in the town who on the same night tossed a file through the window into the cell. The escape was discovered at dawn. We felt sure that they would make for the Abyssinian frontier, the nearest point of which was a hundred miles away. They would certainly have been supplied with water skins by their friends, but it was unlikely that they would be able to carry enough to support them that far. Sooner or later they would have to get water from the river, the Bahr As Salam, or from one of the few village wells, and because they would need to avoid roads and tracks they would have to make their way through the bush. And at that time of the year the bush was waterless.

The police tracker had already succeeded in following the route taken by the five men to the outskirts of Gedaref but had then lost the trail. Small parties of mounted police set out first to warn all the village sheikhs between Gedaref and the frontier; and then to scour the countryside with local help. I took the district truck to the nearest point on the Bahr As Salam and followed the river up to the frontier, warning the villages on the banks. Being foreigners the fugitives were unlikely to find aid or refuge on the Sudan side of the border. And so it proved. They tried to make their way back to Abyssinia through a dry wilderness of thorn bush. By the third day, when they had covered half the distance, their water had given out. They had attempted with little success to find moisture from the roots of shrubs. On the fifth day a police corporal saw a group of vultures circling in the sky and he noticed that their numbers were steadily increasing. He saw too that they were losing height. He and his party of two men rode all afternoon. At sunset they found what they were looking for. These relentless and ever watchful scavengers were already on the ground lumbering, ungainly, silent and watching.

Nearby, four of the Abyssinians were already dead. The fifth was alive and conscious. He died on the gallows in Kassala a couple of weeks later.

Baily, the Governor, visited us in March and as a result I was sent off on my first independent camel trek. I was to ride east to the Atbara river, cross to the Setit at the point where it enters the Sudan on the Abyssinian-Eritrean border, and then follow the river down to a point south of Khashm El Girba. I was to make a survey of the possible crossings on the two rivers. From Khashm El Girba or thereabouts I was to ride east to the Eritrean frontier and thence to Kassala. I was to keep a diary, make a route report with sketches and compass bearings, and survey a trace for a motor road to connect Kassala town with the Atbara along the line, if I could find it, of the old Italian road which had existed forty years before when Italy had administered all this area of the frontier. I was, of course, to take every opportunity of seeing the people who lived in the country I would be passing through. This expedition, which took several weeks, improved my spoken Arabic and gave me my first taste of sitting over a fire at night listening to the elders of the village talking of the past, and of the trials and uncertainties of life in the days before the battle of Omdurman. Their lined dark brown faces were full of resignation, and their eyes bright with humour and kindliness. We would sit late drinking sweet tea from little glasses, and as the embers died, fresh logs would be thrown on to the fire. Beyond the circle of light lay the camels. The sky was bright with stars, Orion overhead, the Plough low on the horizon. And when we woke, as we did each morning at 5 or earlier, there was the Southern Cross.

Although we had brought a few basic supplies with us — tea, sugar, coffee, flour, onions and some tins of sardines — we relied for fresh meat on what I was able to shoot. There were plenty of gazelle. But I found little pleasure in shooting these graceful and gentle creatures great numbers of which were to be found all over this part of the country. I preferred to keep our party supplied with guinea fowl, but these are difficult to bring down on the wing and being swift runners are often unapproachable on the ground. But at dusk they will congregate in the thorn trees with much clamour and it was often easy to secure several with a single shot as they sat silhouetted against the sunset. I used to give my 12-bore to one of the police escort and he seldom returned with less than four birds for every cartridge he had fired.

At Gira, which lies on the Setit, lions had taken a number of cattle and I was pressed to shoot one. They frequented the thick bush and high grass along the river banks and we had heard their calls at night, that deep coughing repeated bark which cannot fail to send a small chill down one's spine. The rifle I had was really too light for lion, but with the support of a policeman armed with a .303 I felt that it would look bad to refuse. I remembered those stern-faced men looking down from the picture frames on the staircase at Griffiths McAlister's, this was the least they would expect. We set off just before dawn; there were four of us, myself, the corporal policeman, a villager carrying an enormous axe on his shoulders like a mediaeval executioner, and a guide. The guide, like General Gordon campaigning in China, was content with the protection of a light cane. Either he was sceptical of finding a lion or he had great confidence in our marksmanship. From sunrise till nearly midday we pursued our way, whispering, on tip toe, pausing to listen and peer from time to time, and in single file along a maze of paths which ran up and down the cliffs and ravines and dry water courses that fringed the Atbara. It was difficult country, thick with high grass and bush and creepers. We found fresh lion tracks and lost them. It grew increasingly hot. After five hours we had had enough. I shot two crocodiles. They had been taking the village goats and although honour was thus not perhaps entirely satisfied it was not completely lost. In all the time I spent in the Sudan I never, to my regret, saw a lion.

The rivers were full of crocodiles. Flying in an open plane over the Settit and Bahr As Salam in 1932 I could see them in scores, lying side by side in regular ranks on the mud at the edge of the water. They frequently took men or women washing in the shallows, or children filling their water jars, and I was once lucky not to become a victim. I had spent the night in a village on the Settit, and after breakfast I sought a retired and secluded spot. The only decent cover was on the river bank half a dozen yards from the edge of the water. I lit my pipe and settled down facing the river. It was fortunate that I chose that direction of outlook for as I gazed towards the water, my mind on other things, I saw a very slight ripple. A moment later, there in the shallows just off shore like a small periscope was the tip of a snout and just beyond, the two projections that marked the eyes. The tactic that crocodiles adopt when seeking a human or animal victim close to the water's edge, as I knew, is to approach stealthily and submerged and then suddenly to launch themselves ashore and fling their prey into the water with an encircling and enormously powerful lash of the tail. Conscious only of my safety I beat an immediate and undignified retreat.

On the last day of our exploration of the river banks south of Khashm El Girba we gave ourselves a holiday. The frontier and Kassala lay four days ride away and for the first three we would need to take our water with us. We spent the day by the river bathing and watching the baboons, and a family of hippos that basked in the centre of the stream showing only the tips of their noses and ears. Where the tangled green thorn bushes lay along the banks, their lower branches touching the water and creating a thin wake, hundreds of small birds clustered at mid-day. Here they jostled for places from which, perilously, they could dip their beaks and drink. And here too the crocodiles glided silently below, swiftly and suddenly raising their long jaws to snatch a mouthful of a dozen small victims.

The men washed their shirts and drawers and laid them out on the rocks to dry. The country was thinly inhabited here, and there were no villages within a dozen miles. Next morning an hour before dawn we climbed, leading our camels, through the sandy cliffs bordering the Atbara and made our way up on to the tableland. I glanced back at the river in the clear early light as it flowed gently, fringed with palms and wild figs, on its way northwards to join the Nile. Half an hour later the sun came up into our eyes. Ahead lay a wide expanse of yellow grass and beyond that a long line of thorn scrub. A hundred miles to the north stood the grey blue domes and peaks of Jebel Kassala. Four days later we rode into the town at sunset.

Baily kept me in Kassala so that I might gain more experience of magisterial work. The examinations in Higher Arabic and Law were held in Khartoum every January and a pass in both was necessary before a Political Officer could be confirmed in his appointment and qualify for his first salary increment. One failure was allowed, but a second one meant an end to one's service. A pass in Law was also essential before an officer's magisterial powers could be extended to qualify him to sit as a President of a Major Court, which had authority to try all cases including murder. I felt confident that my Arabic was making good progress, but without the experience of trying minor cases and preparing more important ones for trial, I was unlikely to pass Law. So I welcomed this opportunity.

In appearance Kassala was more an Arab than an African town. Many of its buildings were of sun-dried brick, rectangular and whitewashed. The streets were sandy, shaded by palms and by avenues of *neem*, a swift-growing evergreen which smells sweet when it is in summer flower. The market provided for the needs of visiting tribesmen. The merchants, light-skinned men from the North, from Dongola, Halfa and Berber, sold salt, sugar, coffee, soap and cotton piece goods. There were makers of camel saddles and of scarlet leather slippers. There were the stalls of corn merchants and the booths in which the ironsmiths worked. The market smelt of burning incense and the shops of spices. Above the town the vultures and kites circled endlessly. I was allotted a small house beside the prison, more comfortable than my Gedaref quarter and it had something of a garden. There were oleanders and bougainvilia, and a bed of red cannas and pink periwinkles which was irrigated by the bath water outlet. But the house had one disadvantage in that there was a lunatic in the prison who howled all night like a dog, and so long as the weather was hot and I had my bed on the roof this poor man's sad clamour made sleep difficult.

The Deputy Provincial Governor was Douglas Newbold,* a man under whom I was later to serve for nearly five years. I had first met Newbold after I had applied for the Sudan but some months before I was selected. He and Martin Parr had invited me to lunch in London and to see the film of *The Four Feathers* which had recently been shot in the Red Sea hills where Newbold had been serving as a District Commissioner. Perhaps the invitation was part of the initial process of vetting and assessment. Newbold was a bachelor, a scholar and an administrator of great imagination and humanity. When he died in Khartoum as Civil Secretary in 1945, worn out by the pressure and anxiety of the war years, he had done more than any single man to create the framework of the modern Sudan and to establish a close and friendly relationship with the educated and politically minded Sudanese. And perhaps more than any other man he symbolised the spirit and mystique of the Sudan Political Service. Seeing him for the first time few would have taken him for a colonial administrator. Short, but strongly built, walking with a slight limp, resulting for a First World War wound, with dark eyebrows and dome-headed, Newbold was a brilliantly witty talker and a master of the written word. I know no one who gave his friendship so generously or who had a greater gift for inspiring those who worked under him, both British and Sudanese. I was fortunate in seeing much of him during those few months, and even more fortunate in coming later to serve under him in Kordofan.

Those who have lived in desert or in semi-arid countries preserve for the rest of their lives a very different attitude to rain from those who have dwelt elsewhere. For rain, be it on the desert, on dry hillsides or on sand-dunes, can mean the difference between near-starvation and, for a season or two, comparative prosperity. As the long summer runs its course and the first clouds begin to build up, men grow restive and anxious. First come the dust-storms and then there is the sound of distant thunder and a tantalising smell of rain. If at dusk the clouds melt away and there is no rain, you are left feeling exhausted and irritated. The first falls bring immense relief,

* Sir Douglas Newbold, KBE, *b.* 1894, *d.* 1945. Civil Secretary, Sudan Government 1939–45. His achievements and many of his brilliant letters have been recorded in J.K.K. Henderson's *The Making of the Modern Sudan.*

but thereafter the concern is that the rain will come at regular intervals, and sufficiently heavily, to ensure a good harvest. Will the grazing be rich? Will the open water holes fill? Will the underground sources be enough to ensure that the wells will last through the coming year? The whole appearance of the countryside changes dramatically after two or three heavy falls. Where there was sand or baked clay, yellow and brown, harsh and barren, suddenly there is meadowland and wild flowers and shallow open pools reflecting the sky. Where there was a rock-strewn ravine fringed with dry thorn there is a brown tumbling torrent, and the thorn has become a burgeoning shrub. Where there was a heap of black boulders there is suddenly a carpet of deep grass and creepers. It is all a miracle. Small wonder that men in countries such as these have seen in the rain the act of a male sky god fertilising a mother earth. The first rains, incidentally, brought to us the migrant Abdin storks, circling gracefully through the air. They built their nests and raised their young in every village, and no one molested them, because they brought good fortune.

The first storm came to Kassala in mid-July, the rain tearing through the palm trees and flooding the streets. Further south the rains had come earlier and the nomad tribes from the Rahad and the Dinder, the Rufaa, the Kenana, the Lahawin and others had begun their annual migration north in search of fresh grazing. An area of over ten thousand square miles, flat and featureless save for a few rocky outcrops, lies between the Blue Nile and the Atbara. This vast plain, known as the Butana, had been set aside by agreement among the tribes as a common grazing area in which boundaries, movements and other conditions had been accepted. Disputes and conflicts were not uncommon during the months when these pastures were shared, and so that differences might be more quickly settled and peace preserved, it was the custom for a Political Officer to move and live among the tribesmen for a month or two. To my delight I was selected for this task, and Baily gave me the following instructions:

> You will tour the Butana for two months between mid-July and mid-September. You should call upon Sheikh Awad al Kerim Abu Sinn, the paramount Sheikh of the Shukria, at Khashm-el-Girba and discuss with him where he would like you to go and what he thinks you should look out for particularly. You should arrange liaison between his patrols and yours. You will make yourself word perfect in the regulations governing the use of patrols in the area. If the grazing is good it will be best for you to travel slowly and let your camels graze as much as possible. You should take with you Acland's treatise on camels, a work crammed with information, and his

notes on the Butana.* You should also take your Arabic copy of the *Thousand and One Nights*, stories from which you should learn by heart and repeat to your camp fire circles. You should live chiefly on camels' milk which, when the grass is fresh and green, is delicious. You should do a lot of topography and look at water holes, existing and potential. You must of course keep a detailed diary. Finally you must go to the top of Mundera Hill and enter alone into the cave, and there you must wish, but you must never tell your wish to a mortal person.

I left Kassala towards the end of July with seven camels and an escort of three camel policemen. I took a tent and a camp bed, a large box of medical stores and a rifle. For reading matter I had the Bible, Shakespeare, the *Arabian Nights* in Arabic and an Arabic Grammar. In the weeks that followed I rode over 500 miles. I learnt to drink camel's milk warm from the mare, and to eat sitting on the ground and using my fingers with sheikhs and herdsmen. I did a great deal of rough and ready medical work. Although there were few disputes or problems, at times it was hard going. We would move off from our host's encampment an hour before dawn, and we rode till dusk — or walked if the camels were tired — halting only for meals. There were rain storms nearly every afternoon and we had difficulty in deep mud and in crossing wide and swift-flowing spates. Few days passed without our baggage and ourselves being soaked. Snakes and scorpions were a constant menace. But there was much to compensate for all this. At times the scene was intensely beautiful. We would ride for miles through deep grass, white with convolvulus blossom, seemingly richer than any English meadow, and across these pastures moved immense herds of grazing camels and their young. We enjoyed the hospitality and comradeship of warm-hearted, humorous people. I followed Baily's instructions and read much of the Old Testament; and I made my wish at the top of Mundera Hill. I returned to Kassala early in September to learn that I had been posted, temporarily, to act as District Commissioner in Khartoum.

Although I was glad at being free, after three months, to return to Gedaref, Khartoum provided a useful experience. As I sat in the comfortable railway carriage which took me away from Kassala I was rather apprehensive about this new type of work. I was pleased to feel that after a year in the Sudan I had been judged sufficiently capable to be given a job which, if not particularly arduous or difficult, was more responsible than anything I had done hitherto;

* P.B.E. Acland, OBE, MC, joined the Sudan Political Service in 1924 and after service in the Sudan Defence Force during the war retired in 1946. His second son was to serve with me in Kuwait twenty-four years later, and as Sir Antony Acland is now Permanent Under Secretary of State at the Foreign and Commonwealth Office and Head of the Diplomatic Service.

but I wondered how well I would be able to adjust myself to a new set of tasks and problems. I had no experience of work in a large town and Khartoum was a city with trams, cinemas and European-type shops and restaurants, with a cosmopolitan community and its social life.

I was given an impressive office. I found myself involved in assessing business profits taxes, evaluating rates on private and commercial property, and issuing motorcar, trading and bicycle licences. I was responsible for the censorship of cinema films. My office with its correspondence and its many callers kept me busy. I spent an hour daily on my law books and took every opportunity to sit on the bench with Tom Maclagan,* the Police magistrate. Tewfik Khabbaz, a member of a prominent Khartoum Lebanese family, taught me Arabic for three afternoons a week, giving me hand-written petitions to decipher and proses to translate.

The Arabic and law examinations were to be held early in January, but my temporary spell in Khartoum came to an end late in November and I returned to Gedaref, glad to be away but satisfied in the thought that I had run Khartoum District alone. I had made some mistakes but none so serious that I had been unable to rectify them when told. And in January I came back to Khartoum for the examinations and passed in both the Arabic and the Law.

Although I was later to be invited to join the Legal Department, it was Arabic which, since I had started to learn it under Dewhurst at Oxford, remained an enduring and indeed a lifelong interest. I was to be fortunate in the next twenty-five years or more to find myself in circumstances where a wider knowledge of the language came almost automatically my way. And because I found it so fascinating and rewarding, I took as many occasions as I could to improve it. Not that one can ever say that one knows Arabic. The vocabulary is so vast, the grammar so complicated and the sounds so difficult, that unless one works at it steadily and continually one goes backwards. As an indication of the difficulty of the language, perhaps one cannot do better than repeat a distinguished scholar's remark that every Arabic word has at least five meanings. First there is the word's original meaning; then there is a meaning which is the exact opposite of that; then there is a meaning which is generally only used in poetry and has nothing to do with either of the first two; fourthly there is a meaning that has some sort of connection with a camel, and finally, he suggests, there is a meaning too improper to be translated. And there is something in the thought which he also suggests that perhaps

* T.A. Maclagan, *b.* 1904, *d.* 1978. Joined Political Service 1926. Legal Dept. 1936. Chief Justice 1947–50. Invalided 1950.

one of the reasons why many Englishmen get on well with Arabs is because they find Arabic so difficult that trying to master it knocks some of the conceit out of them.

I was beginning to think of my leave. I was due to go in March, and I had been told that on my return I would be posted to Kordofan Province. Kordofan, which lies west of the Nile, had an enviable reputation. It had almost become a tradition that a spell there was an essential foundation to a successful career and that the Governor of Kordofan became, in due course, Civil Secretary. There had just been a change of Governor and Douglas Newbold had taken over the Province from J.A. Gillan,* who was about to succeed MacMichael as Civil Secretary.

I had come out to the Sudan by way of the Red Sea and Port Sudan, and returned to England by the Nile Valley. From Khartoum there was first of all a train journey of twenty-four hours to Wadi Halfa, which marked the Sudan-Egyptian frontier. This was the route, in reverse, that Kitchener's army had taken in 1898, leading to the battle of Omdurman and the reoccupation of the Sudan. It was a route that consisted of three hundred miles following the course of the Nile and then another three hundred or so across the Baiyuda desert in which the stations had no names but merely numbers. The long white-painted Sudan trains running on a narrow gauge of three feet, six inches, seldom went faster than thirty miles an hour. At times the heat was severe and the dust all-pervading, but one enjoyed a comfortable sleeper with a washbasin and an electric fan. The dining car served excellent meals and the menu always included Nile perch — as one normally did not taste fish from one year to the next, this was a great luxury. The compartment attendant went up and down the corridor pumping away at his 'Flit' gun ('Flit' was an early insecticide). The endless desert or the unbroken view of thorn scrub slipped slowly past. There were leisurely stops at every station, where crowds of passengers got on and off laden with their household goods. Sellers of eggs, bread and fruit held their wares up to the passengers at the carriage windows, and always there were a few travellers who hurried to fill their tea-pots with hot water from the engine. If the train came to a station around sunset, it would wait while the pious stood and knelt at prayer beside the track. In the rains there were times when the earth embankments were washed away, or the culverts damaged, and then there could be a wait of a day or more while gangs got to work to put things right.

At Wadi Halfa one left the train and took the stern-wheel paddle-steamer. This stage of the journey took two days — of peace and

* Sir Angus Gillan, KBE, CMG, *b*. 1885, *d*. 1981. Sudan Political Service 1909–39.

great comfort. Beyond the green banks of the dark silt-laden river, half a mile wide in places, narrower where cliffs took the place of dunes, was the desert. To the east it stretched unbroken to the Red Sea, and to the west lay the Sahara.

Aswan provided a striking contrast to the calm and order and dignity of what lay behind us, we were now in Egypt with its noise and dirt and flies and confusion. At Aswan beggars and touts pestered one to buy fly whisks and souvenirs and antiques. But once the train set off north the flat countryside was green and rich in corn fields and palm groves. The sun would be setting as we left Aswan; we reached Cairo soon after dawn.

Ten days after leaving Khartoum I met my parents at Naples.

3
THE WESTERN SUDAN
(Kordofan and the Nuba Mountains, 1933–1938)

And so, in the summer of 1933 and at the end of my first leave, I found myself posted to Kordofan, which differed from Kassala principally in that its southern districts were closer to the Equator and were therefore less arid and more African than Arab in character. But like Kassala it stood on the direct pilgrim route from West Africa to Mecca, and thereby constituted a meeting place between the African and Arab worlds. A distance of 450 miles separated Kordofan's northern and southern boundaries. The northern boundary ran along the 17th parallel, and in the south it was marked by the Bahr Al Ghazal river on the 10th parallel. The northern part of the Province was sand-dune and desert, and was the home of nomadic camel-owning tribes. The southern part consisted for the most part of a series of grey granite massifs, rising to 2,500 feet above the plain; a tumbled mass of vast boulders, honeycombed with caves, and populated by pagan tribes. The latter were heterogeneous in physical type, and consisted of more than fifty different ethnic groups who spoke twenty or more languages and followed widely varying customs. These were the Nuba Mountains (at one time an independent administrative Province with its headquarters at Talodi, but incorporated with Kordofan in the late 1920s). Between these northern and southern sections of the Province ran a wide belt of thorn scrub, a country of nomadic and sedentary farmers, Arabic-speaking and largely Arab in custom and culture. Centrally placed in the Province, and at the western terminus of the railway line from Khartoum, was El Obeid the administrative headquarters and trading centre. Kordofan had roughly the area of pre-war Germany, and its population numbered around two million.

Newbold had decided to send me to the Nuba Mountains, but as a start I was to spend two months in El Obeid. Here I would be able to gain some experience of the working of the Province as a whole, some idea of what the educationalists, veterinary officers, agriculturalists and doctors were doing and aiming to do. They had few professional representatives in the districts and relied on the administrators to keep an eye on their work.

El Obeid was an attractive place, cool and green in the midsummer rains. There was the cantonment, which contained the Province headquarters, an old rambling Turco-Egyptian mudbrick building dating back to the previous century and still bearing bullet marks from its siege by Mahdist forces in 1883. There was the town with its single-storeyed shopping and residential quarters built of sun-dried brick in the better areas, and grass hutted in the sections reserved for the less well-to-do. The straight tree-lined streets were wide and sandy. Separated from the main town was the West African quarter where ten thousand Nigerians lived under the day-to-day control of their own chief.

In 1933 the Nuba Mountains consisted of two administrative districts, Western Jebels and Eastern Jebels. I was to go to Eastern Jebels, which had an area equal to Scotland and the Isles, and contained a quarter of a million people. The administrative headquarters was at Rashad, and there were Government posts at two other places, Delami and Talodi. At Rashad, Geoffrey Hawkesworth,* who was twenty-eight, was in overall charge, with Robin Elles,† who had rowed in the Cambridge boat for three years and stroked it to victory in 1929, as his assistant. At Delami there was a *Mamur*, Mohammed Abdel Raziq. A hundred and fifty miles to the south lay Talodi, a long day's journey by truck in the dry weather, while in the rains it could only be reached by pony and mule, and that took most of a week. Talodi was to be my station. The only other British officials there were an Agricultural Inspector and an Engineer in charge of the cotton ginnery. As we all travelled a good deal, it was seldom that any of us met each other more often than once a fortnight.

From the time of the Turco-Egyptian conquest of the Sudan in 1821 until the overthrow of the regime sixty years later, the Nuba mountains formed a slave-raiding reserve in which both government and private enterprise enjoyed a profitable share. Ignatius Pallme, an enterprising Austrian merchant, spent two years in Kordofan between 1837 and 1839, and wrote a horrifying account of the atrocities for which the administration was responsible. While many thousands of grown male and female slaves were marched down to Egypt in conditions of great hardship and suffering, a far worse fate awaited young boys selected for the duties of guards and servants in

* G. Hawkesworth, CMG, *b.* 1904, *d.* 1969. Sudan Political Service 1927–54. His identical twin Desmond was serving at the same time in the adjacent district of Western Jebels. Their exact similarity of appearance caused the Nuba much amusement as well as confusion.

† R.J. Elles, OBE, *b.* 1907. Joined the Sudan Political Service 1929. He resigned in 1934, but came back to join the Sudan Defence Force in the war. He was twice decorated for distinguished service in North Africa.

the harems of Cairo and elsewhere. The operation of castration was performed in El Obeid by a sheikh who was particularly experienced and adept. The victim was firmly secured to the ground by sacks of sand laid upon his arms, feet and chest. The lad's testicles were removed with a razor, haemorrhage was arrested with an application of melted butter, and palm fibre was used as a dressing. The patient remained under treatment for several weeks if he survived the operation — half are believed to have succumbed. Very few of them ever reached Egypt where their sale price greatly exceeded that of a male slave entire in body.

Under the pressure of constant and well-organised raids, the Nuba were driven from the plains into the fastnesses of their hills, defending themselves against their mounted and better-armed assailants with great courage and tenacity. They sited and built their villages with an eye to defence, perfected the use of the throwing knife, the spear and the mace, constructed defensive walls across the valleys to hold back mounted raiders and learnt to terrace their hill slopes and make use of every square yard of cultivatable land with great ingenuity and economy. Harried and oppressed, they developed a fear and suspicion of both Government and Arabs, and an independence of character which subsequently made the establishment of an administration and co-operation with their neighbours a slow and difficult process.

My two months of temporary duty in El Obeid completed, I set out in late September for my new district. At that time of year the only means of travel was by animal and on foot. It was to take me just over a month to reach Rashad, by way of Dilling, Kadugli, Talodi and Delami. The distance was four hundred miles. In Kassala I had learnt to travel with camels, and I was now to have my first experience of trekking with ponies and mules. September is a bad month for movement in Kordofan south of the 12th parallel. Along that line the sand dunes and laterite gradually give way to wide areas of heavy black clay and to numerous watercourses which, during and immediately after rain, form impassable obstacles. Throughout September rain is liable to fall every two or three days, and so it proved that year. We left El Obeid on a clear sunny morning, a party of twelve in all — my two servants, the grooms, and a policeman as escort. We were mounted on four riding ponies and eight pack mules. The first eighty miles were fairly easy; the countryside was broken, lightly wooded and green. The new corn was beginning to ripen, and the open rain pools sheltered migrant duck and geese. The early mornings were misty.

Half way between El Obeid and Dilling there was a rest house close by the village of Sunjikai. Rest houses in Kordofan were sited three and a half or four hours' ride apart and consisted of a number of round grass huts. Normally, when touring with animals, one would leave early, stop for a late breakfast and a mid-day halt at the rest house that lay ahead, and then move on to the next, aiming to arrive well before nightfall in order that the animals might be unloaded, allowed to graze for a while and then tethered and fed before dark. As we came over a slight crest and approached the Sunjikai Rest House, which lay in a hollow with hills on three sides, we could see smoke and the movement of men and animals around the huts. There were mules tethered and several soldiers and policemen were busy with their loads. I dismounted and was met by Hugh Boustead* and Russell Salmon. They were on their way from Dilling to El Obeid. Salmon, who was the Assistant District Commissioner at Dilling, I knew. We had been at Winchester together and he had joined the service a year before me. He was to die serving with the Army in Eritrea eight years later. Boustead I knew of as a legendary character, and he was to become even more of a legend during the next forty years. At that time he was commanding the Camel Corps in El Obeid and two months before he had returned to the Sudan after spending his leave playing a notable part in the 1933 Everest Expedition. Their tea was ready and I joined them. Before the light went, Boustead and I climbed one of the hills overlooking the rest house. Northwards lay the country I had just covered, deeply carpeted in lush grazing.

In the opposite direction stretched a succession of rocky outcrops, low to the immediate south but rising and developing into longer ranges in the far distance; the thorny scrub was thicker and the grass higher. The rains had been heavy around Dilling and were reported to be particularly heavy further south. Boustead and I watched the sunset and he talked of Everest. Warmhearted and twinkling with humour and fun, he was intensely interested in everything and everyone, and gifted with a great capacity for friendship. After that first meeting our paths crossed time and again — in the Sudan, in Jordan, in the Gulf, in Switzerland and in England. When he died in 1980, he had lived a more adventurous and colourful life than almost any other Englishman of this century. The three of us spent the night in the rest house, and early next morning, Boustead and Salmon left for the North.

After Kadugli we ran into constant rain. The road was overgrown with grass, higher than our heads, and infested with ticks, which lodged themselves on us and our beasts. We were plagued

* Colonel Sir Hugh Boustead, KBE, CMG, DSO, MC, *b*. 1895, *d*. 1980. Author of *Wind of Morning*.

throughout the hours of daylight by biting flies which tormented the mules beyond endurance. We spent hours unsaddling our animals, carrying their loads through waist-deep water courses, and then coaxing, leading and swimming the reluctant beasts across. The mud was black, clinging and evil-smelling. At night we sheltered in rest houses which were alive with mosquitoes and the abode of scorpions and snakes. But there were places where the road ran through the granite hills and the track was firm. And here there were the sounds of goat bells, shepherds' pipes and the cowman's horn; and the Nuba came down from their villages to crowd about the rest houses as we unloaded for the mid-day halt or for the night. I had a medical chest equipped with simple drugs, and was kept busy dressing tropical ulcers and dispensing for malaria and other easily recognisable ailments. I never travelled without keeping handy in my pocket a scalpel and permanganate of potash crystals for snake and scorpion bites. I used them a number of times. At sunset we lit smoke fires to keep the animals free of flies, and there would be the smell of cooking and the sound of voices calling from hill to hill. Little groups of women and girls passed on their way home from the fields, stopping to stare and laugh and talk.

We reached Rashad, having spent a week in Talodi on the way, thirty-two days after we had set out from El Obeid; and within a couple of days I was down, perhaps not surprisingly, with my first attack of malaria. I was given two quinine injections in the buttocks by Ali Abdel Kerim, a cheerful 'Sanitary Overseer', and was lodged and looked after by Robin Elles who was acting in charge of the District. I made a quick recovery, my convalescence being marked by a craving — easily satisfied by Elles's cook —, for fried onions. In the years to come I was lucky to escape with less than half a dozen attacks of fever. I never took a prophylactic but was always careful to sleep under a net, wear mosquito boots at sunset and keep my shirt sleeves buttoned at the wrist. My successors were less fortunate. John Rowley,* who took over Talodi from me at the end of 1937, nearly died of blackwater fever, Reggie Dingwall,† who followed him, was lucky to recover from yellow fever in an epidemic which swept the Jebels in the second year of the war and caused a great number of deaths. Ben Arber,‡ who succeeded Robin Elles,

* J.V.d'A. Rowley, *b.* 1907. Joined Sudan Political Service 1930. Retired as Governor of Darfur Province 1954.

† R.G. Dingwall, *b.* 1908. Joined Sudan Political Service 1931. Retired as Commissioner of Prisons 1954.

‡ H.B. Arber, *b.* 1906. Joined Sudan Political Service 1928. Retired as Governor Northern Province 1954.

developed an acute appendicitis travelling in the rains south of Rashad and was lucky to survive.

After a fortnight in Rashad, I made my way back to Talodi, took up my duties and settled into my new house. The Assistant District Commissioner's house in Talodi was a habitation of some style for it had been at one time the residence of the Governor of the Nuba Mountains Province. It consisted of a wide open verandah in front, approached by a set of cement steps. Covered verandahs lay on either side of the four rooms, each of which led into the other. Fifty yards away in one direction stood the earth closet, a hundred yards away in the other direction the stables and the pig sty, the latter a stone hut surrounded by a stout thorn fence. Although the pigs roamed at will, and safely enough during the day, they needed to be protected at night from leopards. At times my herd grew to a hundred or more and very useful they were as gifts to be made on suitable occasions. They scavenged and cost me little to keep, apart from the wages of a young swineherd. The house stood on a slight eminence with a spectacular view over the flat plain that stretched away north and east. Apart from a few flowering shrubs I had no garden: it was all stone and gravel. But bleak as this garden was, half a dozen frangipani trees broke into blossom when the rains came and filled the air at night with a scent of great sweetness. Behind the house rose the great solid circular mass of Talodi mountain, grey and black in summer, green and black in the rains. As soon as the rains ended and the roads became passable for trucks, I had the few pieces of furniture I had acquired in Gedaref sent down from El Obeid. To these I now added, bought at an auction of the effects of a Greek merchant who had recently died of blackwater, a large wooden cupboard, a settee and two wooden armchairs. They served me for the next five years.

My office — a quarter of a mile from the house — was also, by our standards, large and impressive. The floor was of black tiles, the ceiling high, the walls white-washed. Hanging above my desk was a khaki cloth Indian type punka, a *marwaha*. This fan was connected to the adjacent verandah by a rope which ran through a hole in the wall. On the verandah, his back resting against the outer wall of the office, reclined an ancient convict charged with the easy and envied task of pulling the rope gently to and fro. At times, when his arms grew tired, he would attach the end of the rope to his toe, and with one knee crossed over the other, a simple up and down movement of his leg would keep the fan going and a gentle breeze circulating about my desk. As the heat of the day increased — and in the summer Talodi was like a furnace — this aged man would grow drowsy and his movements slower and slower. '*Marwaha*,' I would shout through the mosquito wired window, '*marwaha.*' The movements of the rope would be violently increased in speed and intensity and the papers on my desk would fly in all directions.

The walls of the office were festooned with relics of the Lafofa patrol which had taken place some years before. It had been the last military expedition against a Nuba mountain stronghold held by a small group of recalcitrant tribesmen. There was the rebel leader's sword and his flag, an old Remington rifle or two, and the spears and throwing knives of his followers. To embellish this display, I later added an impressive set of campaign medals which an aged and long-retired Nuba soldier had given me for safe keeping. Mounted and framed by Spink in London, they made a significant addition to these other momentos of a minor and very remote campaign. From time to time the grizzled owner of the medals would visit me and survey them with satisfaction. Finally, high up on the wall facing my desk, there were three large photographs in dark heavy frames. One was of King George V, bearded and in naval uniform. One was of King Fuad of Egypt, the waxed ends of his moustache turned ferociously upwards, wearing a frogged uniform with the Order of the Nile on his chest and a tarbush on his head. The third was of Sir Reginald Wingate who had been Governor-General from 1899 to 1916. His many medals, stars and Orders covered almost the whole of his uniform. He too had the ends of his moustache waxed, but unlike King Fuad's they projected horizontally. Of the three he appeared the most awe-inspiring, but when I chanced to meet him in London a year or so later he seemed entirely human and kindly. These three formidable figures hovered in effigy and spirit over my office hours.

At the far end of the verandah, on which visitors and petitioners gathered waiting their turn to see me, were the prison, the police orderly room, the treasury and clerks' offices, and beyond them the police parade ground, where two plain marble columns stood each surmounted by a replica of a tarbush. They marked the site where many years before, an Egyptian officer, deranged by the heat and loneliness of Talodi, had shot a comrade and then turned his revolver on himself. At the far end of the parade ground were the post office, the officials' club and the police lines; and a quarter of a mile beyond lay the town.

Talodi town had little to boast of. There was a wide open market place surrounded on three sides by single-storeyed and verandahed shops where the Nuba gathered to watch in wonder as half a dozen local Arab tailors treadled away detachedly in the shade at their Singer sewing machines, turning out cotton shirts and drawers. These shops supplied sugar and tea, and printed cloth, and beads and brightly coloured dishes, and kettles that hung on strings suspended from the ceiling. There were two or three Greek merchants and two or three Lebanese. The rest of the trading community were Arabs from the north. They made little more than a modest livelihood. On the fourth side of the market, beneath the shade of half a dozen fine wild fig trees, stood the hospital which had at one time been an Egyptian military barracks. Alongside the market, I created over the years a public garden with shrubs and young mahogany trees protected by thorn fences from the marauding goats, with pathways and benches and an open cement bandstand. Behind the hospital were the grass houses and the compounds in which the three thousand inhabitants of Talodi had their being.

My predecessor in Talodi, Matthew Wordsworth,* was a keen horseman who drove a trap in tandem and had revived a defunct interest in polo. I kept it going, and throughout my time we played once or twice a week during the winter months, and we held an annual match against Kadugli a hundred miles away. Our regular players included the British Agricultural Inspector, the Sudanese Police officer and three or four of his men, the Market Clerk and the Office Accountant. We played on a hard bare ground which was kept smooth and free of dangerous holes and cracks by a simple sort of grader consisting of a heavy triangular iron frame to which were attached thorn branches weighed down with stones. This contraption was drawn by a mule. The polo ground lay alongside the market and our afternoon games were attended by a regular crowd of amused and interested spectators. A fall or a spectacular collision or a runaway pony was what they best liked to see, and they often saw all three.

Talodi was a lonely remote place but as a sub-district it was an ideal post for a young man and particularly for a bachelor for it offered a great deal of independence and scope not only in the administrative field but also in the study of Nuba culture. The ethnology of the Nuba had attracted the active interest of a number of District Commissioners, as forming part of the business of administration, and the lectures on anthropology I had attended in our year's course at Oxford had fired my own enthusiasm. But we were all amateurs and no doubt we all drew wrong conclusions from some of the information we gathered and the observations we made. Douglas Newbold saw the value of a proper appreciation of the social structure of the Nuba as a help to the practical tasks of

* M.C. Wordsworth, CBE, *b.* 1905, *d.* 1976. Joined Sudan Education Department 1927. Retired as Commissioner of Co-operative Societies 1954.

Government and he was instrumental in 1938 in getting Dr S.L. Nadel appointed to conduct a full and professional survey. The result of his researches was the publication after the war of *The Nuba Investigation 1938–41*.

To help me run the Sub-District I had a *Mamur*, who dealt mainly with day-to-day routine and office problems, except when I was on leave, and then he was in command. A Sudanese Police officer was in charge, under my general supervision, of our sixty or so foot and mounted police, all locally enlisted men and all illiterate except for three or four.

In Kassala and Khartoum, I had learnt the basic rules of a District Commissioner's work. What I had yet to learn — and this would come only by experience and by making mistakes — was how the rules could best be applied and, if necessary, modified to suit particular circumstances. Above all, I had yet to learn the danger of impatience. This and similar lessons were to come to me partly through day-to-day contact with the people among whom I was now to work, partly from half a dozen men in particular whose wisdom and warm-heartedness I soon learnt to admire.

One of these, Sherif Osman, had been a policeman reaching the rank of warrant officer, and on retirement had been appointed as 'Regent' of Eliri, to rule until the rightful chief, a lad of fourteen, came of age. The people of Eliri were the sons and grandsons of runaway slaves. They were a feckless and at the same time aggressive lot, and Sherif had a difficult task. He was fifty or so when I first met him: twice my age. Of Northern origin, he was light-skinned, tall and thin, with a sparse beard and a deeply lined face giving an impression of great strength of purpose and of patience. He was a fine horseman, wise and charming as a companion, a man of great loyalty who gave the last seven years of his active life to the service of Government and a troublesome people. During the time in which I served in Talodi, I paid many visits to Eliri and Sherif Osman, and we made many tours together, usually by horse and for two or three days at a time. We would visit the villages and I learnt much from him. He was an easy talker, and he had many stories of the events of 1924 when the Egyptian Army detachment in Talodi supported their fellow-mutineers in Khartoum, and of the part he had played in keeping the Sudan police steady. For this he had been awarded the British Empire Medal. In 1938, when I was no longer in the District, his reason deserted him. All medical advice and aid availed nothing, and when I called to see him in El Obeid he was a tragic wreck of the man he had been. He was being cared for, as best they knew how, by his two devoted sons, but pathetically chained to a post in a darkened inner room. The most gentle of men, he had shown signs of violence and it was their great fear that he might do some mischief that would bring embarrassment or shame to the family. No mental hospital existed in the Sudan and the alternative would have been the lunatic ward of the El Obeid prison. Fortunately for himself and for those who admired him, he was soon to die.

The second of those to whom I owe a debt was Mohammed Abdel Raziq, the *Mamur* of Delami. Delami lay in the northern part of the District and Mohammed was the administrative officer, responsible — as I was — to the District Commissioner in Rashad. His bailiwick consisted of an area of country as large as an English county, containing fifty thousand primitive and at times most difficult and potentially violent people. He came from Dongola, in the Northern Sudan and had had an intermediate education, some years of service as a primary schoolmaster and then a year's training as an administrative officer. He knew no English. When I first met him he had a few more years' service than I had, but was considerably my junior in rank. Mohammed Abdel Raziq's knowledge of and influence over the Nuba were both wide and profound, and no one could fail to be captivated by his perpetually beaming smile and his unfailing cheerfulness. He was short and stout and wore a large overshadowing sun-helmet which added to a general effect of Pickwickian rotundity. And yet he was a man of great energy, and a surprisingly hard walker in the hills, for his sub-district was heavily infected with tse-tse fly and in consequence he was unable to use either horses or mules. Although we lived over a hundred miles apart, we saw a lot of each other in the four years when we served together. I never saw him put out or apparently worried despite the trouble which the people for whom he had responsibility were constantly causing him by their refusal to pay taxes, the murders they so frequently committed and the cattle raids they carried out against their neighbours. He was a strict Muslim, essentially conventional, and the nakedness of the Nuba must have disturbed him.

He was markedly conscious of both propriety and rank. Once, during the rains, he asked me to afternoon tea at his house in Delami. I was staying in the rest house and he came to fetch me shortly before four o'clock. It was raining heavily and he brought with him a large green umbrella sufficiently capacious to shelter us both. As we crossed the police parade ground there was a flash of lightning, followed immediately by a deafening crash of thunder. Largely in jest, I asked him, against the clamour of the storm, whether he thought that lightning could strike the metal tip of an umbrella such as ours. His normal beaming smile was suddenly metamorphosed into deadly seriousness. 'By God,' he answered, 'indeed it could.' How prudent and how right I was to draw attention to the peril in which his thoughtlessness had placed us; such pointless danger should be avoided; and with both hands grasping the crook handle he swung the open umbrella in a half circle and flung it from us. It bounced and slithered in the mud, and a gust of wind spun it over and over and bore it away. Despite my protests that I had never seriously thought that we were in danger, we hurried on unprotected against the driving rain. Later, his servant retrieved the umbrella and shut it away in a cupboard with instructions that it was never again to be used during a thunderstorm. Mohammed Abdel Raziq was a good horseman, but had abandoned polo after an accident. He had fallen, and his helmet had been dashed, he said, into a hundred pieces; he had been fortunate to escape with his life, and his children might have been left orphans and his wife a widow. He had no false pride, and his cautious approach to life and eager deference to seniority might well have seemed to some to denote a lack of enterprise and even of character and courage. But he showed plenty of both in his dealings with the Nuba. He too, like Sherif Osman, was infinitely patient, and although he differed from Mr Jorrocks in all but figure, he shared his belief that more people are flattered into virtue than are bullied out of vice. He too, alas, died at quite a young age.

Throughout the 1930s, it was the view of a number of most senior British officers in the Political Service that it would be a mistake for Sudanese to be promoted above the rank of *Mamur*. The proper future of the administration lay, it was believed, in the development of local government; traditional in the countryside, Western in style in urban areas. Sudanese officers would come increasingly to fill the role of executive officers to rural and town councils. It was argued that a Sudanese officer could not in fairness be expected to exercise in his own country and over his own people the authority and influence which British District Commissioners were able to wield, free as they were from local pressures — any more, it was said, than an Englishman could be a District Commissioner in Sussex. No one, it would seem, had studied the French system of local government under the control of the *Prefet* and the Mayor of the *Commune*. In the event it was unfortunate, for in less than twenty years it became necessary, at very short notice, to hand over entirely to Sudanese officers. By then a few had indeed been given full District Commissioner rank, but the number of trained and experienced men fell far short of what was needed. Mohammed Abdel Raziq and a dozen or more like him were deemed fit, by the time the war came in 1939, to do the work that I was doing in 1933. Although the Government in Khartoum was slow to recognise that the Sudanisation of the Political Service was in the nature of things inevitable, and that the future lay less with the tribal leaders than with the educated product of the towns, it was ahead of other overseas administrations in its view of this particular problem. During the 1920s and '30s, *Mamurs* were being well trained at a school of administration in Omdurman. And because leave for British District Commissioners and their assistants was generous and frequent, all *Mamurs* regularly enjoyed the experience of increased responsibilities while their British senior officers were summering at home.

And finally, among those Sudanese who helped at that time to teach me my job, was Radi Kumbal, Sheikh of the Awlad Himeid, a small cattle-owning Arab tribe that moved with the grazing on the eastern fringe of the Nuba mountains. Radi Kumbal was a conservative and an aristocrat, courteous and gentle and greatly respected by his tribesmen. Because he suffered from a severe goitre, he wore the end of his turban swathed about his throat and chin; only his grey moustache, thin hawk nose and shrewd eyes showed between the folds. He had seen young District Commissioners come and go for many years and had helped to foster that sympathetic relationship between the representatives of a foreign race and his own people which stood us in good stead, especially in the war years, and which gradually, and in the nature of things, changed as an age of nationalistic battle cries supplanted an age of personal relationships. Sheikh Radi was a strict Muslim, and when touring with him or staying with him in one of his encampments we gave our servants instructions to serve us with lime juice in the evenings, and to put the whisky bottle away. He exemplified all the best features of a system of administration based on tradition and respect for traditional authority.

Keeping the peace, ensuring the exercise of justice, raising the scope and standards of local government, improving the level and variety of agricultural produce, expanding health and educational services and improving communications — these were our principal tasks. We aimed to achieve them mainly through the co-operation of the traditional chiefs and elders. There was really no other way. But the funds at our disposal were never enough. There did not exist a World Bank, international loans or rich Arab states to provide help in those days.

For the first twenty years after the turn of the century the Nuba presented something of a military problem, and the administration was principally concerned to prevent conflict among the Nuba themselves, and between them and their Arab neighbours on the plains. Against the background of their history it is not surprising that they had no reason to suppose that things would change with a change of government. Until the early 1920s therefore Nuba administration was essentially direct, and little attention was paid to such traditional authority as existed. It was known that in most communities power resided in two persons — the *Mek*, a secular chief with a council of elders, and the *Kujur*, a religious leader possessing certain supernatural powers, including control over the rain and locusts. It became necessary in this early period of government to discover the relative importance of these two traditional leaders, each with his own sphere of influence and authority, in order to employ them to maintain the peace and welfare of their people. At the same time the administration was concerned to work towards the grouping together of those tribal units which were small and weak, either in direct amalgamation where this was generally acceptable, or in some looser form of federation. A start was made with federated courts, and gradually closer administrative groupings followed. By the end of the 1920s the military problem had ceased to be of any real significance, and some progress had been made in establishing both courts and local government units. The process took time, because it could only be achieved by agreement, and when I came to serve in the Nuba Mountains there was still much to be done in persuading the smaller tribes that if they were to play an effective part in the management of their own affairs, both judicial and administrative, closer and more effective co-operation with their neighbours was essential.

One of the main duties that fell to the administration was, as I have said, to keep the peace and prevent tribal conflict, particularly between the Nuba in the hills and the Baggara — the cattle-owning Arabs — who occupied the plains. In the chaos which followed the end of Turco-Egyptian rule in the Sudan, the Nuba had acquired a considerable quantity of firearms of various patterns. In the rest of the Sudan the possession of guns and rifles was closely controlled by licence, but the Nuba were privileged: they were allowed to carry firearms and they did so. There were probably 20,000 rifles in the Nuba mountains, nearly all of them Remingtons dating back to a series of disastrous defeats suffered by the Egyptian forces fifty years before. Ammunition was hard to obtain so the Nuba made their own crude gunpowder and caps and refilled their old brass cartridge cases over and over again.

I found myself obliged at times to lead a small party of police, accompanied by Chiefs and their retainers, to arrest men who had committed crimes and defied the local courts. We would move by night, climb the hills in the dark, surround the house and hope to surprise and arrest the men quietly. Usually it worked. But there was an occasion in the Moro Hills when the fugitive put up a great deal of resistance and before we could get him away his relations and friends came to his assistance. We were surrounded, but we had our man securely handcuffed. We refused to surrender him but equally the village refused to allow us to move. It was just before dawn. We parleyed for several hours without either side yielding. The village had arms and so had we. We sent for the Chiefs of the neighbouring villages. The discussion went on till mid-day. I insisted that the man must be tried for his offence but I undertook that the sentence would not be unduly severe. Reason eventually prevailed and we led away our captive. He served his three months and went back home.

On another occasion when it became necessary to arrest a wanted man in the hills, he broke away and raced off. He was stark naked, and looked like a Greek athlete in a vase painting as he sped away, long-legged and agile. We pursued him, a newly-enlisted policeman leading the field. On the hillsides around were scores of running figures, some of them friends of the fugitive hoping to see him escape, others out for the fun of watching a good chase. The hills echoed with cries of encouragement and excitement. There was a touch of gaiety and good humour in it all, but also an undercurrent that could have led to sudden violence. He was caught and subsequently served his spell in prison, but I have a fancy that having made the representatives both of his own Chief, whom he had defied, and of the Government pound and sweat for several miles over the hills, he may well have felt that it was worth it. I like to think that he now tells the story to his grandchildren and with much satisfaction and embellishment.

It was also our responsibility to see that the local courts dealt justly with complainants and offenders, and where cases lay beyond their powers, we dealt with them ourselves. Court work brought one, whether one was simply making a magisterial enquiry which would decide whether a *prima facie* case lay against an accused or actually trying a case, into closer and more intimate touch with the people than any other activity. The evidence that one listened to — that is, the day-to-day and intimate circumstances that lay behind the case, and the actual events that led directly to the crime — gave a very close understanding of the lives of these people. The great majority of cases were dealt with by the traditional courts following tribal law and custom or, in the towns, by the Benches of local magistrates which operated the Penal Code and the Code of Criminal Procedure. It was therefore only the more serious crimes that normally came to the District Commissioner or his assistant — murder or attempted murder, grievous bodily harm, robbery and brigandage (the two latter were rare) and in the trial of cases such as these one sat as the President of a Major or Minor Court with two Sudanese magistrates to assist, both in the matter of the verdict and the punishment. It was unusual for the accused in murder and manslaughter cases to deny the charge. A Major Court had the power to condemn to death, but the finding and the sentence of all Major Courts were subject to the approval of the Governor General as advised by the Chief Justice. I presided over many such courts.

I found Maines '*Criminal Law of India*' a great help in all my legal work, particularly when it came to setting out the reasons for the finding. In fact our codes were based on the Indian system. The Sudanese were not a cruel or a vengeful people, but circumstances moved them to great and sudden violence at times. Most murders were committed as a result of a love affair or an unfaithful wife, or through rival claims to farmland, or the destruction of crops by trespassing herds. And these cases could easily lead to tribal fights resulting in a number of killed and wounded. Throughout Kordofan, as indeed in most areas of the Sudan, there existed the age-old conflict of interest between the cultivator and the herdsman. Only in the extreme north where the sparse rainfall prevented farming to any extent did the vast herds of camels graze at will. Elsewhere animals were a constant menace to crops, and the cause of a greater amount of violent crime than almost anything else. With or without the connivance of the herdsman, animals would enter upon and destroy or damage a crop. The infuriated owner would seize or kill the trespassing beasts. The herdsman would then appear, a fight involving perhaps a dozen supporters of either side would follow, and wounds and, often enough, death would be the ultimate outcome.

When the accused was a tribesman, legal regulations provided in some circumstances for the payment of blood money. In these cases the court would impose the sentence that would have applied had the accused not been a tribesman, but would add a recommendation that if the relations of both the deceased and the convicted man agreed to blood money, and if in the event the blood money was duly paid, then the sentence should be reduced. The principle behind the system was that in a case of homicide both the Government and the dead man's family had certain accepted rights; the Government's right lay in imposing a period of imprisonment, the right of the family lay in receiving the blood money. By this compromise arrangement both rights were met.

Every Arab and Nuba chief responsible for a tribal area, an administrative unit and a court of justice had his own small band of rural police or messengers. The chiefs took some pride in these manifestations of their authority and they dressed and equipped them as impressively as their slender budget resources allowed. We helped them by letting them have written-off ('boarded') items of our regular police kit; puttees, belts and sandals. From a small reserve fund I gave the Nuba chiefs' police brightly-patterned turbans and kilts. They provided their own firearms, which were more decorative than lethal. Once a year we had them in to Talodi for a few days' course of drill and basic police duties. They performed an invaluable public service at a minute cost.

We were responsible for ensuring the collection and payment of a simple annual tax which was basically a rudimentary combined wealth and income tax. Having made a broad assessment of the number of able-bodied men, cattle and goats in the tribe, together with the expected value of the main cash crops, it was left to the Chief and his elders to allot the amount due from each family. On average it worked out at about seven shillings. And here it was that my herd of pigs came in useful, for the Nuba bred pigs and ate them at times of festival. Chiefs who were prompt in their tax payment were given two or three pigs as a reward, and their subjects then enjoyed a communal feast.

We were responsible too for the maintenance of roads, bridges, rest houses, dispensaries and schools, for there was no Public Works Department in the district. So we imposed a certain amount of communal labour, and every year we were obliged to record the details which were duly incorporated in a report which went from the Government to the League of Nations. Opening the motor roads after the rains was the main *corvée* that was thus levied. Each village in the vicinity of the road was made responsible for a stretch, the distance depending on the number of able-bodied men. The annual repair of the grass rest houses was another form of communal labour. Our District budget allowed us a small sum for road repairs and rest house maintenance, but it was not enough to cover a daily wage to the scores of men required, and we used it to buy bulls or goats which were slaughtered and fed to the men on the work. I suppose that on average every villager did five or six days of communal work a year, for which he received a satisfying meal or two, and also a decent motorable road and a dispensary somewhere near his village from which he would certainly be able to derive some benefit.

We never had any difficulty getting our *corvée* operating. A single mounted policeman, usually a local man, would be in charge of perhaps a twenty-mile stretch, and he and the chief knew how to keep their gangs effective and content. Not that it was light work. The thick tall grass had to be cut, deep scouring had to be filled and patched, drainage ditches dug and log bridges replaced or strengthened. With all that it was a pretty cheerful communal affair.

There would be much singing, especially when the women came out in the afternoons bearing on their heads large earthenware jars of foaming home-brewed beer. It was all very friendly, very paternal and of course it was the easiest thing in the world to misrepresent. Our ability to do this sort of thing sprang from an authority based on reputation rather than upon power. I suppose that one could claim that in the last resort — and despite the fact that the Nuba were well-armed — it was a case of 'whatever happens we have got the Maxim gun and they have not.' But the ratio of administrative officers in outstations, British and Sudanese combined, to the population was roughly three or four to a quarter of a million. The Sudan, with a population of possibly eight million, had a police force of 6,000.

In addition to our hospital in Talodi — the only hospital in Eastern Jebels — there were dispensaries in half a dozen other places in the District, but the Sudan was a poor country and medical services, like others, were limited by the funds at our disposal. Cerebral-spinal meningitis came to the Nuba Mountains twice while I was there, and in the winter of 1934/5 and in the following year the death toll, especially among the young, was heavy. The disease started to show itself in the cool dry weather, and once it began to spread there was little we could do except urge the people to avoid crowding together and encourage them to sleep in open shelters rather than close together inside their huts. When the weather was cold it was difficult to persuade them to do this. I spent long and exhausting days travelling from village to village, talking to chiefs and elders and gatherings of people, trying to explain how the disease was transmitted. There was nothing that could be done medically once the disease struck. There was no prophylactic. The epidemic had come to us from the west, from Darfur. Having taken its heavy toll over two winters it ceased to menace us, but two years later it was followed by yellow fever. Leprosy was widespread and we ran two leper colonies, but that was before the days of Dapsone and we could offer no treatment.

There were many areas in the Jebels which had never been completely or accurately surveyed, and it was possible to do a certain amount of useful work in the course of one's walking in the hills — using a compass, making sketches and route reports, and recording the names of features. These items of information the Department of Surveys checked and subsequently incorporated in the excellent district maps which it revised and reissued every few years. It gave a satisfaction to feel that one was recording details of remote and hitherto unmapped areas, however relatively small their importance.

As the cool north wind of December and January gave way to the breathless and blistering heat of the summer months, the bush fires began. By night they showed as a sinister glow on the horizon, by day as pillars of dark smoke fanned by the spiralling *dust devils* that marked the hot weather. They brought a sharp pungent smell that lingered for days. The ground over which the fire had swept was like a blackened stubble field on which lay smouldering logs and smoking tree trunks. While the fires were at their height, hawks and kites and vultures circled above waiting for the fugitive birds, hares, lizards and rats. Often these fires were started by hunters who waited down wind for the gazelle and other game in flight. It was strange to see how within a few days after the fire had passed and the ground cooled, a crop of fresh green grass would appear as if miraculously through the baked and blackened earth. But although the fires brought profit to some, they often led to a loss of valuable grazing and subsequent soil erosion. So tribal rules imposed penalties on those responsible for them.

There was only one way of ensuring that the many tasks one was trying to fulfil were being attended to, and that was by constant travelling; not only in the dry weather when movement by truck along the roads, and on foot in the hills, was comparatively easy, but in the rains too. Trekking in the rains was hard work but it was relieved by the beauty that so quickly showed itself after months of drought and heat. As a rule the clouds built up about mid-day and the rain would come before nightfall. When one set out at sunrise it would be cool and sparkling after the previous day's downpour. The country smelt fresh and clean-washed. Sometimes there would be short-lived waterfalls cascading down the granite hillsides; sometimes a veil of white mist would hang around the tops. But it would soon grow humid and by around nine one would halt for breakfast. One aimed to reach the night stop before the afternoon storm. And when the storm came, it came with great fury. Grey sheets of rain would lash the hillsides and thunder would roll and drum around the peaks. Then if the rest house had a good roof, one could get into bed under a mosquito net and read by the light of a pressure lamp. But there were many grass rest houses that leaked, and when they did the night could be miserable for the men, for the animals and for oneself. There were days when if the watercourses were in full spate, it was impossible to move from where one had spent the night.

Perhaps a paragraph from a letter I wrote to my parents in June 1937 gives an indication of the sort of life and the sort of tasks that fell to all of us in remote stations, particularly during the rains.

I reached Rashad at mid-day yesterday after spending a night in an encampment of the Awlad Himeid, where the district truck met us, and where we left our horses and mules to follow. For the last two hours of the journey we were ploughing our way slowly through deep mud. It was raining. I drove, with a sheikh whom we were bringing into hospital beside me. He seemed very weak, and the poor chap fell dead against my shoulder before we reached our destination. In the back, besides the Corporal driver, the cook, his boy and my head servant, there were a Camel Corps soldier returning from leave, two school-boys, the Sheikh's wife, a policeman's wife, a tribal policeman, and a handcuffed lunatic who wept and banged his head on the floor of the truck. During a halt he slipped his bonds and escaped into the long high grass and thick bush. We searched, but never found him.

But walking in the hills in the dry season was a pleasanter and more rewarding task. The high villages contained generally the shyest and most primitive people of the district, people whose fathers and certainly whose grandfathers would seldom have ventured down into the plains for fear of mounted raiders. Their neat stone-built thatched-roofed houses clustered like swallows' nests along the ridges, or grouped themselves around a mountain well or stream. Three or four huts would be joined together in a circle forming a small central court which was entered by a low single doorway. Each homestead thus formed a kind of miniature *château* which could if necessary be closed to outsiders and defended. The separate huts each had their particular purpose; one for sleeping, one for cooking, one for storing grain, a fourth for the pigs and goats. Inside, the walls were plastered, outside they were decorated with coloured patterns and geometrical designs, black, ochre and white. Against the outer walls the firewood stood in neat stacks; inside the courtyard rested the water jars and the farming implements. Within the sleeping quarters their spears and throwing knives and perhaps a rifle were ready to hand. Everything was in its place and their houses were kept constantly swept.

Moving on foot by narrow winding and often precipitous paths meant that porters were needed to carry a bedding roll, the cook's box, a folding table, a camp chair and such like. As a rule it was the girls and young married women, accustomed to carrying grain baskets from the plains, who came forward as volunteers. Unashamedly the men would say with a laugh that it was too burdensome for them. Up the stony hillside the dark column would wind its way in single file, each girl with a load on her head, graceful and erect, each carrying a long stick to preserve her balance. The oil on their bodies had an odd smell, not unpleasant but pungent and clinging. They chattered like birds as they picked their way among the rocks. We paid them according to the time taken to do the climb, two or three hours, and I usually added a handful of coloured beads or salt to the fee. Again, it was all very paternalistic; of course it was. It was also very friendly and cheerful. It is nonsense to condemn practices and relationships of this sort that were without malice or resentment, coercion or fear. It is nonsense to pretend that this was oppression or that there was anything undignified about it.

The Nuba felt no shame at all in their sexual organs save perhaps when they visited Talodi. Here a vague respect for this fringe of civilisation, and possibly a fear of Arab criticism, obliged the men rather than the women to make some gesture towards covering themselves up. The unmarried girls normally went completely naked apart from a string of beads about their necks. The older women wore leaves or leather thongs about their loins. But all decorated themselves in numerous other ways. The girls in particular underwent a painful cicatrisation during their first pregnancy that consisted in cutting complicated scar patterns on chest, stomach and back. They bored a hole in their lower lips and filled it with a long stone cylinder and sometimes with a .303 bullet. The edges of their ears held a score or more of brass rings. At puberty both boys and girls submitted to having the centre tooth in the lower jaw prized out with the point of a spear. The young men pierced their noses and decorated them with porcupine quills or rats' teeth, and many plaited their hair and covered it with white cheese in complicated starfish and other designs. They decorated their bodies with oil and ash and red ochre. Circumcision had previously been unknown, but among a few, and particularly those who had served in the army or police, it was a growing practice. I once ran into a party of three young men who two days before had circumcised each other with no other instrument than one of the light axes they habitually carried. They had sharpened it and used a rock as a chopping block. They were all in a bad way and it was fortunate that I was able to get them into hospital that night. However in some of the hills circumcision was an honoured privilege limited to old men of particularly distinguished status. Once the operation had been performed these greybeards were entitled to the privilege of carrying their tobacco in a cat-skin bag. It was fortunate that female circumcision, which was practised throughout the Muslim North, was scarcely known in the Nuba Mountains.

In the Northern Sudan Muslim modesty meant that even if one were spending the night in the centre of a village or encampment one was left alone while dressing, undressing or bathing. The Southern Sudanese had no such inhibitions. Here in the Nuba Mountains, a dozen or more silent but deeply interested faces would crowd under the grass eaves of the rest house as I sat, dimly displayed by the light of a hurricane lamp, crosslegged in my folding canvas bath. As I emerged to dry myself their interest would manifest itself in a prolonged murmur of amusement.

Often I would visit a village, get through whatever there was to do in the way of discussing law cases, tax collection, the crops or the water supply and then there would be an afternoon or evening free. I would wander about the houses or climb a nearby hill and talk to whomever I met. One such afternoon I was sitting alone on a hillside near the police post at Heiban, seventy or eighty miles north of Talodi. The place boasted a small lock-up, a police garrison of six men under a Corporal, a rest house and a grass hut which I used as an office whenever I came to inspect. I sat and looked at the view. An old man came towards me. With typical friendliness he smiled, greeted me in quite good Arabic and sat beside me. He wore nothing but a necklace. I was smoking a pipe. He took out his own from a small leather bag attached to his wrist. It had an earthenware bowl and the wooden stem was decorated with bands of brass wire. He scraped out the bowl, looked at it and looked at me. Then he sighed and gazed at the distant horizon. I needed no second hint and passed him my pouch. He lit up, filled his own pouch, savoured deeply the fragrance of Players Navy Cut and smiled again in gratitude. He was, he told me, an old soldier and he had served in the 10th Sudanese battalion of the Egyptian Army. He had been on the Suez Canal during the 1914–18 war. 'Ah yes, those were the days.' He had been in the band, he said. And then quietly and rather shyly he began to sing. For some moments I was completely puzzled both by the tune and by the very strange words of the song. Could they be English? And then suddenly I recognised both. It was 'I love a lassie', which the band had learnt in 1916. Harry Lauder would have been pleased. What an odd legacy our civilising influence had bequeathed to this old man. What strange dead leaves of Imperialism.

The routine of day-to-day life, much as the circumstances and the environment varied, seldom altered greatly. Mohammed, my butler, woke me and brought me a cup of tea shortly before dawn. The sky would be limpid, the air cool and still, the sun not yet quite risen. I would be conscious of the smell of dry grass and of the nearby stables. By half past six I would be up and dressed and Ali and Hassan, the grooms, and the three ponies would be waiting at the foot of the verandah. I kept a handful of dry dates in my bush tunic pocket as a titbit for the ponies at the end of the ride. We jog-trotted down the hill with its avenue of cotton trees planted by one of my predecessors ten or fifteen years before — now they were thirty feet high. We all planted trees, and provided they were watered and protected by thorns against the goats, they generally thrived and matured quickly. My ride usually took me past the office and into the town. Once a week there would be a police parade to watch, once a week a town inspection. Sometimes I rode to see how things were going on at the Agricultural Department's Experimental Farm, or to the hospital for a word with Dr Akasha and to visit and enquire after patients, or I rode to the District garden where two or three good conduct prisoners worked to produce a few rather poor vegetables. But limes, bananas, guavas and pawpaws grew well and these were distributed daily to the office staff.

By eight I was back at the house and an hour later, after a quick cold bath and a breakfast of fruit and eggs and tea, I would be in my office until about half past two when I lunched: cold consommé, cold meat and something of a salad followed by a cup of sweet Turkish coffee. The house was shuttered against the heat and in a refreshingly dim light I usually read until half past four when I would be out again walking or riding until sunset. And then a bath. I had tried the habit that some people followed of an afternoon sleep, but I found that I woke up feeling so lethargic that I preferred to avoid a siesta unless I had had a particularly tiring morning. I got through my evening work between seven and perhaps half past eight. There could be a criminal case to prepare, tribal notes to write up or a report to draft. Much of my time in the office was taken up with seeing people, and it was easier to do all but the purely routine written work after office hours. From time to time I would have members of the office staff or leading merchants to tea. Occasionally I might have a guest for a night or two, or someone visiting Talodi and staying in the rest house would come over for dinner armed with an electric torch — and a stick, for there were snakes. But for six nights out of seven I was alone. Such was the pattern of life in Talodi.

On trek — where I expected to be for more than half of every month — my times of waking and feeding and sleeping did not vary greatly, but there was no question of keeping any office hours and I worked and moved from village to village or hill to hill as circumstances required. In the evenings I was seldom alone, for with the work of the day over, the village elders would come and sit around my fire — in the winter and in the rains it could be cold in the hill-top villages — and drink sweet condensed-milk tea, and talk.

Return from trek usually meant that one had picked up on the way two or three patients in need of hospital treatment. Throughout the Nuba Mountains varicocele was a common complaint among older men, manifesting itself in a grotesquely enlarged scrotum. The operation necessary for the cure of this condition was comparatively simple, and it was often watched with awed interest by convalescent patients peering through the window of the operating theatre. Here they could see Dr Akasha and the one-eyed Al Jak, his chief dresser, at their mysterious and fascinating work. Recovery was quick and restoration to normality came as a delight to the patient and his family, who as often as not would have followed him into Talodi on foot. As a public relations exercise, if nothing else, this particular operation did much to bring credit to the Government.

By the early 1930s we were turning our attention increasingly towards the economic and social development of the Nuba. The introduction some years earlier of rain-grown cotton as a cash crop had been popular, and its cultivation increased rapidly. Government buying centres were set up during the picking season at various points throughout the District to which the crop was brought in, graded, weighed and purchased. In Talodi John Colman, the Agricultural Inspector, and his Sudanese assistant ran an experimental farm in which improved types of cotton and food crops were tested, and from which seeds were distributed. In education too, we were beginning to meet a slowly developing demand. Elementary schools were already in existence in the main Government centres, and were being reinforced by Primary schools in rural areas and at tribal headquarters.

What, one may well ask oneself, lay behind the means by which we exercised the considerable powers and responsibilities entrusted to us? First, I suppose, common sense and secondly a measure of idealism combined with a warmth of feeling that few, living so closely with these people, could fail to experience. A people who succeeded in combining rascality with honesty, a sense of the ridiculous with dignity, and bluntness with a natural courtesy; all in a remarkable amalgam that somehow showed itself in the deeply lined gravity as well as the quick impish humour of their faces.

The Nuba were greatly attached to tobacco. They grew it, they smoked it and they chewed it. As a harvested crop it served also, in many of the hills, as a part of the bride price. Fashioned into the shape and size of large currant buns it was the portion due to the bride's mother. It was smoked in little stone or earthenware pipes by the middle-aged and the old of both sexes. And the elderly also chewed it, together with a piece of rock salt, and a wad of these two ingredients would be held in the mouth for hours together, creating a great deal of brown saliva, as a result of which the chewers became adept at long-range and accurate spitting. The young and newly married avoided tobacco. They would laughingly explain — and how sensibly — that it contaminated the breath, and that they found the smell inhibiting. Pipes were an excellent present to give to chiefs and elders, and every year when I was on leave, I would buy two or three dozen at Woolworths at 6d each. I also used to bring out coloured combs. Old men liked to hang them round their necks and when they had nothing to do they would gently comb their thin scraggy beards. They were not a hirsute people.

The Nuba enjoyed and showed great skill and dash in a variety of manly games. They wrestled, they threw spears with wooden points at one another, they fought with single stick and shield, they ran cross-country races, and at Kau, Nyaro and Fungor they fought one another armed with metal bracelets on their wrists. This last was a dangerous game despite the rules that governed it and the care of the referees, and I have seen a man kill his opponent. An English Sunday newspaper recently published some remarkable and beautiful photographs of these people, described in the accompanying article as a tribe whose existence had hitherto been known only to a handful of anthropologists. The people of Kau, Nyaro and Fungor were in my Sub-District and I visited all three hills frequently, as did a number of my predecessors and successors. The article also said that these people did not believe in the existence of any other Nuba tribes — which sounds very odd to me when in fact their young men came every year to Talodi and attended the two-day gathering and Agricultural Show which, as an element in our administration, aimed at bringing the Nuba together. Even more surprising was the claim in the article that the body and facial painting enjoyed by these people was thought to be uncivilised, primitive and repulsive by the British Colonial Government. We thought nothing of the sort. It is true that some of the educated Sudanese criticised us for allowing the Nuba to go about naked; they felt it was shameful in that it made their country appear backward and uncivilised. One can understand this, but how could we have imposed an order on the Nuba obliging them to dress? There were half a million of them. As education spread, friendly contact with their Arab neighbours grew closer, and as the Nuba developed economically they began to wear clothes, in a somewhat bizarre fashion at times, but gradually more conventionally, and the forms of dress they adopted were happily Arab rather than European.

They had a great sense of fun and humour, and being a simple people were highly amused by simple things. I had two clockwork mice which I used to take with me when I toured and these, if surreptitiously set off, never failed to evoke a moment of alarm followed by gales of laughter. But they once got their own back on me by releasing a snake as I sat talking with a group of greybeards who may well have been privy to the plot, and everyone was doubled up with merriment at my alarm. I didn't know that the snake was harmless. They were not an aggressive people, but they could seldom resist the comedy provided by other people's misfortunes. When an old woman was killed and eaten by hyenas, this was the funniest of accidents. I often carried round with me a small portable gramophone, for the Nuba loved martial music, and I had a laughter record which would make them roll about with merriment. They would listen with fascination to the ticking of my watch, and they were simple enough in those days to be amazed by the novelty of motor cars. Whenever in the District truck I came on a party of young men on the road they would race ahead of or alongside us, setting their speed of foot against ours with shouts of merriment and challenge. They were heavy beer drinkers, especially at harvest time and after funerals, and I often visited a village and found the entire population so merry and witless as to make my remaining there a waste of time. 'Come back in two days,' they would cry rumbustiously, 'and we will then be ready to talk sense!'

In the winter months the weekly mail came through from El Obeid by truck. A letter from England would arrive in ten days if it came by air and in a month by sea. But once the rains started and the main roads were closed, the postal contractor changed over to bulls as a means of transport. A bull, though slower, can make his way through deep mud far more surely and reliably than a horse or a mule. So in the five wet months the mail to Talodi came regularly enough but it took longer, and not infrequently the letters showed signs of submersion. On the other hand the mail to Rashad was carried in the rainy season by a runner from the railway at Rahad eighty miles to the north. If one was feeling homesick one could climb Zib Abu Anga, the granite peak that commands Rashad, and possibly glimpse the smoke of the twice-weekly train as it passed through Rahad station, and if one was up there at the right time one could see the mail runner trotting along the track with his mailbag over his shoulder.

My nearest neighbour to the south of Talodi was the Assistant District Commissioner Eastern Nuer. I never, in fact, met him for we were separated by at least a hundred and fifty miles of country which was partly under water for nearly half the year, and he was based not at an established Government post but on a river steamer. But from time to time he would send me a messenger with a note asking me to supply the man with tea, sugar and a few other necessities, which I did. His name was Wilfred Thesiger.* We were to meet again in the war, and frequently thereafter.

No visitors came to Talodi or indeed to any other part of the Nuba

* W.P. Thesiger, CBE, DSO, *b*. 1910. Sudan Political Service 1935–40. Explorer and writer.

Mountains during the rains, when the roads were under water. During these months I saw few Europeans apart from the two or three missionary families whose stations I occasionally visited. There were times when for many weeks on end, and once for three months, I saw no fellow-countryman. This never bothered me. There was always so much to do, one was always active or on the move, and the time passed quickly enough. But in the winter Douglas Newbold would come twice or perhaps three times and spend a few days touring round the hill villages, and the Deputy Governor would come and inspect the offices, and there would be visits from departmental officials, although the only Departments represented in both Talodi and Rashad were the Medical and the Agricultural. The Sudan Defence Force Nuba Infantry Company from Kadugli, a hundred miles away, marched over once a year to do a week of mountain exercises, to show the flag and to look for likely recruits. I enjoyed these visits for they would bring Eric Palmer, a seconded Royal Marines officer who was good company, or Jacky Hackett-Paine who was later to serve in Palestine, or Hugh Boustead or Etienne Boileau. And in 1937 I had one particularly interesting visitor from outside the Sudan, Margery Perham. She stayed with me for several days and I took her round and showed her how our administration worked and what we were hoping to achieve. She was an expert — informed, perceptive, sympathetic and stimulating. We kept in touch thereafter and were to meet again in the years to come in El Obeid, Khartoum, Nigeria and Oxford. Once a year around Christmas there would be a two-day meeting at Delami near Rashad of all the District Commissioners in the Province, together with the Agriculturalists, to discuss economic and agricultural development. And from Khartoum would come Guy Foley,* who was Director of Economics and Trade, to give us a wider picture of our economic problems and aims.

Every year in January or in February we would hold a Tribal Gathering lasting two days to which would come men from all the hills, and from the nomadic and the settled Arab tribes. There was a grand parade on the first morning, the hillmen and their Arab neighbours drawn up by tribes, dressed in their traditional finery, carrying their ancient firearms, their spears and swords, with their banners flying and their chiefs mounted on tough country-bred ponies. Some of the Arabs wore chain mail. The Governor and his pennanted outriders and his attendant staff would arrive on the parade ground and ride along the ranks to *feux de joie* and shouts of welcome. Rank after rank, they numbered anything from seven to

* Major G.F. Foley, CMG, OBE, MC, *b*. 1896, *d*. 1970.

ten thousand men; it was an impressive scene. The inspection over, the Governor would repair to the grass-roofed dais decorated with red bunting and over which the two Condominium flags would be flying. Beside and around and behind him were seated the town elders, the merchants, the administrative and other officials, the Greek and Lebanese shopkeepers with their wives, and visitors from other parts of the Province. An important element in all this splendour was the Talodi town band, which performed under the direction of ex-Sergeant-Major Al Jak (whom we have already met). Al Jak was a tall, warm-hearted, but exceedingly sinister-looking one-eyed Dinka, long since retired from the Army, and now for many years the senior medical orderly at the hospital. His instrumentalists, except for the drummer and the triangle player who were schoolboys, were likewise retired soldiers. In their white turbans, long shirts and red cummerbunds, wearing old police puttees and 'boarded' police sandals — for we could not afford better ones — they would render their full repertoire of ten pieces. We never knew, nor did they, what these tunes were — with one exception which I had managed to identify: it was Waldteufel's *Estudiantina*. Some must clearly have been Turkish, at least in origin. All the pieces were referred to simply by numbers from one to ten. Al Jak would glare myopically at his strangely assorted group, tap and raise his baton: 'Number Six', he would call, and away they would go. They played for an hour in the market place every Thursday evening.

There followed the presentation of medals, robes and swords of honour to half a dozen or more chiefs and others for service to their people and to the Government. The robes of honour were dark purple and embroidered with gold thread. The swords, of scimitar type, had red velvet scabbards and ivory handles. The medal which was usually presented on these occasions was the King's Medal for Chiefs, which was oval and hung from a heavy chain. The obverse bore the image of King George V, and the reverse a complicated representation of a battleship throwing up a heavy bow wave, a lighthouse and an early type of aeroplane. Competition for these rewards was keen, and they served a useful purpose. Finally came the march past. The tribesmen were well drilled by their leaders. As the columns passed by, they blew their horns and beat their drums and shouted and stamped. Al Jak and his men would do their best to complete with this wild cacophony. The red dust rose thick and stifling. By mid-day the last contingent had passed and we would ride home for a cold bath. The tribesmen dispersed to their camps under the trees on the outskirts of the town. The fires would be lit and the oxen, the pigs from my herd, and goats — all of which we had distributed the previous night — would be cooking. The locally brewed beer would be waiting in earthenware jars.

In the afternoon and on the following day there would be an agricultural show with prizes for the best cattle and horses and goats and crops. Committees under the leadership of the Veterinary Officer and the Agricultural Inspector would have had a hard task making their judgements. There would be wrestling matches and races, on foot and horse back, and possibly a polo match. The schoolboys would give a display concluding with a gymnastic pyramid on the top of which the smallest boy of all would clamber to wave two small representations of the Condominium flags, an achievement that would be greeted with applause and later with congratulations to the young bespectacled headmaster. These durbars, which in various forms were held all over the Sudan, were a popular institution. The tribes vied with one another in the size and splendour of their turnout. They served the purpose of bringing together men who, less than a generation before, had regarded one another as natural enemies. They gave us and the chiefs both the opportunity and the right atmosphere for the discussion of mutual problems and the settling of inter-tribal affairs.

Throughout the winter which began in late October and ended in May, I kept to the southern part of the District. In the rains I normally moved up to Rashad for a spell and took my turn in charge of the District for a month or two while Hawkesworth and Elles were on leave.

I enjoyed these annual spells in Rashad. The rolling countryside was softer and the air cooler. The town lying in a shallow saucer in the hills consisted of little more than a market, the District Headquarters built of stone in the form of a small square fort, the police lines and half a dozen officials' houses. Robin Elles had built a series of dams which held the summer rains against the winter shortage. He had also created a garden which provided the station with fruit and vegetables throughout the year. In the afternoons when I was free I would teach the mounted police tent-pegging, or walk or tend the garden, and in the evenings I often spent an hour or so at the Officials' Club. There was seldom another European in the station. On Fridays, our weekly holiday, I used to walk down to the little market and sit and chat and drink coffee with the merchants in their shops. We drafted the District annual budget in the rains, and as I was nearly always there at that time the task fell to me. The Chief Accountant, the *Mamur* Nasr Ed Din Shaddad and I would wrestle with the figures over two or three weeks, incorporate those that came to us from Talodi and Delami and send off the final document to El Obeid. And then with the budget done I would set off with my ponies and mules back to the south or, if my leave had come, up to the railway at Rahad.

My four and a half years in the Eastern Jebels, based on Talodi, ended in December 1937. Khartoum had planned to move me the year before, but I had pleaded to be allowed to stay and see through some of the plans I had developed, to which Newbold had agreed. So I had been given an additional year. By then it was probably right that I should move on to something new. I was fortunate to have enjoyed so much varied responsibility and experience, to have served under and with men whom I liked and admired, and to have worked among a people who, although difficult at times, gave me the reward of their good humour and friendliness. I left with a feeling that I had made a start, and that even perhaps those other and more senior customers of Messrs Griffiths McAlister, whose photographs hung on the stairs, might one day accept me among their number.

4
PALESTINE
(Galilee, 1938–1939)

I knew, when I left Talodi in December 1937 that the coming year would be one of change. I had no idea how far-reaching the change would prove to be. I was due for a move out of the Province by the middle of 1938 but it was Newbold's idea that until a posting came I would benefit from a spell of Headquarters work in El Obeid. I found myself therefore at the beginning of the year working as his personal assistant, and acting as Commandant of the Province Police. This latter duty gave me an insight into police administration that was to prove useful in the years to come.

Although both of these were temporary appointments I enjoyed them and I enjoyed working with Newbold. There were no more than about a dozen British officers, political, military and departmental, in El Obeid and I therefore saw a great deal of him in and out of the office. The Deputy Governor was away for most of the time and so I worked directly under Newbold, 'putting up' the files, the letters and the telegrams, and drafting the replies. We played polo or squash in the afternoons or rode over the scrubby sand-dunes that surround El Obeid. And often in the early evenings there would be small informal tea parties in Newbold's house with a handful of Sudanese officials, or merchants or tribal leaders in from the districts. From time to time we went to the Sudanese officials' club, and because the menace of Nazi Germany was growing and there seemed a possibility of war, this naturally led to discussion and debates on current affairs.

One of my duties was the weekly inspection of the Province prison with about 300 long-sentence convicts. Along with this responsibility went the obligation to be present at executions. I attended my first during those months and in subsequent years I was obliged to officiate at half a dozen more. It was an unpleasant duty relieved only by admiration for the extraordinary courage of the condemned men. I never saw one who failed to go to his death bravely. These men were murderers whose sentences would have been commuted to life imprisonment had there been any grounds for a reprieve. But theirs were crimes of particular brutality or callousness or premeditation. In their condemned cells, where I had to visit them on the eve of their execution to tell them of the failure of their appeals, they showed nothing but resignation. Although I am sure that it was right in these extreme cases for the death penalty to be carried out, the mechanics of execution undoubtedly lacked imagination and thought for the condemned man. The man would be pinioned and hooded, and there was a walk to the scaffold which included a shuffling and awkward climb of ten or twelve steps to the platform in the prison courtyard. This was in view of the rest of the convicts who crowded the barred windows of their cells and shouted encouragement. When all was ready I would give the sign. After the man had dropped there was an appallingly macabre and gloomy wait of fifteen minutes while the body, its head shrouded in a linen bag, pathetically revolved slowly round and back again; a motion which somehow gave the impression that it still held a thin thread of ebbing life. And then at last we descended into the pit below the trap door where the doctor drew up the man's shirt, listened for his heartbeat and pronounced him dead. I hated these mornings. When it was all over I would mount my pony at the prison gate and ride slowly through the early sunshine of the wakening market.

The stoicism of the Sudanese, their capacity to bear bodily pain as well as mental distress, and their physical toughness and resilience were extraordinary. One year returning from leave I was travelling by train from Khartoum to El Obeid. Early in the afternoon we drew into the station at Rahad, a small market town of perhaps two thousand people, with a primary school and a dispensary. Among the passengers in the crowded third-class carriages was a middle-aged man. He had the usual handful of two or three spears that most Sudanese carried when travelling, together with several bundles, his bedding and his clothing, a kettle and a cooking pot. There was a jostle of other passengers at the end of the coach; and whether the man was inadvertently pushed, or being unused to rail travel misjudged the speed, he jumped to the ground while the train was still moving. Rahad station, like many others, had no platform. Encumbered with his possessions he slipped and fell on to the track between the coach in which he was travelling and the next behind. The wheels passed over his legs just above the knees crushing them both. The train came to a halt.

The only other official travelling apart from the normal train staff was George Bredin who was Deputy-Governor Kordofan.* We were sharing a compartment and were soon aware that some kind of incident had occurred. The ticket collector was the first to inform us. We hurried out and along the track to see whether we could help. An

* G.R.F. Bredin, CBE, *b.* 1899. Joined the Sudan Political Service after war service 1921. Retired 1948. Fellow and Bursar Pembroke College, Oxford 1950–66.

inquisitive group stood looking silently at the wretched man. He was quite conscious and he sat between the rails beneath the carriage under which he had fallen with, I remember so well, a sad puzzled look on his face. His spears and his other possessions lay scattered pathetically about him. At this moment the stationmaster in uniform and sun helmet appeared. He was a solemn self-important man. He gave the impression of thinking more of the report he would have to write, and of the subsequent enquiry, than of the victim of the accident.

'We must get this man to the dispensary at once,' we said. 'Have you a stretcher in the station?' 'No. There is, alas, no stretcher.' 'Any first-aid equipment?' 'Unfortunately not.' 'Then someone must take a donkey and gallop to the dispensary.'

The dispensary was not far, a quarter of a mile perhaps. A boy and a donkey were found and despatched. There was little that any of us could usefully do. The man was pinned by the wheels which for the moment were acting as a tourniquet. He continued to sit silently regarding his disaster. And we and the others around regarded him in shocked silence. The stationmaster spoke to a young bystander who hurried away. A few minutes later he returned. On his head he carried two upright chairs taken from the stationmaster's office. These chairs were placed facing the train and immediately opposite its victim, and we were politely invited to occupy them. It was a hot afternoon, and 'doubtless we were fatigued.' Fortunately at this incongruous moment the dispenser, a calm efficient young man, arrived with a stretcher and other equipment. The train was manoeuvred just sufficiently to release the victim. He was dead before they got him to the dispensary.

I recall too a somewhat similar but fortunately happier incident a year or so before. I had stopped half way between Kadugli and Talodi in order to meet the *Mek* of the mountain village of Koko Limon. His own name, likewise, was Koko Limon. I was to drive him back to Talodi. I was travelling in the District truck and in order to give him the position of precedence which was his due, and likewise to his *Wazir* who accompanied him, my driver took his place with the servants on top of the luggage in the rear of the truck. The *Mek* and the *Wazir* mounted beside me, and I took the wheel. As I did so the *Mek* showed me with some pride a walking stick he had recently acquired, embellished with fine intricate poker work designs: the Nuba seldom travelled without a stick and some were cleverly made and attractively decorated. It was customary in the Sudan to remove the doors of our trucks and box cars: it gave more room and was a lot cooler. The *Wazir* sat between me and his master who thus enjoyed the breezy outside seat. We set off for Talodi. The roads in the Jebels, although only seasonal, were on the whole good. Nonetheless one was wise to avoid driving at much more than thirty miles an hour. Anteaters were liable to dig holes that were not always visible until the last moment. We were travelling at just about this speed when the *Mek* lost hold of his walking stick. He made a grab for it. As in the case of the man in the train at Rahad he no doubt misjudged the speed, and imagining that he could step to the ground safely, he fell. The hub cap of the rear wheel hit his head with a horrifying and sickening thud. We stopped and ran back. The *Mek* lay in the road, unconscious. He looked very bad. He was bleeding from the top of his head and it seemed to me as if part of his brain was oozing out too. The *Wazir* turned to me: 'You have killed the *Mek*,' he said. I rather feared I had, although inwardly I made the reservation that the fault was not entirely mine. We bound Koko Limon's head tightly round with several turbans, and laying him as comfortably as was possible in the back of the truck drove swiftly into Talodi and straight to the hospital. Dr Akasha was non-commital. The *Mek* was still unconscious and his dark skin looked grey. We would have to wait until tomorrow and see how he was. I went anxiously to bed and scarcely slept. At half past six next morning I was on my pony and down at the hospital. On the verandah, his head neatly bandaged and leaning on his precious walking stick, was a smiling Koko Limon. He walked back to his village the following afternoon.

Once or twice a year, on a public holiday, the Governor held a levée in El Obeid. This function, which I was responsible for arranging, involved two hundred or so of the leading townsmen and officials — both in the Service and on pension — assembling at the old mud-brick Turco-Egyptian building which still served as Provincial Headquarters. There, on the verandahs, at nine in the morning, the Governor's visitors would pay their respects and then sit at small tables to drink tea and coffee and eat biscuits and cakes. The Sudanese merchants came in their robes, the officials in European suits, and the pensioned officers — some lean and wizened, others well-favoured and rotund — appeared in their old uniforms carefully preserved for this occasion, with Sam Browne and sword, tarbush or topee. On their chests were their brightly polished campaign medals and on some a British or an Egyptian decoration, the MBE or the Order of the Nile. They were colourful occasions, modest manifestations — soon to disappear — of imperial pomp.

In the early spring my posting came through. I had been appointed Commandant of the Police and *Mamurs*' Training School at Omdurman, together with the Assistant Directorship of Public

Security and Intelligence. I was to succeed W. O'B. Lindsay* (my contemporary) in the autumn after my leave, and was delighted at this prospect. I felt that my Arabic would need to be improved if I were to meet the challenge of this sort of work and I persuaded a friend, Hassan Ali Karrar, to give me lessons twice or three times a week. Hassan was headmaster — and an outstandingly good one — of the Elementary boys' school in El Obeid and he was later to rise to high rank in the Ministry of Education. He is one of those for whose friendship I am grateful and the richer. His father, Ali Karrar, had carried the camel post, before the advent of cars, between El Obeid and Darfur in the west, and I remember him as a very old man resting on hot afternoons in a deck chair set up in the sandy street, on the shady side, outside his house in El Obeid. I often used to greet him and have a word with him on my way home from an early evening ride. Hassan had ten daughters, and his clever and jovial wife, who was one of the few Sudanese ladies who would dine in mixed company, accepted this fate with as much merry resignation as her husband. As Hassan would say, 'I only need one more to make a ladies' cricket team.' And at last in 1949, and in triumph, a son arrived. Hassan was a great admirer of Douglas Newbold and modelled his own English handwriting, which in any event was excellent, precisely on Newbold's clear script. Twenty-five years after his death in 1945, Hassan wrote to Newbold's niece in England: 'I hope you will come one day to the Sudan and visit us and the tomb of the late Sir Douglas Newbold and see for yourself how he is remembered by his large circle of Sudanese friends. I keep his photograph in my bedroom and often visit his grave and talk to him, with no reply from him. He was very kind to me and to all the people of this country. And', he added, 'please give my best wishes to "young Bell" as Sir Douglas used to call him.'

Hassan was a dashing polo player who rode quite uncontrollable and entirely unpredictable ponies. There was a match in El Obeid when, from the moment the ball was thrown in, Hassan's pony executed at terrifying speed not only half a dozen circuits of the ground but at times a diagonal course, missing the other players by inches. He contributed, alas, nothing to our team's efforts for he was as much a threat to us as he was to our opponents. Not surprisingly he made no contact with the ball, for all his efforts were concentrated on his desperate struggle to manage his mount. I can see him now leaning back in the saddle and gritting his teeth, his boots thrust forward in the irons to give him greater leverage. And

* Sir William Lindsay, KBE, *b.* 1909, *d.* 1975. Joined the Sudan Political Service 1932. Transferred to Legal Department 1944. Chief Justice 1954–5.

then in the last chukka with the score at three-all it came about by sheer chance that Hassan's pony and the ball coincided somewhere near the half way line. Hassan, his shirt tails flying, his helmet held to the back of his neck by the chin strap and almost exhausted by his efforts to stay on, let alone direct his pony, shifted the reins to his left hand and took a desperate swipe. Stick and ball met in perfect unison. The latter under the combined impetus of the stroke and the speed of the pony flew high into the air and directly between the posts. We won by a goal! Hassan saw problems in their proper proportion and perspective, and with a vast fund of good humour. He contributed much to the Sudan. He died, alas, in 1982.

We worked away at Arabic in the afternoons, and under his enthusiastic teaching I made progress. Meanwhile I was planning to spend the first part of my leave in the Gulf, Iraq and Palestine, returning to England in time to have a fortnight's shooting at Bisley in mid-July. But my leave date was put forward. I was able to make my Arabian trip, but I had to return to the Sudan without getting to Bisley. In August there came a circular letter from Khartoum offering two members of the Political Service secondment to the Government of Palestine. They were to be bachelors and under the age of thirty-five. The appointment was to be for two years. The situation in Palestine had deteriorated during the spring and summer; Arab desperation at the unchecked flow of Jewish immigration had developed into open rebellion. Two Assistant District Commissioners had already been assassinated, and members of the Palestine Police and the Army had been killed in action against armed bands. The Germans, with the co-operation of neighbouring Arab states, had given the Arab 'nationalists' or 'rebels' or 'terrorists' — however one regarded them — both material and moral support. Sir Harold MacMichael, after a spell as Governor of Tanganyika, had recently been appointed High Commissioner and he had turned to his old Service in the Sudan as a means of reinforcing the administration. Despite the attractions of my Omdurman posting, this seemed a far more exciting and challenging prospect. With Newbold's backing I put in my application.

Palestine, and indeed the whole of the old Turkish empire, had interested me for some time and although I had felt bound to spend a part of my leaves with my parents, and I had tried to get to Bisley for a fortnight in July whenever possible, I had succeeded in travelling in the Middle East every summer between 1934 and 1938. I had sailed in a pilgrim ship to Tor, visited St Catherine's Monastery, crossed Sinai, and travelled up to Amman from Akaba. I had been to Palestine and Syria three times, and followed the North African coast from Cairo to Carthage, visiting Mersa Matruh and the oasis of Siwa on the way. I had been to Aden, Baghdad and Istanbul, though an attempt to join an expedition to the Libyan desert had failed. But Palestine had drawn me more powerfully than any of the other countries. On all these journeys I had travelled alone and generally stayed in small hotels and rest houses, but by way of contrast I had sought once or twice to enjoy rather more exalted company and a brief taste of imperial grandeur. In all our Embassies and Government Houses formality was impressive, but nowhere more so than in Jerusalem when General Sir Arthur Wauchope was High Commissioner, and where I was once able to engineer an invitation to dine at Government House. I borrowed a dinner jacket and a stiff shirt, and presented myself at the exact hour. The dozen or so other guests and I were received by a uniformed Aide-de-Camp, and a servant offered us each a glass of sherry. A clock struck and the Aide marshalled us into line. The High Commissioner appeared, walked slowly along our rank shaking hands as our names were called, and then led us into the dining-room. The meal over, the High Commissioner seated himself in the drawing-room with an empty chair beside him, and in turn, and in order of seniority, we were invited by the Aide for a brief talk with His Excellency which lasted just five minutes, and which was brought to an end by a glance and a movement from the hovering officer. At 10.30, when the last of the guests had concluded his interview, the High Commissioner offered us a final handshake and retired. The guests thereupon departed. This was protocol of a high order, and when Sir Harold MacMichael came to succeed Sir Arthur the atmosphere grew a good deal less formal and ritualistic.

With some first-hand knowledge of Palestine I felt I had a fair claim to this secondment, perhaps reinforced by the fact that on my recent leave a month or two earlier I had served for a short while during a period of emergency as a Special Constable with the Palestine Police in Jerusalem. I waited anxiously, and to my delight I was chosen. The second man selected was A.E.S. Charles who had joined the Political Service two years after me.* He too had served in Kordofan, and we were friends; we were to be ready to go in the autumn. The Munich crisis intervened and it looked for a while as if the whole project might be off. I was still in El Obeid, and while the crisis lasted I was heavily involved helping to prepare the Province for the possibility of war. But it passed and I made plans to leave.

It was late September. Munich was past but few doubted that war

* Sir Arthur Charles, CBE, *b.* 1910, *d.* 1965. Joined the Sudan Political Service 1932. Retired as Establishments Adviser 1967. As Speaker of the Aden State Legislative Council, he was assassinated in 1965 while playing tennis.

lay ahead. My last day in El Obeid was a Sunday. I had sold all my household possessions except for a few rugs. That evening Douglas Newbold conducted our usual weekly service in All Saints Church. It was a converted army hut. We prayed for peace in Palestine and for wisdom and understanding to be granted to those engaged in the administration. And he read the prayer for the peoples of Kordofan, which he had composed when he had first become Governor of the Province. 'Almighty God, the fountain of all wisdom', it ran, 'whose Divine Providence ordereth all things upon earth, we pray thee in thine infinite mercy to preserve the peoples of Kordofan. Let the shadow of thy protection be over them in town and countryside, in mountain, forest and desert. Guard them, we beseech thee, from all disaster of famine, sickness and bloodshed. Pour into their hearts and minds thy precious gift of understanding, so that they may bring peace into feuds, justice into their councils, loving kindness into their homes, and may cast away the works of darkness from their lives, through Jesus Christ our Lord.' I was moved by the thought of this opportunity that had been given me, and by the good wishes of friends whose opinion I valued. Afterwards I dined with Newbold and we sat in the garden talking until midnight. My camp-bed had been set up in the open alongside the railway station, and I slept there until six when the twice-weekly mail train left on its twenty-four hour journey to Khartoum.

Two days later Arthur Charles and I were on our way to Port Sudan and Port Said. We had dined with Sir Stewart Symes, the Governor-General, the evening before we left.* He had been a member of the Palestine administration after the 1914–18 war, and he talked of the north of the country where he had served. I remember him saying, as we sat on the flat terrace roof of the Palace, that he did not believe partition would ever commend itself to the British Government, and that it would not be long before an end must be put to further Jewish immigration. The position at that time was that despite the suggestion by a Royal Commission in the previous July that partition appeared to offer a solution, the British Government, in October 1938, had in fact rejected the idea, and decided to invite representatives of both Jews and Arabs — together with delegates from a number of Arab states — to a Round Table Conference in London. The conference was to consider future policy, including the question of immigration; however, immigration was the factor on which Jewish and Arab views were completely irreconcilable. How different the history of the world would have

* Sir Stewart Symes, GBE, KCMG, DSO, *b*. 1882, *d*. 1962. Resident Aden 1928–34. Governor-General of the Sudan 1934–40.

been if the Governor-General's prediction had been correct.

At Port Said we joined a night train coming up from Cairo. It was full of troops: Inniskillin Dragoons and the Black Watch. At dawn we crossed the Egyptian frontier into Palestine. There were long delays. The troops sang and played mouth-organs and drank beer. At Lydda Arthur Charles left us, since he had been posted to Jerusalem where the situation was particularly tense. I travelled on to Haifa, for I was to go to Galilee. All along the way there was plenty of evidence of how serious the situation was. Most of the railway stations had been burnt; much of the track had been damaged and repaired and damaged again, and the telegraph lines were down. Near Lydda there were two locomotives lying at the foot of an embankment with their wheels in the air. 'Wolseley'-helmeted British troops were occupying sandbagged and wired-in posts alongside bridges and culverts. More than half the country was in the hands of Arab gangs. They were poorly armed but their morale was high. Although after the Munich crisis the British forces in Palestine had been increased to eighteen Infantry battalions, two regiments of armoured cars and some artillery; and although RAF help was also on hand, the authority of the Government was mainly confined to the principal towns, and even there the control was marginal. Hebron and Beersheba had fallen to the southern gangs and been abandoned. In Jaffa the official town crier was daily making his rounds calling for recruits to the 'National Cause'. The Arabs issued their press bulletins and held their own courts. Orange and olive groves owned by Jews had been cut down and standing crops burnt. Movement by day, even on main roads, required an escort of at least in armoured car. Secondary roads were regularly mined. By night the country belonged to the gangs. The intelligence services, as always in a situation of this kind, received little information and in any case much of it was useless or misleading.

There were in fact two authorities controlling Palestine. There were the Arabs, who knew clearly enough who their opponents were: the Jews first and the security forces next. The second authority was the Palestine Government and the Army, who groped in the dark. Any innocent looking farmer driving his donkey along a village track might well be carrying arms or explosives and returning from, or on his way to, a raid or an ambush. A shopkeeper could easily be a gang leader or an agent, watchful to report police or troop movements. The Arab members of the Palestine police found their loyalties under intolerable strain, and village headmen or *Mukhtars* were in an impossible position too, between the representatives of the Government or the Army who occasionally visited them by day, and the gang leaders who controlled them at all other times. Some suspected of active sympathy with the gangs were in detention, but some suspected of active sympathy with the Government had been kidnapped or executed as 'traitors'. This was a deeply rooted peoples' revolt and the seeds of its success, in so far as it had succeeded, lay in the fact that thousands of simple and normally peaceful villagers were prepared to risk their lives to fight what they regarded as oppression and injustice as represented by aggressive Zionism supported by British imperial interests. Ironically all this was precisely what the American King Crane Commission, from which Britain and other Allied Governments had disastrously withdrawn, had foretold twenty years before. The Jews watched the situation with anxiety for the safety of their own people — many of them in exposed and remote settlements — and with determination to turn every development and every incident to their long-term advantage. Groups of Jewish Commando-type men — Special Night Squads — had been enlisted to combat the Arab gangs, and were led by Orde Wingate, and their imaginative training and deliberate ruthlessness had brought them some success. These encounters and the Arab casualties that resulted — often innocent villagers — left a bitterness that was to grow ever deeper with the passage of time.

I spent a night in Haifa and a morning in the District Commissioner's office. He and his Arab Chief Accountant were drafting their budget proposals, and when they came to the expenditure item 'Officials' funerals' the accountant deferentially suggested that the figure should be doubled. The District Commissioner readily agreed. I was issued with a .450 service revolver. This would have been impossibly awkward to draw and use in an emergency and I soon exchanged it for a light Italian automatic — a 'Biretta'. In the Sudan I would never have considered carrying a firearm, nor did any of us, but I did so throughout my time in Palestine. I never cared for the Biretta which was difficult to cock in a hurry and had little stopping power, but its advantage was that it was light and easy to carry. When I went to Beersheba the following year, I was glad to exchange it for a .38 Smith and Wesson revolver. By regular practice and constant handling, and by a course at Police Headquarters in Jerusalem, I made myself fairly handy with the .38.

I reported to Alec Kirkbride,* the District Commissioner in Nazareth, the following morning. Kirkbride had been with Lawrence. Heavily built, taciturn, a first-class Arabist, he gave an impression of vast reliability and strength. No other administrative officer in the country had the same extensive knowledge of the

* Sir Alec Kirkbride, KCMG, CVO, OBE, MC, *b.* 1897, *d.* 1978.

personalities and politics of Palestine and Trans-Jordan, in both of which he had served for the past twenty years. Kirkbride posted me to Tiberias and he drove me over there with a police escort to introduce me to my District and to the Military Commander. Half the culverts were blown and the telegraph wires lay entangled among their posts along the road. There were groves of olive trees, and the brown newly-ploughed fields waited for the first winter rains. It was an Arab area and the square stone-built villages, each with its mosque and minaret merged into the background of the hills. On these same hillsides pines, prickly pears, arbutus and mountain oak formed a *Maquis* which, combined with outcrops of limestone, were ideal sites for snipers and watchmen. But the countryside was beautiful and every mile of the way called to mind the Old and the New Testaments and all the march of later history: we passed through Cana of the first miracle, we could see the Mount of the Beatitudes, we passed Hittin where in 1187 Saladin had destroyed the Crusader army and thus brought to an end the Christian kingdom of Jerusalem. We came to the edge of the escarpment and there, over 1,200 feet below us and 700 feet below sea level, lay the Sea of Galilee, still and blue in the autumn sunshine. To the north lay Mount Hermon and beyond it Damascus; eastwards were the Hauran, the Jebel Druze and the Syrian desert, and to the south stretched the Jordan valley. And there too was Beisan, an area for which I would also be responsible. Beside the lake stood the Arab town of Tiberias (founded by Herod Antipas but named in honour of the Roman emperor), partly enclosed by the ruins of its black basalt crusader walls. On the outskirts and over the surrounding hillsides that ran down to the lake were scattered the modern villas and apartments of the Jewish community. How tranquil it looked, yet only a week before a number of Arab groups had broken into the town and held parts of it for most of the night until the garrison, the South Staffordshire Regiment, had dispersed them. During those hours a score of Jews, men, women and children had been killed, some with great brutality. The District offices had been burnt and every file and record destroyed.

As Assistant District Commissioner Tiberias/Beisan I had two District Officers to help me; one an Arab, the other a Jew. Each kept to his own community and neither dealt with his colleague except through me. The Army was responsible for public security which meant, in the existing circumstances, responsibility for almost everything that would normally be dealt with by a civilian district administration. The 'South Staffords' covered Tiberias and the surrounding Arab villages and Jewish settlements. The northern end of the Jordan valley and the eastern part of the Vale of Esdraelon, which included the purely Arab town of Beisan, were patrolled by the Trans-Jordan Frontier Force. This was a British force enlisted locally from a variety of nationalities and including a majority of Arabs but also a good many Circassians; the senior officers were British. It was effective and reliable. The Police — British, Jewish and Arab — fulfilled the role of supplying the Army with such information as they could obtain, providing escorts and making such criminal investigations as were feasible. But many serious crimes went undetected and even unreported. What role could I best fulfil in all this confusion? I thought I could at least be a useful co-ordinating link between the armed forces and the police on the one hand and the Arab and Jewish populations on the other. The Jews were only too ready to keep in touch. For the most part relations, certainly friendly relations, with the Arabs had been lost, but the Army constantly patrolled the Arab areas and I could accompany them. At least I could speak to elders and villagers in their own language.

My intention that I should find a house in Tiberias was vetoed by the security forces. It would have involved an escort of strength and I therefore accepted, as a temporary arrangement, the South Staffords' invitation to join their mess. They could not have been more friendly. They gave me a room in a commandeered hotel containing a bed, a cupboard and a table, and there I lived to the sound of boots clattering on the stone stairs, mouth-organs playing and vehicles coming and going at all hours. They also gave me a cheerful soldier servant who whistled a great deal. His arms and chest were covered with tattoos including a representation of a gravestone and beneath it the sad inscription 'In memory of my dear mother'. Contact with the South Staffords involved working closely with their Intelligence Officer John Commings.* Quick and aware, he had a great fund of humour and an acute sense of essentials. We rapidly became friends, and have remained so ever since.

Life was full. Shortly after my arrival the Jewish Mayor of Tiberias was shot and killed in the centre of the town. A week or two later the Arab Mayor of Beisan was abducted, carried off into the hills, imprisoned in a cave for a week and beaten up. Soon after that my Arab District Officer, Nejib Bawashi, was shot in the back as he left his house. His successor, immediately on his arrival, departed on a long spell of sick leave. On the way to Beisan in the dusk of a late afternoon, accompanied by my orderly John Laws who had joined the Palestine Police from the Rifle Brigade, we were ambushed. The Frontier Force escort vehicle was shot up and a man was wounded. For several minutes there was confused firing. The hired car I was

* Brigadier J.C. Commings, CBE, *b*. 1913.

driving stalled and the self-starter would not work. There was an Arab behind a bush at the side of the track four or five yards away, his face half covered with his headcloth, a rifle in his hand. We were a very easy target — and so was he. 'Shoot him,' I shouted at Laws. 'Drive on, Sir,' Laws shouted back. He and the Arab fired several rounds to no effect. Mercifully the car at last responded to the self-starter and I drove on. We reached the Police Station at Beisan with our escort unscathed and rather pleased with ourselves.

That same afternoon a squadron of the Frontier Force had been engaged in the hills of Gilboa. Although on a small scale, it had been a successful encounter and in exchange for two men wounded the Force had killed or captured the greater part of a gang of some size. And so it was, during the latter part of that winter and the spring of 1939, throughout most of Palestine. There were still numerous incidents — ambushes, sniping, abductions and murders. British troops were engaged in constant small actions, villages were searched and fines imposed, and sometimes a house found to have been used as a hide-out was destroyed by explosives. Men were held in detention on suspicion. At first the British forces were at a marked disadvantage in attempting to deal with terrorists and saboteurs operating on ground with which they were thoroughly familiar, and among their own people. But now the Army were learning how to bring the gangs to action and when they did so their superior weapons gave them an overwhelming advantage. Thus gradually but surely the tough dedicated men of the gangs, with their unrivalled knowledge of every rocky hill, wooded valley, cave and watercourse were slowly forced to yield to numbers and fire power. In March they shifted the focus of their activities to Trans-Jordan, and the Arab Legion was involved in an action in Gilead.* Although a British officer serving with the Legion, Lieutenant Macadam, was killed, the Legion with the help of the RAF, inflicted severe losses on the infiltrators who eventually withdrew to Syria. But in the extreme south, the country around Hebron and Beersheba still remained firmly in the hands of the gangs. Meanwhile in London during February and March 1939 the Round Table Conference, attended by Arab and Jewish representatives and delegations from Iraq, Saudi Arabia, Yemen and Trans-Jordan, failed to reach agreement.

Throughout the spring I accompanied the South Staffords on their patrols and searches of villages. I interpreted and tried to keep relations between the soldiers and the Arabs as friendly as possible, which in general was not difficult. There were times certainly when over-zealous soldiers surrounding an Arab village before dawn to

* The Arab Legion was commanded by Major John Glubb (Glubb Pasha). Unlike the Trans-Jordan Frontier Force it was not an imperial formation but the Emir Abdulla's army, and owed its loyalty solely to the Emir.

search for arms or explosives or wanted men would shoot a cordon-breaker, often a shepherd lad or some old man driving a donkey who understood nothing of what was afoot and to whom the pamphlets dropped by the RAF by way of warning meant even less. I did my best to avert incidents of this sort and, if they came about, to pacify as far as I could the relatives of men killed or wounded. But mostly the troops behaved with exemplary restraint even when they suffered casualties. I never saw or heard of a case of looting or brutality; every party which searched a house or a village was accompanied by a local witness, and I knew no case of a woman being molested. Although mosques were sometimes used as arms stores they were scrupulously respected.

The combing of a village entailed all the men and boys being collected and lined up. There would then be a search for wanted men. This meant that these people would be obliged to file slowly past a police armoured car in which a Government informer was concealed. This character peered through a chink in the vehicle, seeing but unseen, and indicated to the CID officer beside him if he recognised or thought he recognised anyone on the wanted list. It was a system open to abuse, and although there was no other way whereby the identification of elusive gunmen and saboteurs was normally possible, few of us cared for the use of what was bound to be a frequently corrupt and, as it seemed, somewhat unsporting way of doing things. And for all that the gangs were guilty of inexcusable methods on occasions and the troops were sometimes over-zealous, there did exist nonetheless a flavour of fair play and a sense of humour between the two sides. There were occasions when facetious messages were exchanged in the same spirit as in the Boer War. Roads particularly village tracks, were always liable to be mined, but, in the paradoxical way things work in the Arab world, there was never any shortage of volunteers among the local taxi owners prepared to drive immediately ahead of a military column and thereby, in some degree, to ensure its safety. The financial rewards were considerable, but so were the risks.

I tried to divide my time equally between the Jewish and Arab communities. In number they were roughly equal. Dropping in at short notice on Jewish settlements presented no problems. They were always eager to see me, indeed they were constantly inviting me to meals, when immediately the conversation would turn to demands for increased protection, a larger establishment of Jewish Supernumerary Police, and above all additional weapons. In the face of frequent attacks both on the settlements and on individuals the Jews generally showed remarkable self-restraint — but not always. For the fact is that the Jewish Agency, which answered for the Jewish community, was not always master in its own household. Numerous acts of terrorism were carried out by Jews against Arabs during this period and earlier, and in particular bombs were planted in Arab vegetable markets and other places and dozens of innocent people were killed or wounded. The Jewish case was that these acts were the work of two paramilitary organisations — the Irgun Zvai Leumi, command of which was soon to be assumed by Menachem Begin, and the Stern Group — which refused to respond to the Agency's appeals for moderation; and that the Agency was powerless to prevent them. This may have been so but it is worth remembering that as soon as the Mandate came to an end the Israeli Government had no hesitation in controlling these extremist groups. And of course we knew that in all these settlements they were busy training their men — and their women — in the creation of an underground army, the Haganna, and clandestinely acquiring supplies of arms from numerous sources, arms which in time they were to use to great effect not only against the Arabs but against us. Sometimes I would spend a night in a settlement. The *Kibbutz* aimed to combine in its agricultural setting three objectives; social equality, sexual equality and national aspirations. The atmosphere of these *Kibbutzim* was always the same: neat, regimented, efficient and austere. The food and drink were institutional. The men and women were mostly dressed alike, in light-blue shirts and skin-tight shorts. There would be stimulating evening entertainments when the young men and girls would enliven the bare assembly hall with their traditional songs and dances. The feel of the place would be heavy with a combination of gaiety and sadness — confidence in the future and nostalgia for the past. Behind the stockade and the barbed wire fence the settlement searchlight slowly swept the surrounding countryside.

Visiting Arab villages and encampments meant going with a sizeable escort, and the atmosphere, although superficially sincere and friendly, would contain an element of hazard, restraint and caution on both sides. But the hospitality was always warm and generous even if the village had been recently subjected to an army search or possibly a communal fine. The unhygienic food was delicious; the host tattered, dignified and courteous. In the background the women, shrouded, dark fluttering figures, would hover and disappear. With smiling protestations of loyalty on one side and equally hypocritical expressions of confidence on the other, we would depart before mid-afternoon. An evening ambush on the road home, to which our host might just conceivably be privy, was always a possibility. And in that event our host would be embarrassed.

In common with the great majority of the British serving in

Palestine at that time, in whatever capacity from private soldier upwards, I admired but found it very difficult to like the Jews, settlers as well as townspeople. And again in common with most of my countrymen, I liked and sympathised with the Arabs but in general had less admiration for them. So often — as we saw it — they failed to realise where their best advantage lay, and cut off their noses to spite their faces. The soldiers, who called their opponents *Ouzlebarts* (a corruption of the Arabic word *Asabat* meaning fighting groups), instinctively felt a preference for the wild men who sniped at them from the hillsides to the seemingly friendly Jewish settlers who over-keenly entertained them with food and beer. The cause for which the Arabs were fighting was, to us, understandable and just. Their methods and the means they employed, particularly against unarmed and innocent Jews and frequently against their own people, were often barbaric and inexcusable; but as a general rule when admiration and liking are in conflict, the latter will prevail.

The Jewish people may well have made the most tragic of mistakes in believing that their unique gifts and their remarkable genius lie in a territorial entity rather than in their traditional international role, a role that has always been essentially economic, cultural and social, and which embraced the world. For centuries, despite all their sufferings, their genius enriched the greater part of civilised mankind with great achievements, and in many of the highest realms of human endeavour. Where have their nationalistic and political ambitions now led them? The answer is into what has simply become a new kind of ghetto of their own creation, more and more inward-looking and menaced from without by ever-increasing bitterness and hatred. As a small, embattled and besieged nation, they have sacrificed a position of stateless but nonetheless world influence for what they appear to believe is a divine title-deed giving the land of Palestine to the people of Israel. It is sadly ironic that a people whose sufferings have shocked the world so often in the past are now imposing comparable sufferings on another people. The Arabs of Palestine were not responsible for what Europe did to the Jews, yet it is they who are paying the price. But however much one may deplore Zionist aims and practices the fact is that the initial responsibility for what has happened lay with Britain. The Balfour Declaration and all that sprang from it do not constitute a creditable part of our history. The United States too must accept its share in supporting Zionism morally and financially for more than thirty years. In doing so it has encouraged Israel on a course which, unless it is radically altered, must sooner or later lead to even greater tragedies than those we have seen already.

By the beginning of December things in Tiberias town were sufficiently quiet for me to be able to move out of the South Staffords' wired-in area and into the Tiberias Hotel. The place was practically empty and I took a small suite consisting of a bedroom and a sitting room with a hallway. In spite of the hospitality of the mess, I preferred this arrangement for it gave me much greater freedom of movement. I felt sufficiently confident to go about the town, varying the time of my movements and my route, and I came to know a few of the townsmen, both Arab and Jew. And from Beisan I got an occasional ride with the Trans-Jordan Frontier Force. They had a detachment of sixty mounted men and six armoured cars in the Jordan valley north of Jiflik, commanded by 'Shan' Hackett.* Shan had been at Oxford with me, had joined the 8th Hussars from the University and was now seconded to the Frontier Force. I went to stay with him and his men and they took me with them on their patrols. He was a stimulating host, and no one who knew him then can have been surprised at his later distinguished career both as a fighting soldier and, after retirement from the Army, in the academic world. We spent days visiting the Sugr, the Zinati and the Ghazzawia, semi-nomadic tribes that moved up and down the Jordan valley following the grazing. Most of their able-bodied men operated with the gangs from time to time but that did not prevent them entertaining us to lunch with roasted sheep, rice and sour milk, and with the greatest courtesy.

The mountains of Gilboa overlooked us, the vale of Jezreel stretched away to the west, and across the Jordan lay Gilead; and as the winter rains, intermittent but heavy at times, and the cold winds from the north gave way in February to warmer weather, spring came to the Jordan valley, and a little later to the Galilee uplands, with incredible beauty. The fields and hillsides became covered with white, purple and pink cyclamen and scarlet anemones, which are St Matthew's 'lilies of the field'. There were yellow crowfoot, marigolds, lupins and sky-blue sea lavender. As the spring progressed there emerged narcissus, sweet-smelling mustard and pink flax. The farmlands showed green with young wheat and barley, and the stony stream beds were pink with oleander blossom. Only those who have seen it can understand the Solomon's Glory of spring in Palestine.

And with the spring I developed bacillary dysentery which put me into the Scottish Mission Hospital in Tiberias for a fortnight. As I had scarcely taken a day off since arriving in Palestine, I rather enjoyed the enforced idleness. Perhaps I was fortunate in falling ill

* General Sir John Hackett, GCB, CBE, DSO, MC, *b.* 1910.

when I did, for although I knew nothing of it at the time, a 'rebel' court had decided that I should be done away with. I was to be shot from a window as I left the Tiberias hotel on my way to or from my office. My retirement to hospital threw the operation out of gear, and by the time I was up and about again, an informer had disclosed the plan and I was able to take the necessary precautions. It was then seemingly decided that a bomb should be thrown into my office. The bomb was thrown all right, but it bounced off the wire that protected the window and exploded harmlessly. Several anonymous written warnings were sent to me. It surprised me how used I became to this sort of thing: I now automatically looked both ways immediately before passing through a doorway and chose the corner seat, wherever I happened to be, with a clear view of the door.

These incidents were reported to the Major-General who had recently arrived in Haifa to take command of the 8th Division operating in Northern Palestine, and he came to Tiberias. He was a lean, wiry, dynamic man who spoke in clipped staccato sentences. He strongly advised me to move back, for a short while at least, into the South Staffords' mess. I pondered what he had said and, conceding that in the circumstances it was a sensible idea, I agreed. His name was Bernard Montgomery. I never met him again.

A far more frightening and dangerous incident occurred some weeks later when two South Staffordshire officers and I were swimming from a rowing boat in the sea of Galilee. The sudden storm so dramatically and accurately described in the New Testament caught us and we had the greatest difficulty regaining our boat. When we did so the wind and the waves were such that we would certainly have been swamped and drowned had a group of soldiers on shore not seen us purely by chance. We were rescued, just in time, by a Palestine Police launch. I don't think I have ever since felt quite the same terror.

The London Round Table Conference of February and March 1939 had failed. War with Germany, which had already occupied Prague, and possibly with Italy, which had invaded Albania in April, became an increasingly ominous likelihood. German press and wireless bulletins poured out, in Arabic, violent anti-British propaganda. Palestine was a vital link in the line of Britain's communications with India and the Far East. Against this background of growing tension the British Government produced on 17 May a White Paper embodying its own proposals for a settlement. It fixed a quota of Jewish immigration for the next five years at 10,000 annually plus a total of an additional 25,000 as a contribution towards a solution of the Jewish refugee problem. At the conclusion of this five-year period any further immigration would be subject to

Arab consent. It justified this restriction on the admission that the Balfour Declaration did not intend that Palestine should become a Jewish state, or that the whole of Palestine should be converted into a Jewish 'national home'. Furthermore it proposed the creation of an independent Palestine state at the end of ten years. This was explicit enough, yet events were to show within less than ten years the complete invalidity of all that the White Paper contained. Not surprisingly these proposals were rejected by the Jews who immediately intensified their campaign of clandestine arming and training. For the Arabs the White Paper held out the promise of an independent state with an Arab majority in population, effectively removing their basic fear of being outnumbered. In some quarters the White Paper was accepted, but from no part of the Arab world did any positive agreement emerge. I believe that in thus failing to respond the Arabs made a wrong judgement; had they been more realistic and ready to accept something less than their complete demands, history might well have unfolded differently. In practice, however, they showed an increase of goodwill in contrast to the rapid diminution of Jewish co-operation. Indeed from now on, despite lip-service to the contrary, a considerable section of the Jewish population of Palestine gave greater support to the eventual creation of the state of Israel than to the defeat of the Axis. This measure of Arab goodwill was to stand us in good stead throughout the war years.

My own fortunes too were about to change. The High Commissioner came to Tiberias. He told me that he had thought of sending me to Trans-Jordan as Assistant Resident but had decided instead to move me to Beersheba. I was to take over the Sub-District as Deputy District Commissioner Gaza/Beersheba, and in addition was to reconstitute the *Hajana* — the Camel Gendarmerie — which had disintegrated when the gangs had occupied Beersheba the previous September. I was to create a force similar to the Desert Patrol of the Arab Legion. 'I want someone,' he said to me, 'with Kordofan ideas, someone who knows one end of a camel from the other, someone who can meet and talk to these people, these Bedu, on the basis of gentleman to gentleman.' Here was good fortune indeed. This was exactly the sort of job I felt qualified to do both by experience and by inclination. I moved south to Beersheba late in June, and was delighted with all that I saw and by the prospect of what I hoped to be able to achieve.

5

PEACE IN THE DESERT

(Beersheba, 1939–1941)

The Gaza/Beersheba District covered nearly half the total area of Palestine, the southern half. But in population it represented no more than a tenth, something like a hundred thousand people out of a total of a million or more. The district was triangular in form, the shape of a long narrow wedge. The northern boundary ran westwards from the Dead Sea to the Mediterranean coast north of Gaza, and followed the line of the foothills of Judea. The eastern boundary marched with Trans-Jordan and ran from the Dead Sea to the Gulf of Akaba. On the western side the frontier left the Mediterranean coast at Rafah until it too struck the Gulf of Akaba. This was our frontier with Sinai, undemarcated and of small significance to the nomadic tribes who moved across it at will. In the Judean foothills, and along the Mediterranean shore, were neat stone or mud brick villages housing a settled population of farmers. They prospered from the produce of their citrus and olive groves, their vineyards and their vegetable gardens. When the winter rains came they planted barley and wheat. The rest of the District, the exclusively desert area that fell under the administrative control of Beersheba Sub-District, supported a nomad population of perhaps seventy thousand Bedouin tent dwellers, who bred and depended on their camels, sheep and goats, and who in the years when the winter rainfall was good ploughed the stony ground with camel or donkey and harvested a meagre grain crop. For water they counted on their ancestral wells and a few ancient rock cisterns. And with their tents, their families and their animals they followed the grazing, crossing sometimes into Trans-Jordan and Sinai and sometimes, in dry years, moving into Judea and even as far as Samaria. Their homeland was a wilderness: the Biblical wilderness of Zin, Paran and Shur: the Arabian El Negeb. They were a thin birdlike people, gaunt and stringy. 'Very spare, sadly shrivelled, poor over-roasted snipe, mere cinders of men', Kinglake had said of them in *Eothen* a hundred years before.

This southern area of Palestine had always been lightly administered by the Mandatory Government. The Bedu sheikhs had been given delegated powers to administer justice in all but serious crime in accordance with tribal law and custom. Apart from a handful of British Police stationed in the town of Beersheba, public security was maintained by a force of Camel Gendarmerie locally enlisted and hitherto under the command of a British Palestine Police officer. Its most notable commander had been John Faraday.* The administrative officer responsible for the peace and welfare of the Bedu had for many years been a Palestinian Arab. Left to themselves the tribes, apart from their own local feuds, had given little trouble and had scarcely concerned themselves with the various outbreaks of anti-Government activity that had been so much a feature of the rest of the country over the previous twenty years. But the circumstances of 1937 and 1938, the influence of neighbouring Arab countries, German and Italian radio broadcasts and a general growth of political awareness had all had an effect, partly on the Bedu but more particularly on their sedentary neighbours around Gaza and Hebron. Great violence and destruction had marked the year 1938, and throughout Palestine the number of killed and wounded on the Government side, among civilians and among the gangs had totalled well over three thousand. Southern Palestine and Beersheba were not immune. The period leading up to the Munich crisis brought things to a head, and on 9 September 1938 Beersheba was raided by a large gang which probably consisted principally of men from the area of the Hebron hill villages, but may also have contained elements from the Bedu and from Gaza. Working with great precision, the gang destroyed the wireless post, broke into the prison and released the prisoners, and after killing a British Police Sergeant raided the Police Station and got away with a Lewis gun, rifles and ammunition. The Arab District Officer was left unmolested. Later in the month all Police and Government buildings in the town were set on fire and destroyed. Government representation was thereupon withdrawn, and Beersheba and the whole of southern Palestine apart from the town of Gaza remained for the next nine months outside Government control. The half-dozen desert posts which had been manned by the Camel Gendarmerie were abandoned and destroyed, and the men melted away taking their arms with them. Road culverts were blown up and telegraph lines were torn down. But saddest of all in this catalogue of violence was the complete destruction of all the few medical dispensaries that existed. They had been set up in remote areas solely for the welfare of the tribesmen and particularly their families. The roofs were torn off and the windows broken and every bottle of medicine was smashed. The dispensers fled. And in consequence, for almost a year, the Bedu

* Group Captain J.A.M. Faraday, MC, KPM, *b.* 1899.

were left without medical aid, and people, and particularly children, died.

A detachment of British troops moved into and occupied Beersheba in the spring of 1939. At the same time the Police Station was re-established and a start was made on repairing the burnt-out Government offices. But administration was confined to the town, and the desert areas remained without a Government presence until the early summer, when the District Officer was able to make a number of visits to the tribes. This was the position when I arrived in Beersheba in June.

I had got my first sight and initial impressions of this arid but romantic land, in which I was to live for the next two years, in 1934, when I had spent part of my leave exploring Sinai and Trans-Jordan, and had then driven down the desert road to Egypt through Beersheba. And in the following year I had been up in the Judean Hills on an archeological site at Tel Duwair, the ancient Lacish, and had looked southwards to where the hills fell away to this same desert. Much as I had been drawn to this part of the world I had never imagined that within a few years I would be there in administrative control.

It was a drab landscape, in places monotonously flat and in others gently undulating, its harshness and general uniformity relieved here and there by patches of camel thorn and areas of low scrub. The sand and gravel surface of the land was marked by dry shallow watercourses which once or twice a year became, for a few hours, brown tumbling torrents. South and east of Beersheba this even and gently rolling country gave way to the barren hills and ridges of the escarpment that overlooked the southern edge of the Dead Sea, and the Wadi Araba. Beyond lay Trans-Jordan. Southwards in spectacular desolation stood a series of deep canyons and rugged cliffs. Along the Sinai frontier rolled the waves of windswept sand dune. In the summer the sun glared through the haze, and the heat struck back from the silent sand and rock. There was little shade apart from the shadows cast by cliffs or thorn trees. It was a land of constant mirages, of lakes and trees and buildings that were without existence. From time to time the deserts were swept by dust storms. But in the winter and spring the air was cold and invigorating, and along the watercourses and on the plains the land was green and welcoming.

One narrative imputes the origin of Beersheba to Abraham, the other to Isaac, both of whom are said to have dug wells there. Throughout the succeeding centuries it remained the centre of a sensitive border area on the edge of the desert that led to Egypt, to Moab and to Edom. It marked the southern frontier of Israel and

Judah under David and Solomon. In Roman times Beersheba was a garrison town and later the seat of a Christian bishopric, and in the seventh and eighth centuries nomad tribes from Central Arabia moved into the Negeb, and it became a well centre for the Bedu. The Turks garrisoned the town and built a railway to it which was extended to aid their attack in 1915 on the Suez Canal. It marked the eastern flank of Allenby's advance in 1918. So Beersheba had seen peoples and armies come and go. Yet few could have imagined in 1939 that it would so soon be under Israeli rule, and that by 1949 both Yigal Allon and Moshe Dayan would, in their turn, as officers commanding the Israeli Army's 'Southern Command', be responsible for that precise area in which I had been the civil administrator ten years before.

In 1939 Beersheba was no more than a small market town. There was a single street of simple shops and shaded booths that met the needs of the Bedu; cotton clothing and bright headcloths, cloaks, camel furnishings, coloured enamel kettles, brass and copper coffee pots, and the few luxuries that they could afford in good years: coffee, tea, sugar and rice. The merchants had their square featureless stone houses on the fringes of the town and it was in half of one of these, consisting of a central chamber with two rooms leading off it, that I lived for my first months there. The other half of the house was occupied by Michael Hankin-Turvin, the Assistant Superintendent of Police.

Gaza by contrast was a town of size and substance, and a certain amount of my work had to be done there. It had a British District Commissioner to whom I was nominally subordinate. He had been seconded from an African territory and, not surprisingly, knew no Arabic. But he suffered from other disadvantages, not least of which was a disturbing habit of keeping much of the secret correspondence under his bed and forgetting that it was there. Within a few months of my arrival he departed, and I was not altogether sorry. For nearly a year no one replaced him and I was on my own in charge of both Gaza and Beersheba. This meant that the Gaza area took up time that I would have liked to give to the desert and its problems, but Arif Al Arif, who had previously served in Beersheba for many years and was accorded the courtesy title of *Bey*, was in Gaza as District Officer. Arif Bey combined wide and colourful experience with a great deal of shrewd judgement. He had served in the Turkish Army, deserted and escaped to Russia, and returned to Palestine by way of Vladivostok; in the 1920s he had been an anti-British political leader, but had subsequently been pardoned and joined the administrative service. I was happy to leave most of the work in Gaza to him. Nonetheless first the threat and subsequently the outbreak of war in

September brought us new problems: we had to consider supplies and rationing, and the possibility of air attack. Every week we had a meeting of a locally appointed Security Committee. This Committee consisted of the British Police Superintendent, the Mayor Rushdi Bey Esh Shawa, Arif Bey Al Arif, and one or two others. We were appallingly ill prepared to deal with the problem of air raids; we had no sirens, no shelters, no wardens nor any funds that might provide these essentials. But we formed an Air Raid Precautions Committee which after careful deliberation issued the following admirably simple instruction to a not very interested public: 'The approach of enemy aircraft will be signalled by the Muezzins of the five principal mosques. From each minaret they will cry out a loud warning. The arrival of enemy aircraft will be made known to the people by the firing of the Ramadan gun. A 50lb barrel of black powder will be ordered for this purpose.' Fortunately no raids came and in the months that followed an advance party of the Australian Sixth Division arrived, and the Australian Commander took over the chairmanship of the Local Security Committee. Our resources and our preparations thus became less primitive and I was able to revert to the duty of Secretary. I tried, as far as I could, to do my Gaza work at the weekends and to spend the rest of the week dealing with Beersheba and its problems. Although the road was rough, I could get from Gaza to Beersheba by car in an hour and a half.

It seemed to me that three things needed to be done as soon as possible to restore the authority of the Government among a people who were not basically hostile to our administration, but who needed to see evidence that it was both effective and sympathetic. The first — which was what I had been instructed to do — was to reconstitute the Camel Gendarmerie, a force of something over a hundred men, and rebuild and re-establish the half dozen or so desert posts which had been abandoned and destroyed. The posts would need to be defendable and equipped with wireless, and we would require two or three trucks with sand-tyres to enable us to make constant inspections. The second essential was for me to visit the areas where the principal tribes lived and get to know them and particularly their Sheikhs. Thirdly, we needed to re-establish a working liaison with the neighbouring Trans-Jordanian tribes and with the Arab Legion which had a post at Akaba and another at Gharandal half way up the Wadi Araba. Furthermore it would be necessary to re-establish contacts with our neighbours in Sinai where Colonel J. St H. Hammersley, one of the last British officers to serve in the Egyptian Frontier Defence Administration, was Governor. I was anxious to know how the administration of the desert area of Trans-Jordan worked and how the forts, which had been built by

Major J.B. Glubb,* and the men in them functioned. I had been told by the High Commissioner to create a force along the lines of the Desert Patrol of the Arab Legion. All this had to be done quickly and against the background of the storm that was gathering in Europe. The French were in trouble in Syria, and Syrian nationalists and agitators were in close and constant touch with some of our own Palestinian political leaders.

Akaba in the extreme south of the district was one of the places I visited during those first weeks. Here Trans-Jordan and Palestine shared a common frontier, and here for the first time I met Glubb. I took an immediate liking to him, to his disarmingly quiet and almost diffident manner, to his evident friendliness, and to the sympathy and help he was clearly anxious to give me in restoring and keeping the peace between the Trans-Jordan and Palestine tribes. I also came to admire increasingly his tireless enthusiasm for his command, and his unique knowledge of the Bedu and their ways and of their written and spoken language. He had time for everyone and infinite patience with the problems of any tribesman, however trivial, and would listen endlessly to complaints. And later, when I went to serve under him in the Legion, I saw day after day the steady queue of visitors to his office and evening after evening the groups of petitioners who preferred to bring their problems to his house. He received them all with apparent and doubtless real sympathy. At this our first meeting he suggested that I might usefully visit the Legion's desert posts as soon as possible, which was exactly what I wanted to do. So I went over into Trans-Jordan in August and spent the inside of a week with Norman Lash who was in command of the Legion's Desert Patrol. I met him in Amman and he took me round the Desert area visiting the forts at Bair, Jeffar, Wadi Rum and Mudawara, where the rusty corpses of the trains destroyed by Lawrence and his men still lay beside the twisted tracks, and Al Guwaira which the Romans had once garrisoned. I came back to Beersheba eager to try and make use of what I had seen.

That autumn I was able to make an extensive camel tour that covered almost the whole southern area of the District. With a party of eight I rode down to Birein on the Palestine-Sinai frontier intending to cross the two thousand foot watershed between the Mediterranean and the Wadi Araba, and then ride northwards up the Wadi Araba to the post at Ain Hosb that had been abandoned and subsequently burnt. From there I would make my way back to Beersheba. It would take ten days. We followed the main track to the

* Lt.-Gen. Sir John Glubb Pasha, KCB, CMG, OBE, DSO, MC, *b*. 1897. Soldier, author and Arabist.

Sinai frontier past the abandoned Gendarmerie posts of Asluj and Auja Hafir. This was the Biblical Wilderness of Paran and the land of the Amalakites, that lay astride the great trade route from Petra to Gaza linking the Mediterranean with South Arabia. It was a harsh, dry, flat and featureless landscape and we covered the distance in two and a half days. After half a day's rest we set off from Birein at mid-day and four hours riding brought us to a small Serahin encampment consisting of a single tent. Here with our poor but welcoming host we spent the night wrapped in our sheepskin cloaks and in such meagre space as we could find on the tent floor amid a confusion of saddle bags, cooking pots and goats. From this point the character of the country began to change. We left at six the next morning in thick mist, following a path which climbed steadily upwards through broken and rocky country. The mist turned to rain and we were soon wet and cold and miserable. The camels hated it. Early in the afternoon we were fortunate to come upon another isolated Serahin encampment, where our hosts gave us damp refuge but warm hospitality, and a goat for our dinner. Once again we were away soon after dawn and once again through heavy fog. After an hour's riding we lost our way and stumbled on, leading the camels through driving rain and unable to see more than a hundred yards ahead. We were still climbing. Then at mid-day the rain lifted and we halted for a meal of bully beef, raw onions, olives and bread. We got a slow smoky fire going and made a kettle of tea.

It was while we were sitting drinking our tea, the camels grazing on such meagre shrubs as they could find, that a very aged Arab emerged from the mist and accepted our invitation to share our refreshment. He was looking for a lost camel. We poured him a glass of tea and enquired whether he would care for milk. He looked at me and then suspiciously at the tin of condensed 'Carnation'. In his mind tins were identified with Christians and the contents of tins with what he understood to be Christian taste. 'No', he said, 'I never touch pig's milk.'

The weather showed signs of clearing and we rode another two hours to camp in the open just short of the watershed. It was very cold. The next morning dawned fine, but still misty, and we reached a ridge of high ground after less than two hours slow riding. Here we made tea, and as we sat, the mist suddenly lifted, and there far below us lay the Wadi Araba with the blue line of the mountains of Edom and Moab in Trans-Jordan beyond. We moved on and began to make our way downwards. It was a rocky deserted scene. We stopped at midday for a brief meal, and by sunset we were down on the plain in comparative comfort. Behind us, now clear of cloud and rain, stood the impressive looking range we had crossed. We slept under the tamarisk bushes in the sand, warm and dry for the first time in three days. Eight hours of riding northwards on the following day along the dry sandy bed of the valley brought us to the Arab Legion post of Gharandal.

Gharandal was built on the model of all the Trans-Jordan Arab Legion forts; high stone walls surrounding a central courtyard with twin towers at opposite corners commanding a clear view over miles of country. Two peacocks provided an additional alarm in case of a stealthy night attack: every post had a pair. The garrison, consisting of a sergeant and half a dozen men, welcomed us warmly, dined us with a sheep and rice and sent us on our way next morning. Seven hours' easy ride brought us late in the afternoon to the ruined Gendarmerie post of Ghaur. Here again we camped among the tamarisks. There was plenty of firewood and the men cooked fresh bread in the ashes and we dined on a tin of milk, olives, red peppers and sardines in oil. We slept early and moved at four next morning.

By mid-day we were at a another abandoned Gendarmerie post, Ain Hosb, whence a rough motorable track climbed the escarpment, and led over the watershed back to Beersheba. Here we slept in the ruins of the post.

Commanding the only road from Beersheba to the Wadi Araba and thence eastwards to Trans-Jordan, north to the Dead Sea and south to Akaba, it was essential to get Ain Hosb rebuilt and garrisoned as soon as possible. As with most of these abandoned posts, the buildings had not been structurally damaged. All that was needed were roofs and windows and doors, and a defensive surrounding wall. Next day we made our way up the escarpment and that night camped at Al Kurnub, the site of a Byzantine town, a church and the ruins of an impressive work which kept the flood waters of the Wadi in check by means of three great dams. In the bed of the ravine were numerous wells, for Kurnub was a watering point for many of the Arabs in the area. A further two days' ride across a featureless plain brought us back to Beersheba.

The Inspector-General of Police, under whose general guidance I was working in my capacity as Commandant of the Camel Gendarmerie, was Colonel Alan Saunders,* and as soon as I had had a look round the Trans-Jordan desert posts and my own area, I went up to Jerusalem to tell him of my ideas for reconstituting the Gendarmerie, and of what we would require. He could not have been more helpful, and I was gazetted a District Superintendent of Police

* Colonel Alan Saunders, CMG, OBE, MC, KPM, *b.* 1886, *d.* 1964. He was present at General Allenby's entry into Jerusalem in 1917, and joined the Palestine Police the day it was founded in 1920. Inspector-General Nigeria Police 1935–7 and of Palestine Police 1937–43. Commissioner of Police Tripolitania 1946–52.

for the purposes of this side of my work. Because it would have looked incongruous and been physically uncomfortable to do otherwise, I wore the uniform and Arab head-dress of the Camelry whenever I was in the desert.

Alan Saunders gave us all the arms, kit and equipment we needed to re-establish the Force and the authority and funds to set going the rebuilding of the damaged and abandoned posts. Most of the men who had been in the Force before its disintegration came in to offer their services anew. We weeded some out and kept others, including most of the NCOs and in particular men from leading families. We set up a training camp in Beersheba. A number of the men wanted to be allowed to wear their long hair in ringlets and grow their beards. This had not been allowed previously but it was the custom in the Legion and I felt that there were strong arguments in favour of it on our side of the border where the way of life and the duties we would demand of our men were so similar. I also wanted the men to be allowed to carry their personal daggers. All this was asking a good deal of the Inspector-General but he accepted it and we went ahead. We needed to establish wireless communication between our posts and Beersheba. Alan Saunders gave us the sets and we trained as operators a dozen lads who could read and write. The small force of regular Palestine Police in Beersheba, both British and Arab, were co-operative; their duties were confined mainly to the town and to criminal work unconnected with the desert and the tribes, but they were able to help us in our training programme and in many other ways.

As each Gendarmerie post was re-established, I spent three or four days in the nearby encampments feeding and sleeping with my hosts, and I completed each visit by giving a lunch party for fifty or more sheikhs and tribesmen at which the post commander acted as host. Thus I hoped to re-establish the good relations between our local security forces and the tribes which had existed before the disturbances. In all this I had the help of Michael Hankin-Turvin, who had come to Palestine from the Metropolitan Police in London, and was now Assistant Superintendant in charge of the regular Police at Beersheba as well as my Second-in-Command in the Gendarmerie.

If pressed for time and if a motorable track existed, I used an open Ford car but whenever I was able to do so I continuted to tour the desert by camel. I normally took an escort of two or three men. I had no servant, and no kit apart from what I could carry in my saddle bags; two blankets and a sheepskin cloak. We depended on the encampments we visited for food, but as a reserve we carried tea and sugar, flour and dried cheese, and a few tins. In Tiberias, in the South Staffords' mess, I had lived in considerable comfort; now except when I was in Gaza or Beersheba, I lived a good deal more simply.

To trot on an easy pacing camel for hour after hour with half a dozen companions is a memory that I hope I will never lose. It is an activity that few have experienced nowadays, when not even a great number of Arabs habitually ride camels. I had ridden for many hundreds of hours in the Eastern Sudan, and during the years I served in the Beersheba area I must have covered over two thousand miles by camel in the course of constant visits to Arab encampments and on Gendarmerie patrols. I learnt to mount by grasping the lowest part of the camel's neck, scaling up the nearside foreleg and thus clambering into the saddle, rather than making the camel kneel. But I never managed, as some of the younger and more agile men of the Gendarmerie did, to leap into the saddle while the animal was trotting, by making use of the upward thrust of the hock.

The war brought about a strange unnegotiated truce between the rebel command and the Government. During the summer of 1939 the security forces had largely got the measure of the gangs but there were still parties in the hills all over Palestine, little groups who came together when opportunity offered, mounted a small operation and then dissolved, hiding their arms and explosives for the next exploit. In the Beersheba area these activities had practically ceased but around Hebron, where Arthur Charles was now in charge, several small gangs still operated and I was shot at twice while returning from Jerusalem through his District. On the Bedu, the immediate effect of the war was scarcely marked except that on 5 September 1939 a large party of Sheikhs came to see me to affirm their loyalty to the Government. They handed me a list of those who, they alleged, had been responsible a year before for the attack on Beersheba and the burning of the Government offices. The list contained a number of embarrassingly prominent local leaders and several senior officials. This seemed a case in which it was better to do nothing.

In the late autumn the Black Watch moved down from Jerusalem to Beersheba for a week of desert exercises. General Wavell* came up from Cairo to watch them and he spent the night with me in my small Arab house in the town. We rode together all over the low gravel hills which the Australians had attacked in October 1918. The Turkish trenches were still to be seen. He talked of the battle and showed me features I had not previously identified. Housman's poems were among the very few books I had brought with me, and after dinner that night he read them and talked of Housman. He also talked of Winchester. When he left the next day he invited me to

* 1st Earl Wavell, *b.* 1883, *d.* 1950. Viceroy of India 1943–7, Field-Marshal.

come and see him if anything should bring me to Cairo. I had long admired him, and twenty-four hours of his company immensely reinforced that admiration. In due course I made use of his open invitation.

By the turn of the year I had managed to get round the greater part of the District and had come to know most of the leading Sheikhs. I had ridden with them and slept in their tents, and they had fed with me in Beersheba. Two of the Government buildings which had been gutted by fire the previous September were the old Turkish railway station and the stationmaster's house (the line had long since been pulled up). The Public Works Department converted these into a couple of simple but adequate dwellings and I moved into the station and Michael Hankin-Turvin into the stationmaster's house. Once installed, I had an Arab guest chamber built out of what had been planned as a garage, furnished it with mattresses, cushions and rugs, and in the centre of the floor placed a hearth with a set of coffee pots and cups. Here I could entertain in a traditional way. To run my household I found a cook in Hebron and engaged a young tribesman to do odd jobs. I needed neither when I was travelling.

As the cold weather gave way to spring, news of the war began to filter through to the tribes. We did what we could to maintain confidence. The First Cavalry Division had arrived in Palestine with their horses, but a number of regiments were already converting to tanks and armoured cars. Their mounts went to the Palestine Police or were destroyed. The Greys celebrated a sad good-bye to their horses with a point-to-point at Sarafand to which I took a party of Sheikhs and tribesmen. The news grew bad as the spring turned to summer. In Beersheba we gave open air propaganda film shows. It was just as well that most of the Bedu, in their remoteness, showed no great interest. As I went constantly around, I took with me photographs provided for us by the Public Relations Office in Jerusalem — of battleships, aeroplanes flying in formation, troops training and so on. They found these very difficult to fathom. One picture of Mr Chamberlain strolling in St James's Park, an image no doubt intended to convey the confidence felt by the Prime Minister, was examined to my surprise with special closeness. It was passed from hand to hand and turned all ways, held up and placed on the ground. Finally a spokesman, nodding with sudden enlightenment and conviction, commented, 'Ah, yes, of course, that's Mr Jordan. He was in the Public Works Department and two years ago he came to repair the Sinai road.'

But whatever they may have thought of the Germans, and whatever pretty confident expectations they may have had of their eventual victory, the Bedu held no brief for the Italians when they entered the war. We were able to make much useful propaganda out of alleged Italian atrocities during the conquest of the Senussi in the 1920s, and in particular of the fate of the Senussi leader, Omar al Mukutar, who was firmly believed to have been got rid of by being thrown out of an aeroplane. There was also a grim story that went the rounds of an Italian official who invited a Senussi patriot to dinner and served up the patriot's infant son as the main dish. *El Macaroon*, as the Italians were generally referred to, were regarded as an inferior type of European and Wavell's early victories in the desert were well received.

In the year or so during which Southern Palestine had been practically unadministered, many crimes had been committed between the Beersheba tribes and between them and the tribes of Trans-Jordan. Most of these concerned animal theft, but there had also been shootings and stabbings and highway robbery. Furthermore, there were cases going back many years which had been discussed in the past, adjourned, brought up again and never settled. We were anxious to get these potentially dangerous affairs dealt with and satisfactory relations with our neighbours re-established. And so Ishak Nashashibi, my Arab District Officer, and I went down in the spring of 1940 to Ain Hosb where the Gendarmerie post had now been re-established. Ishak and I took with us a dozen or more Sheikhs from among the Beersheba tribes together with one or two neutral tribal judges, men who were respected and whose word could be relied on to carry weight when it came to difficult conflicts of interest. Ahed Bey Es Sukhn, the Governor of Ma'an District, came over with Hamed Bin Jazi, Sheikh of the Howaitat, and many others who had claims to make and cases to raise. Ahed Bey brought with him a number of Trans-Jordanian Sheikhs known for their wisdom and knowledge of tribal law. For three days in the shade of an immense wild fig tree the tribesmen talked and argued, breaking up sometimes into little intimate groups to discuss this or that, coming together again to propose or protest, stalking off in real or feigned indignation or returning placated. They talked far into the night, harshly and loudly at times, in whispers at others. Sheep were killed and eaten, tea and coffee went round the circles of cross-legged and mantled tribesmen. The grey blue mountains of Moab looked down on us across the trough of the Wadi Araba. We were 1,000 feet below sea level. At the end of the third day of a series of long and involved and at times seemingly insoluble discussions, agreements were reached. Some cases would need to be reviewed; the execution of some of our decisions, the payment of compensation for instance, would doubtless take years to complete; but for the most part honour and interest had been satisfied and compromise had been accepted. Everyone had had his say, had had an opportunity, with such powers of oratory as he possessed and the aid of his supporters, to make his case. And that of course had been an essential ingredient to the success of our meeting. Often it was more a matter of creating an atmosphere than coming to clear-cut decisions. Words meant a great deal, the right words and even pious expressions. They created a warmth of feeling. Perhaps one of the mistakes we, the British, often make abroad with foreigners is to shy away from insincerity and flattery and oratorial exaggerations which, however little we may think of them, do at times serve a purpose. The same can rightly be said of those elaborate and repetitive forms of speech that often accompany greetings and other occasions. Much of what is said may well be insincere but a neglect of these rituals can be seen, by Arabs especially, as an indication of vulgarity and insensitivity. This applies too to physical contacts in the form of prolonged handshakes, holding hands and even kissing between man and man. Many Europeans regard these manifestations of friendship and respect with distaste, but no greater distaste than that felt by Arabs and others at what they see as our abruptness and lack of polish and sympathy. For myself I had come to know some of the Trans-Jordan tribesmen and we had established a friendly relationship between our people and theirs which promised well for the future. In the months that followed, meetings in El Arish put our relations with Sinai on a similarly satisfactory basis. And the Sheikhs' Court, which had been formed some years before from a dozen or so tribal leaders to deal with cases under tribal law but which after the events of September had temporarily ceased to operate, resumed its weekly sittings in Beersheba. It would deal with twenty or thirty cases in a morning in an atmosphere which at times seemed chaotic, but which nearly always concluded in concord and settlement.

The war brought a number of new problems to my work in Gaza, and with the fall of France these increased enormously. I was working twelve hours a day and seven days a week, for there was still no District Commissioner, and while I remained based in Beersheba I spent an increasing amount of time in Gaza and the surrounding area. We had already laid the foundations of a system of rationing and supply. The Australians were arriving in large numbers to reinforce our Middle East forces and we found ourselves engaged in the construction of camps along the coast from Deir al Balah on the Sinai frontier to our district border south of Jaffa. Compensation needed to be assessed, a civilian workforce organised and above all a good relationship established between the townsmen of Gaza and the farmers of the coastal villages and our new arrivals. British troops had been stationed in and around Gaza for some time and we had had few problems. But the Australians had a reputation for rumbustious and unpredictable virility and we were anxious. Events proved that we had comparatively little to fear. The first to arrive of the 6th Division, commanded by Brigadier Blamey,* lost no time in establishing a rapport with the administration which apart from a few isolated incidents remained entirely satisfactory. A number of Arab lunches which I gave to introduce the senior officers to the Sheikhs, at which we sat down a hundred or more, led both sides to regard the other with greater understanding. Rushdi Bey Esh Shawa, the Mayor of Gaza, gave invaluable help and boundless hospitality. When units of the Australian artillery arrived it became necessary to find an area suitable and large enough for a 25-pounder range. We chose Asluj between Beersheba and the Sinai frontier, which meant that the Australians would be camping in tribal areas: I was anxious to avoid any sort of incident.

As one means of bringing the Australians and the Bedu together, we decided to hold in Beersheba a combined camel and horse race meeting. We catered for a gathering of almost of five thousand, and it was a great success. The High Commissioner and notables from all over southern Palestine, Australian and British troops and a great host of tribesmen came. And they met in an atmosphere in which all had a common interest, horses. Although fewer Arab than Australians were interested in betting, we organised a tote. The Australians patronised it heavily, and the Bedu lost little time in doing likewise. There was a young man from a remote part of the District who chanced to be in Beersheba on the day of the meeting. He came to watch. A fellow-tribesman, who knew something of the world, explained to him the object and functioning of the tote and persuaded him to place a bet. It was the simplest thing, he said. You chose the horse you thought would win, noted its number and then bought a ticket corresponding to the number of the horse. You paid ten piastres; you might win a large sum. The young man was not altogether convinced. What number was he to ask for? Why, the number of the horse he thought would win of course. But which horse would win? 'Only God knows that,' his friend declared, impatient at this obtuseness. The young man pondered and finally joined the queue at the tote. His turn came. 'What number?' asked the face at the *guichet*. The young man had no idea. 'Number four', he answered in alarm and at random. He paid his ten piastres. He

* Field-Marshal Sir Thomas Blamey, GBE, CMG, DSO, CB, *b.* 1884, *d.* 1951. GOC 6th Div. AEF. Dep. C.-in-C. ME 1941. C.-in-C. Allied Land Forces SW Pacific.

watched the race. The winner was led in. The young man spotted his friend. 'Which horse won?' he asked. 'Why, number four of course,' his friend answered. Had he taken a ticket? 'Yes.' 'By God, you have the winning number; go and draw your prize.' He was hustled to the payout pigeon-hole. The crowd had drifted away from the vicinity of the tote. Most of the Arab punters had put their money on number six. The Australians, with an eye for a horse which in this case had erred, had betted heavily on number two. No one but the hero of this story had a ticket on number four. He presented it. The face in the *guichet* examined it closely and then a hand slowly counted out forty pound notes. The young man gathered them up and pushed them into his purse. But it was all too much for him; he fainted, and his friends carried him away.

This was the second visit of the High Commissioner to Beersheba within a few months, and an invitation which he then gave me to spend a weekend at Government House in Jerusalem led to much speculation among the Sheikhs. They knew that he had two daughters, and that the elder, Araminta, was of marriageable age.* Had I been accepted by His Excellency as a suitable son-in-law? Surely I must have been — to have been invited to Government House. Significant, but of rather less importance, had the daughter expressed agreement? Surely she could hardly do otherwise. My protestations that I had only met Araminta twice, and that although she was very charming she had a great many suitors in Jerusalem, and that no romantic attachment had ever been contemplated by either of us was simply greeted with sly smiles, nods and knowing winks. The more I protested the more they knew better. For some months, until the story died a natural death, I basked in a measure of undeserved glory and, in their view no doubt, was assured of rapid promotion.

Water was a constant problem for the Bedu. Throughout the Beersheba area and particularly in the southern parts of the desert were ancient stone water cisterns designed to collect and conserve the rare winter spates. Some were in need of structural repair but all that was required of most was the removal of sand that had silted them up over the years. We secured a grant of several thousand pounds and started work on several of the more promising cisterns in the summer of 1940. By the autumn the work was done and the subsequent winter rains filled them. Apart from anything else this was a profitable public relations exercise at a time when it was important that the welfare of the tribesmen should be seen to be recognised by the Government in Jerusalem. In this and in many similar problems we

* Now Lady Aldington.

were fortunate to have John Macpherson as Chief Secretary.* He combined great energy and dynamism with sympathy for the man on the spot. I never hesitated to approach him direct and never failed to get as much help and encouragement as he could possibly give me. If necessary he refreshingly swept aside the objections of his less imaginative subordinate staff.

In the course of one of my routine visits to an encampment on the Sinai frontier I found in progress the trial of a case of theft. A hundred or more men representing both the plaintiff and the accused were gathered around half a dozen tents. The accused, although highly suspect, had maintained his innocence and it had been impossible to prove his guilt by means of witnesses or other evidence. He had been asked therefore whether he would accept the ordeal by fire, *Al Bish'a* — to have refused which would have been an admission of guilt — and he had accepted. *Al Bish'a* consists of the heating over an open fire of a flat iron spoon, normally used for roasting coffee beans. A group of assessors, led by the Sheikh of the *Bish'a*, a highly respected elderly man from Sinai, sat around the fire with the accused beside them. Beyond, in a wide circle, were the representatives of the parties. When the spoon was red hot it was handed round the assessors who certified that its condition was satisfactory. The accused, who was watching these grim proceedings with apparently complete calm, was given a cup of water with which to rinse out his mouth, then the spoon was held in front of him and he licked it three times. Each time I heard the clear hiss of moisture in contact with heat. The Sheikh of the *Bish'a* and the neutral assessors then examined the man's tongue. Had they detected signs of burning he would have been found guilty. A clear tongue would have indicated his innocence. As it was his tongue was found to be unmarked and amidst a deep murmur of approval he was declared to be innocent.

On the face of it the ordeal appears to have been a brutal and unreliable practice, open to abuse, and it had been forbidden in Egypt. But the Bedouin argument in its favour was simply that if a man knows he is guilty his mouth will be dry with fright, while a man who is confident of his innocence has nothing to fear and therefore his mouth and tongue retain sufficient saliva effectively to prevent burning. The Palestine legal authorities were not at all happy at the continuation of the *Bish'a*, but I was not prepared, certainly at this particular time, to order its abolition. To have done so would have been to antagonise the Bedu over a custom in which they believed and one which in effect the Government would have been powerless

*Sir John Macpherson, GCMG, *b.* 1898, *d.* 1971.

to prevent. So *Al Bish'a* continued to be practised for some years to come until the Tribal Court in Beersheba was persuaded to use its influence to end it. Under the persuasion of their own leaders the practice in due course ceased to exist.

But the Ordeal by Fire was a practice that existed far beyond the boundaries of Beersheba, and while I had been in Talodi I had found plenty of evidence of its use among the nomad Arabs of Kordofan and the Nuba who may well have adopted it from their Muslim neighbours. The methods used were dissimilar but the principle was the same. The Ordeal, be it by fire or poison or other means, is as old as history and has at times been practised throughout the world.

We are all compounded to a great extent by the influence of those whose lives have been brought into close contact with our own. As in the Sudan, so here in Beersheba, I inevitably learnt much from the people for whose welfare I was partly responsible and with whom I was in constant contact. There were many to whom I owe gratitude, but three or four stand out. Of all the Beersheba Sheikhs, most of whom I knew well, I like best to remember Salman Abu Rabia. He was a young man, respected not only by his own people but by other tribal leaders. He was slim, with a long rather wistful face and a lock of straight dark hair hung over his forehead beneath the edge of his white headcloth. Salman was Sheikh of the Zullam Abu Rabia section of the Taiyaha tribe, and his people occupied and moved over the area of rocky desert that ran eastwards from Beersheba to the escarpment overlooking the Dead Sea and the site of Sodom and Gomorrah. Their northern border exposed them to pressure from the Hebron highwaymen and to demands for sanctuary when police action forced them out of their hiding places among the caves and gullies of that inhospitable wilderness. These freebooters were the residue of the gangs who had occupied and partly destroyed Beersheba in 1938. Their claim was that they were patriots and they thus expected Salman and his tribesmen to aid and comfort them from time to time. The Government on the other hand expected Salman, as a recognised Sheikh and leader of his people, to assist in every possible way in the arrest of these wanted men. I like to think that he and I enjoyed a personal friendship. I had ridden many miles with him and his people, and had spent many nights in his and his kinsmen's tents. In one of the latter, just before we went to sleep, he said to me with a smile: 'Wrap your head up well, the bedding here as I know from experience is full of fleas.' It was indeed. Salman frequently found his loyalties and his interests confused and in conflict. He handled these difficulties with skill and tact, and like Radi Kumbal in the Sudan, he had an ambassadorial gift of rare skill and grace. He was a heavy cigarette smoker and he died of lung cancer shortly before the Israelis seized Beersheba and the whole of the Negeb. It was as well for him that he never saw his tribal lands occupied. He would have taken it very hard.

A very different character but a warm-hearted friend was the Mayor of Beersheba, Taj Ed Din Shaa'th. He was well past middle age when I first got to know him, a slight but dignified figure, bearded and fair skinned. He had been a man of some substance and authority in Turkish times and I think he must have had some Ottoman blood. He had seen the Turks go and the British come. He had watched the subsequent progress of Jewish land purchases around Beersheba. He had seen the occupation of his town and the destruction of the Mandate's authority by gangs from Hebron, with tribal support, in the autumn of 1938, and he had been present when, the following spring, British troops had appeared and Government control had been re-established. He had survived all these vicissitudes unscathed. He must have given a great deal of thought to the possibility of a German victory in 1940 and 1941, and considered what his role would be in that eventuality. He had the skills and the agility of the Vicar of Bray highly developed, and he combined these with a completely disarming charm, great humour, and an endearing absence of false pride. His main object in life was to survive in comfort and to co-operate with whomever happened to be in authority, but with room for manoeuvre. Throughout the difficult first two years of the war his attitude towards the Allied cause was never other than openly loyal.*

He had been Mayor for twenty-five years when I went to Beersheba. He was to remain in office certainly until 1947 and may have survived longer, though I doubt whether he would ever have accepted an Israeli regime. His Mayoralty was not an onerous appointment in itself, for the town contained no more than three thousand people, but his office called for skill in reconciling opposing commercial interests and personal factions.

Taj Ed Din frequently came to tea with me. Our houses were no more than a quarter of a mile apart but the dignity of his office required that he should always arrive on a splendid white Egyptian donkey led by a small boy. He would dismount and it was an accepted pleasantry that he would then say: 'As you see I have come on my bicycle.' We would discuss the progress of the war and he never failed to express his unswerving support of Britain, for at that

* In 1951 he was awarded the King's Medal in the Cause of Freedom for his services to British interests during the war, and invited to Cairo to receive it from the British Ambassador. He accepted the invitation, and I went to the Embassy hoping to see him, but by then the Israelis were in occupation of Beersheba and he failed to appear. Perhaps he thought it prudent to keep away.

time we had no active allies, except for Trans-Jordan, outside the Commonwealth. But he tended to weaken the plausibility of his case a little by recalling gleefully how as a younger man he had outwitted the Turks. He had been most unwillingly conscripted into the Army, but had found no difficulty, he explained, in leaving the trenches between Gaza and Beersheba whenever things became unpleasant — under the necessity, as he put it, of visiting wounded comrades in hospital.

The Arab District Officer who arrived in Beersheba half way through my time there, and with whom I worked closely, was Farid Sa'd. Farid and I were almost the same age. He had taken his degree at the American University of Beirut and gone into teaching first in Iraq, then in Jordan and then in Palestine. He had in fact been Principal of the Bedouin Boys' Boarding School in Beersheba for two years in the mid-1930s, so he was no stranger to the District and its problems. The Palestine Government was wise to offer him an appointment in the administration in 1935, and I was fortunate in having him posted to Beersheba in 1940. Energetic, cheerful, enthusiastic, patient and imaginative, he quickly mastered the problems we faced. Without him I would have found it difficult to persuade the High Commissioner in 1941 that I could well be spared to join the Army. In Farid's competent hands nothing would be likely to go wrong in Beersheba; nor did it. But he was destined for a far more successful career than our administration could offer to a man of his calibre. He resigned in 1943 and after a spell as Manager of the Arab Bank in Haifa and as a member of various Arab delegations, he became first a Senator in the Jordan Parliament and later Minister of Finance. At the time of writing, as Chairman and Director of a number of important Jordanian companies and a generous supporter of numerous charities, he lives in Amman with his charming wife Khadijeh, and with his children and grandchildren around him.

There were no Jewish settlements in the Gaza/Beersheba District. This is not to say that land had not been sold to the Jews and the sales registered: immediately to the east of Beersheba there were several such, totalling something like forty square kilometres, and south of the town a rather smaller holding. To the west, not far off the Gaza road, there were also Jewish-owned lands, and well to the north of Beersheba and close to the Judean foothills they had a number of scattered holdings that came to around twenty-five square kilometres. It was mainly the security situation and the absence of adequate water which had hitherto prevented the Jews from moving in. But it was also a great relief to me that at the end of February 1940 the Land Transfer Regulations placed Gaza and Beersheba within a zone in which further purchase of land by Jews became prohibited. Even so, one of my principal worries was that the more successful the administration was in establishing security the more likely we were to wake up one morning and find, as had happened in other parts of Palestine and despite the advice and warnings of the administration and the Army, that a Jewish settlement complete with stockade, watch towers and armed guards had been established overnight. Had this come about in this exclusively Arab area, attacks on the settlement would certainly have followed and I would not have been able to rely on the men of the Camel Gendarmerie, or indeed reasonably expect them, to help in the protection or defence of a settlement against action by their own tribesmen or neighbours. It is true of course that some local Arabs, even some of the Sheikhs, had sold land. The Jews had the ability and the financial means to be very persuasive.

Later that year Anthony Eden, then Secretary of State for War, came on a tour of the Middle East which included Palestine, and he visited the Australian troops in the camps which we had built for them along the Gaza coast. I was invited to meet him. He asked me about security in the Negeb and whether I felt I could keep the area peaceful while the Australians and others did their training. I said I could do so provided no Jewish settlements were established.

Some miles to the east of Auja Hafir, which was the frontier post with Sinai at that time, there lies the reputed burial place of Sheikh Amri who is believed to have been the ancestor of the Tayaha tribe. Amri was an oppressive and detested ruler and after his death he was buried beside a *Wadi* bed in a remote part of the desert. His tomb, marked by a cairn of stones, soon came to be regarded as a place of ill omen and misfortune. Passers-by protected themselves from the dead man's malign influence by loudly cursing him and by adding to the cairn. It was widely and sincerely believed that failure to do so would inevitably and almost immediately be followed by some form of misfortune. The belief was supported by many stories. It came about that five of us, including two men of the Gendarmerie, were riding in the vicinity when, emerging from behind the steep cliffs that marked the edge of a *Wadi* bed, we chanced suddenly upon this ill-omened pile of stones. It stood six or eight feet high. My companions hastily uttered their curses, leapt from their camels and each hurled a stone or two at the cairn. At the same time they shouted to me a warning to do likewise. I had heard the story and I knew of the belief, but I felt disinclined to curse a dead man, and in any case I was not convinced that the belief had any real validity. However, I swung my camel away from the immediate vicinity of the tomb, circling it at a distance of perhaps fifty or a hundred yards. My companions rejoined me and we continued on our way. They were clearly ill-at-ease on my behalf. We had ridden on for five minutes or less when my camel stumbled. It recovered itself. My friends' alarm was marked. Another few yards and it fell to its knees. I was able to slip out of the saddle but the animal was clearly in distress. It tried to rise, fell again and within half a minute it was dead. An hour earlier the animal had left Auja Hafir fit and fresh. It could not have grazed on any poisonous shrub. No snake had been seen and there were no signs or symptoms of snake bite. I was and still am unable to account for what happened. My companions were never in any doubt.

Despite an occasional day or two of duty in Jerusalem, and once a weekend of duck shooting on Lake Huleh north of Tiberias, it was a lonely sort of life. Sometimes Arthur Charles came down from Hebron and spent a night, but on the whole I had few visitors. In the tents one was for ever surrounded by people and there was no privacy, and conversation was limited to what was of interest to the Bedu. When Michael Hankin-Turvin and I were in Beersheba at the same time we usually dined together and then took an hour's walk before going to bed. We both found we slept the better for it, particularly in the hot weather. There is an Arab proverb which is the exact equivalent of 'After dinner walk a mile, after luncheon rest awhile.' So we followed it. But I was often alone and as the war news grew worse and worse, it was sometimes difficult to feel entirely confident of the outcome. It was essential not merely to conceal any anxiety, but to give the appearance of radiating complete assurance. I knew that the expression on my face each morning would be closely watched by those around me, and that local morale would depend to a certain extent on the degree of cheerfulness I was able to muster. With this partly in mind I made a point of wearing a dinner jacket whenever I was in Beersheba for the evening, and of smoking a cheroot before finally going to bed. My cook, I felt sure, would report this trivial fact to his friends in the market, and that it might perhaps indicate to them that I was entirely at ease and without a care.

From the day that Italy entered the war in May 1940, and hostilities broke out in the Middle East, I began to hanker and then to agitate to be allowed to join the Army. As early as April 1939 Colonel John Crystal, who then commanded the Trans-Jordan Frontier Force, and had previously served in the Sudan, had offered me a commission as an intelligence officer in the event of war. At the time I had been pleased but had put the idea out of my mind. In the early summer of 1940 I went over to Amman and saw Glubb, who offered to take me into the Legion at any time. I made a written application to the Chief Secretary, which was turned down on the perfectly reasonable grounds that I was much more use to the Allied cause where I was than serving as a subaltern or even as a Company Commander in the British Army, or for that matter in the Arab Legion. But although I saw the sense of this I was ill prepared to accept it; I had held a territorial commission, I was in my early thirties and I had no family ties or responsibilities. Southern Palestine, as I saw it, was quiet after the disturbances that had marked the winter of 1938/9. Nearly all my friends were in the Army and I wanted to be there too.

I bided my time for a month or two and then tried a new approach. This was to suggest to the Government in Jerusalem that out of the Beersheba Camelry I could find thirty or forty volunteers for service, under my leadership, in the Western Desert. They would be of great use, I argued, working in small groups behind the Axis lines, supplying information and sabotaging enemy dumps and installations. I thought they could be a valuable adjunct to the Long Range Desert Group. Bill Kennedy-Shaw, a Government archaeologist and a friend of mine, had been released from his appointment and was serving with the Group. I believed that the idea would commend itself to him and, I hoped, to others. This imaginative, as I saw it, and indeed not wholly impractical idea was backed by the GOC Palestine and recommended to the Army in Egypt. The Palestine Government would have none of it.

In July came the first Italian air raids on Palestine. The war was getting a little closer to us, and I was determined to try and play a more active part. There was now a District Commissioner in Gaza, Edward Ballard, and I was therefore relieved of a good deal of work in that part of the District. In September I asked for a week's leave and went to Cairo. It was my first break for two years. Here I called on Colonel Bromhead, who was commanding the Libyan Arab Force, and was taken to see the Force under training near Cairo. I went to call on the DMI and then, on the strength of having had him as a guest for a night in my two-roomed house in Beersheba, I asked to see General Wavell. He invited me to lunch at the C.-in-C.'s house in Gezira. I told him what I wanted. He said, to my surprise, 'We asked for you some months ago but Palestine refused to let you go. The situation may have altered since then.' But he went on to warn me that he would find it difficult to move the High Commissioner. He then took from his pocket a small memorandum pad and made a note. Encouraged and much impressed by his sympathy and thoughtfulness at a moment when his mind must have been full of a thousand problems, I took my leave — more cheerful but without any great hopes of success.

My secondment to Palestine had originally been for two years.

The two years were due to expire in November 1940 and the Palestine Government wanted to retain me for a further year. I was agreeable to this, mainly because I thought I would have a better chance of seeing something of the war from where I was than in the Sudan, despite the fact that the Abyssinian campaign was then in full swing. So I accepted a year's extension, and thought it wise to wait for a few months before agitating again. In due course I went up to Jerusalem and saw the High Commissioner. He had had a note from General Wavell. I reminded him that I had done over two years without leave, and that for nearly a year I had held administrative responsibility for both Beersheba and Gaza. After months of constant patrolling, travelling by car and camel, I felt that I had largely completed what had been required of me. I had re-established the Camelry as an effective peace-keeping force, reopened the desert posts and equipped them with wireless and competent operators. With the help first of Ishaq Nashashibi and then of Farid Sa'd, and with the co-operation of the Arab Legion, all the outstanding cases between the Beersheba and Jordanian tribes had been settled. There was now a senior District Commissioner in Gaza. I tried to make my plea as objective as I could. MacMichael was as kindly and sympathetic as I had expected him to be, and he committed himself to the extent of saying that if things got really bad in Egypt or in Syria and provided the Sudan Government agreed, he would let me go. And he added that he would give my claim priority over any other member of his administrative service. It was some comfort to feel too that I had Wavell's support and also that of an old friend from the Eastern Arab Corps in Gedaref days, Terence Airey.* At that time he was serving in Cairo, as a Lieutenant-Colonel in GHQ. It seemed to me that this was an advance, and the best I could hope for at the moment. I went back to Beersheba and threw myself with renewed energy into a ceaseless round of work: visiting, patrolling, seeing as much of the tribes as I could and, with Michael Hankin-Turvin, further improving the efficiency and morale of the Camelry. I rose each morning at dawn and frequently worked till ten or eleven at night.

The winter of 1940/41 turned into spring. The rains had been good and both the grazing and the wheat and barley crops promised well. The desert was at its most beautiful, the air fresh and clean. In places the rain had left pools around which the Bedu had pitched their black tents. As we rode from one encampment to the next, on every hand there were flocks of young lambs and kids. And further afield were the herds of camels and their young slowly moving as they grazed on

* Lt.-Gen. Sir Terence Airey KCMG, CB, CBE, *b*. 1900.

the green shrubs and thorn bushes. The tribesmen were in good heart. Whenever we stopped for lunch, or to dine and spend the night, there was milk in abundance and sour curds to be poured over the roasted sheep and rice that we shared around the common dish. At Winchester we had sung the Psalms daily for five years and here, in their lovely descriptions of the spring, they became a reality: '*Thou crownest the year with thy goodness: and thy clouds drop fatness. The folds shall be full of sheep: the valleys also shall stand so thick with corn that they shall laugh and sing.*'

Had it not been for the war I would have been content to lead this life almost indefinitely. And there was always something exciting to give object and emphasis to this easy-going side of one's work. The Hebron hills still afforded refuge to several groups of highway robbers, men with prices on their heads, who had belonged to the bands which in 1938 had controlled nearly half Palestine and who had burnt and destroyed Government offices, Police posts and dispensaries up and down the country. We spent many nights lying in ambush, or at dawn searching the remote caves and valleys where they might be lodged. For their part they watched the movements of our patrols closely, and twice we avoided their ambushes only because we seemed to them to be too powerful a party to engage with hope of success. But on the whole these outlaws posed no great problem as compared with eighteen months earlier when they included four hundred 'Wanted Men'. Now the number was down to just over double figures.

During that winter of 1940/41 the war had seemed, for the moment, to be moving in our favour. In November the Italian fleet had been attacked and crippled at Taranto; in December the Italian land forces suffered a severe reverse in Greece and by early February the whole of Cyrenaica had fallen and we had taken 125,000 prisoners.

But these triumphs were short-lived. The summer came. Resistance in Yugoslavia crumbled, Greece was over-run, Crete fell, and the Germans were hammering at Tobruk. Iraq had been held but Syria was in danger. I went once again to Jerusalem to see MacMichael and reminded him of what he had said to me previously about things getting bad in Syria and Egypt. I reminded him too that I had had no leave since the summer of 1938. I was due to return to the Sudan in the autumn. Could I not have leave now and spend it serving in Syria? I knew that a force of irregular Druze Cavalry was being formed at Mafrak in Jordan under Gerald de Gaury with whom I had stayed in Kuwait in 1938. They were to move into Syria. I had seen de Gaury and he had offered me command of a Squadron. Beersheba District, I pleaded, could safely be left in the more than competent hands of Farid Sa'd. The Camelry could pass to the command of Michael Hankin-Turvin. The High Commissioner consented. In delight I hastened back to Beersheba, where it took me twenty-four hours to pack my possessions and settle the rest of my affairs.

6
WAR IN THE HILLS
(Syria, 1941)

I collected a uniform and equipment in Jerusalem and the same day drove over the Jordan, through Amman and north to Mafrak. Mafrak consisted of a few mud huts and a single corrugated iron shed, but the Arab Legion had provided us with tents alongside their fort at the edge of the gravel airstrip. They had also given de Gaury as a liaison officer *Rais* (Captain) Selim Arif Selim, a Druze. Jack Collard of the Iraq Petroleum Company, who had arrived a day or two before from the Trans-Jordan Frontier Force, had been made Adjutant. There was Head, a forestry officer from the Trans-Jordan Government, and Wilfred Thesiger of the Sudan Political Service just back from the Abyssinian Campaign. We each took command of one of the three mounted Squadrons which were being formed. Over four hundred men from the French-officered *Groupement Druze* had been persuaded by various means to join us and had come over the frontier the previous week. We called them the 'Druze Legion'. In the two or three days that followed they were joined by others, most of whom brought with them their horses and their rifles. Two men arrived with a light automatic and a box of ammunition. To the Vichy French all were deserters, to the Free French and to us they were *ralliés*. We were also reinforced by a number of ex-soldiers and a few civilians including two or three Chiefs who had fought the French in the 1920s. By the end of the campaign we totalled nearly 1,200 men.

As a background to the infinitely unimportant but nonetheless agreeable part I was fortunate enough to play in the following four months, it is worth recalling something of the flow of events that led to the launching of 'Exporter', the code name given to the Syrian operation of June/July 1941. Although small compared with campaigns in other parts of the world, where far greater quantities of men and matériel were engaged and losses were far heavier, the Syrian campaign was of great strategic importance and its success was a significant milestone on the way to a change in Allied fortunes. It finally put an end to any further attempt by the Axis to penetrate eastwards from the Mediterranean to the Gulf and India, and by moving the eastern line of defence of the Suez Canal several hundred miles northwards it relieved Turkey of further anxiety over her southern frontier.

During those vital summer months of 1941 Syria was one of four Middle East campaigns that followed one another in rapid succession. The other three were the Iraq campaign, the struggle for Crete and a critical battle in the Western Desert. The dates are worth remembering. The Iraq campaign began on 2 May and was brought to a successful conclusion on the 30th. The battle for Crete, which followed our withdrawal from Greece in late April, began on 20 May and ended in our evacuation of the island and its occupation by the Germans on 1 June. 'Battleaxe', the Western Desert operation from which so much had been hoped, including the relief of Tobruk, started on 15 June. Within three days it had failed to achieve its objective and Tobruk remained invested.

Syria was one of the overseas territories of the French empire which, on the collapse of France, felt itself bound to the terms of surrender by what was considered to be the legitimate French Government. The influence of a French garrison of 50,000 men was strong, and both among the armed forces and the civilian authorities there was little support for Britain's continued resistance to the Germans. Following the visit of von Hentig, Head of the Near Eastern Division of the German Foreign Ministry, to Damascus in mid-January 1941, German agents began to arrive in the country and to direct themselves to fostering anti-British feeling. The steady flow of Jews into Palestine, and the openly expressed ambitions of Zionism, provided the Germans with plenty of material for their propaganda. Iraq was von Hentig's first target. The pro-British Regent of Iraq, learning on 31 March of a plot to arrest him, escaped to the American Legation in Baghdad disguised as a woman. From there he was smuggled out to the RAF base at Habbania in the Minister's car, hidden beneath a rug in the back seat, and finally took refuge in Trans-Jordan. British troops from India landed at Basra in the second half of April. Rashid Ali Al Gailani, who had seized power in Iraq, appealed to Hitler for help against Britain. Admiral Darlan, Commander of the Vichy French Naval Forces, thereupon agreed to the transport to Iraq of large quantities of war material held in Syria. Throughout the Arab world there were few at that moment who were not convinced that within a very short time the British would be overwhelmed leaving the Germans in complete control of the Middle East.

The Iraq campaign was launched by the British garrison in Habbania, which had been surrounded by Iraqi land and air forces some days previously, with a pre-emptive strike on 2 May. At noon that day, although heavily outnumbered and outgunned, the British commander attacked the encircling enemy positions. For a fortnight or more the situation in Iraq was extremely grave. Thinking about the events of the Second World War one is tempted to speculate where and when the balance finally tipped, and to wonder how light, how apparently insignificant at the time, was the touch that set the course of affairs moving towards final victory. It is easy to suggest a dozen possibilities. I like to think that one turning point came in Iraq on 14 May 1941.

The flying column 'Kingcol' that led the main Habbania relief force 'Habforce' across the desert from Palestine to Iraq consisted of the Household Cavalry, two Companies of the Essex Regiment, some artillery, 200 3-ton RASC trucks carrying supplies to the besieged garrison, and 250 men of the Arab Legion. On 13 May, when the column was within striking distance of Habbania, the 200 RASC trucks ran into sand dunes and were unable to move. The column was halted. The Arab Legion contingent had been away on a reconnaissance that day and when they returned to the main body in the evening the situation was extremely hazardous. The column was exposed to air attack, water was short and there was talk of a possible withdrawal. At this critical point the Legion, which knew the desert intimately, suggested a route where the going was firm and they led the column through. The Habbania garrison, which had already broken out but still remained isolated, was relieved and resistance by the Iraqi forces thereafter collapsed. Had 'Kingcol' and, in consequence, 'Habforce' failed to reach Habbania, the Germans would have occupied Iraq.

On the night of 29/30 May, Rashid Ali fled across the frontier into Iran with a group of his closest colleagues. Among them was the ex-Mufti of Jerusalem who had been mainly responsible for leading the Palestine rebellion of 1937/8. Had the Germans secured Iraq, as they so nearly did, Egypt and Palestine would have been outflanked and the Axis powers would have obtained control of the main sources of British and Commonwealth oil. But despite this close-run success we remained in a position of great peril. Syria could still be captured, with Vichy's connivance if not its open co-operation, by a few thousand German airborne troops and would thereafter provide an ideal jumping-off ground for the air domination of Iran, Iraq, and above all of Egypt, and for an invasion of Palestine by an easy flanking movement through Trans-Jordan. French forces in Syria consisted of some thirty battalions and a considerable number of tanks.

As early as February 1941 both Glubb and Kirkbride were given authority to make confidential approaches to the Syrian tribes and the Druzes, and funds were put at their disposal for this purpose.

Their contacts were to pay a dividend before long.

Arising out of a period of widespread and bloody conflict between the Christian Maronites and the Druzes in Lebanon in 1860, France, with the support of the European powers, intervened and created an autonomous regime for Lebanon. The sovereign power was Turkey, but French influence was already strong and thereafter increased in scope. In consequence a large proportion of the Lebanese Druzes migrated south-eastwards into the basalt fastness of the Jebel and established a capital at Suweida. With the defeat of Turkey in the 1914–18 war and the grant to France by the victorious powers of a mandate for both Lebanon and Syria, the French, firmly believing in their historic and unquestionable *mission civilisatrice*, found the Druzes of the Jebel exceptionally difficult first to pacify and then to administer. The events of 1920 when France forced King Feisal to leave Damascus, and of 1925 and 1926 when they were obliged to fight a campaign of considerable difficulty against the tough inhabitants of the Jebel, left a legacy of deep and indeed bitter anti-French feeling. To most of the Muslim communities in Syria and Lebanon and to the Druzes of the Jebel, France was a Christian, colonial, expansionist power and as such essentially hostile.

With England the Druzes of the Lebanon, and subsequently of the Jebel, had established an unusually close rapport. This friendly relationship stemmed partly from their ancestors' alliance with Admiral Sir Sidney Smith during the Napoleonic wars, partly to their remarkable admiration for Lady Hester Stanhope, William Pitt's eccentric niece, and furthermore to their close relations with Colonel Churchill, a relative of Winston Churchill, who had been British Consul in Beirut in 1860 at the time of the migration to the Jebel. During the 1925–6 Druze rebellion Trans-Jordan had provided a clandestine base and refuge.

Throughout April, May and June 1941 the whole problem of Allied intervention in Syria was bedevilled by sharp and at times bitter conflicts of view as to what was militarily and politically feasible. What forces could be mustered? Could the Free French with minor assistance manage the operation on their own? What would be the reaction of the Vichy French to an invasion of Syria by the Free French as contrasted with an Anglo-Saxon force? What would be the response of the Arab populations in Syria and Lebanon as well as in the rest of the Arab world? What view would the Turks take? Should an entry into Syria be conditional upon initial German intervention? Even among the Free French there was no unanimity. De Gaulle was confidently in favour of an almost entirely Free French enterprise which would ensure the continuation of French political and administrative control. General Catroux, his representative in the Middle East, believed that a reinforcement of no less than two British Divisions was necessary if the project was to succeed. The High Commissioner in Palestine had certain reservations. The Air Force's and the Navy's appreciations were not altogether in accord with that of General Wavell. The Foreign Office had their ideas. The Chiefs of Staff in London theirs. Finally there was the British Prime Minister. And behind all these conflicting assessments lay the desperately critical situation developing in the Western Desert and, as we have seen, in Crete and Iraq. In the event, and under strong pressure from London, a bold approach, as opposed to the more cautious one advocated by General Wavell, was followed in Iraq and subsequently in Syria.

By the end of May the German presence in Iraq had been eliminated but German influence still remained active in Syria. One of the question marks that revealed itself with mounting emphasis during this time was whether and to what extent units of the Vichy-dominated forces in Syria could be persuaded to cross the frontier into Palestine or Trans-Jordan and join the Free French. There had been little response, due mainly to the pro-Axis attitude of General Dentz, the military commander in Syria. In late May, Colonel Collet in command of the Circassian Cavalry slipped over the frontier. It had been hoped and expected that he would bring eight squadrons with him, but in fact he came over practically alone. And it was not until the fighting began that the cautious and calculating Druzes showed an inclination to join us.

But whatever the previous differences over intervention, by mid-May the menace of increasing German pressure on the authorities in Syria and an augmented German presence led to a general agreement that unjustifiable as General Wavell might consider the risks to be, particularly in the face of the situation throughout the rest of the Middle East, a military advance into Syria in co-operation with the Free French was essential. As for the Arab attitude the simple fact was that although Vichy French rule was unpopular there was no evident enthusiasm for British intervention, and even less support for the Free French. What was required by the Arab leaders was no less than a clear understanding guaranteeing independence to both Syria and Lebanon. In the latter part of May therefore a proclamation was agreed between the British and Free French and broadcast by General Catroux. It abolished the Mandate, proclaimed the Syrians and the Lebanese free and independent, and declared that their sovereign and independent status would be confirmed by treaty. The British Government added its own guarantee to this declaration. British, Australian, Indian and Free French forces thereupon entered Syria and Lebanon on 8 June.

General Wavell's plan, which was to be carried out by the GOC Palestine, Lieut.-General ('Jumbo') Wilson,* was to advance on a broad front. On the right the 5th Indian Brigade was to occupy Deraa and the line of the Yarmuk railway. A Free French force under General Legentilhomme was then to pass through and advance on Damascus. On the left the 7th Australian Division under Lieut.-General Sir John Laverack was to advance in two columns, one inland by Merjayun and the other by the coast road to Beirut.

The invasion started well enough but soon ran into stiff opposition. The Vichy French were in greatly superior numbers, and in addition they had at their disposal some ninety tanks while it had not been possible to spare any armoured vehicles from the Western Desert. The enemy were thus able to initiate a series of counter-attacks. On our right they sent a column from Damascus which made a turning movement by way of the Jebel Druze and attacked our lines of communication between Deraa and Damascus. Further left and on the coast their counter-attacks achieved some success. These were held, but their effect was to bring the Allied advance almost to a standstill. However, troops from Iraq were made available, and moved from Baghdad up the Euphrates towards Aleppo. 'Habforce' with its Arab Legion detachment advanced across the desert towards Palmyra and Homs. Vichy forces came under increasing pressure on all fronts and gradually withdrew. But throughout the campaign they put up a notably stout resistance, and one of the results of the fighting was that feelings between them and the Free French became extremely bitter. After the armistice the number of Vichy French who opted to join de Gaulle's movement was minimal.

As the campaign progressed the welcome given by the local people to the British far exceeded in warmth their attitude towards the Free French. Nowhere was this more marked than in the Jebel Druze. Sultan Pasha Al Atrash, who had led the Druze forces in 1925–6, kept in discreet touch with those of his countrymen who had joined in open opposition to the Vichy garrisons in the Jebel. He gave us not only his moral support but useful information. He was an impressive old warrior, eagle-nosed, hawk-eyed and heavily moustached (he lived to be nearly 100, dying in 1982).

As we planned our northward move from Mafrak a colourful, flamboyant and dynamic lady, the divorced wife of the Emir Hassan Al Atrash, hereditary ruler of the Jebel Druze, appeared in our camp dressed in a cloak, riding breeches, and a surprising form of semi-military headdress. She had come from Cairo where after her

* Sir Henry Maitland Wilson, later Lord Wilson, GCB, GBE, DSO, *b.* 1881, *d.* 1964. Field-Marshal 1944.

divorce she had made a name for herself as a singer and film actress under the stage name of Ismahan. Although Arabic was her mother-tongue she also spoke fluent French. Like most of her compatriots she was strikingly good-looking. Later she was to entangle a number of very senior officers with her beauty and her intrigues, and like all Druzes, she believed firmly in the principle of keeping in with both sides. In the months that followed a number of scandals of various kinds were connected with her, and she was finally arrested trying to cross into Turkey, her car allegedly filled with contraband, with a British officer hiding in the boot. Be that as it may, her arrival in Mafrak at that moment with her offer to ride at the head of our advance and lead us in the role of a Joan of Arc into the Jebel did not commend itself to de Gaury, and for the moment we saw no more of her. But the Princess was not a lady to let difficulties stand in her way. Within a few days of the armistice she took up residence in Suweida, the Druze capital, with Hassan her former husband now confirmed by the Allies as Prince and Governor. Here she entertained with royal charm and a great show of jewels, including a large gold Cross of Lorraine which nestled in the cleavage of her ample bosom. We had not by any means heard the last of her.

June and July are hot months in Jordan and Syria. A dry burning wind blew across from Saudi Arabia. We lived in clouds of yellow dust. Twenty miles to the north we could see the dark outline of the Druze mountains. By the time that we were sufficiently organised to move north, Allied forces, after their initial setback, had already advanced into Syria and Lebanon along the coast, up to Merj Aiyun and along the Euphrates to the east.

On 3 July units of the 5th Cavalry Brigade, which was then located in northern Palestine, were ordered to move to the vicinity of Deraa thirty miles due west of Suweida. The Vichy French forces in the Jebel which were commanded by Colonel Bouvier consisted of two battalions of Moroccan and Tunisian infantry, four squadrons of the then disintegrating *Groupement Druze*, a small Foreign Legion detachment, and a number of fortress and anti-tank guns. Colonel Bouvier's headquarters was in Suweida, and he also had a Company of Tunisians holding the hilltop fortress of Salkhad — the Old Testament Beisan of King Og — twenty miles to the south-east. Small detachments and patrols were operating in other parts of the Jebel. The troops under the command of the 5th Cavalry Brigade (Brigadier K.F.W.D. Dunn) were a composite regiment of the Greys and the Staffordshire Yeomanry, the Trans-Jordan Frontier Force, two troops of an anti-tank regiment and the Druze Legion. We were all — or nearly all — going to war on horseback. The object of the operation was to contain and deal with Vichy French resistance in the Jebel by reducing outlying posts, and to close in on the two fortresses of Suweida and Salkhad. Both were strongly held and the approaches to Suweida were mined. Brigade Headquarters accordingly moved to Deraa. To the north Ezraa was already in Allied hands. The Druze Legion was to advance north from Mafrak and carry out patrols as widely as possible in the vicinity of both Salkhad and Suweida.

My squadron consisting of 165 mounted men rode out of Mafrak on a burning hot afternoon. I had been given a G (R) Emergency Commission as a Second-Lieutenant/Acting Captain. Some of the men had come over with their French uniforms more or less intact, but we had had to supply the rest with whatever we had been able to lay our hands on in the markets of Mafrak and Irbid, and nearly all Wilfred Thesiger's men were wearing black embroidered civilian jackets from Es Salt which he had bought in Amman. Our weapons were even more varied. We had a number of French rifles but we had had to provide those of our men who had no firearms with material captured from the Italians in the Western Desert — very antiquated and unreliable stuff it was. With French and Italian weapons we had no reserves of ammunition, but then we didn't seriously expect to have to use much. Already the campaign had turned in the Allies' favour and it seemed unlikely that we would be directly involved in an attack on the strongholds of Salkhad and Suweida.

A six-hour ride from Mafrak brought us to Bosra Eski Sham. We met no opposition and moved into the railway station and the huge stone thirteenth-century Arab castle on the southern edge of the town. Bosra is a remarkable place. Originally a Nabataean city, the Romans made it the headquarters of the Third Legion and the seat of the Governor of their province of Arabia. In Muslim times it was an important trading centre; then in the following centuries it fell into decline, caused partly by successive earthquakes and partly by the weakness and decay of the Turkish Government. But its vast black basalt ruins, its ancient gateways, its paved streets and its castle were grimly impressive, and two great stone-lined reservoirs provided ample and easy watering for ourselves and our horses.

Apart from the positions at Salkhad and Suweida we were uncertain whether any of the villages which lay scattered throughout the Jebel were held or what patrols might be operating. It was a rough stony country of shallow watercourses, of fields divided by walls, of small scrubby woods and orchards, and of Nabataean ruins. Wilfred Thesiger's squadron had moved to the east of Salkhad and had been shelled from the fort. I took my squadron to reconnoitre the villages south-east and east of Bosra. We were welcomed wherever we went.

We enjoyed some night alarms and a lot of indiscriminate firing but nothing more. Head's squadron was briefly in action in Mjamer, a village half way between Bosra and Suweida. We were ordered to cut the road linking Salkhad and Suweida, and Wilfred Thesiger and I set off at dusk to do so. We made a night march, crossed the road and took up a position the next day at Sahwat al Khadr. From here we carried out a series of patrols north towards Suweida without meeting any opposition apart from some long-range ineffective rifle fire. And then on 12 July came a standfast order followed on the 14th by the announcement of an armistice. We rode back to Bosra. De Gaury went off to Dair Ez Zor on the Euphrates, Wilfred Thesiger took command of the Druze Legion temporarily and I was appointed 'Political Officer' to the 5th Cavalry Brigade, that is to say adviser to its Commander on local political matters.

The campaign, which had lasted in all just over five weeks and had caused a total of 4,600 Allied and 6,500 Vichy French casualties, had come to an end but its political repercussions were to sour Anglo-Free French relations for some years to come. In the Jebel Druze they were about to become acute. This was an area where French susceptibilities and emotions were always liable to be especially sensitive, because the French had long suspected the British of attempting to undermine their authority there, notably during their campaign against the Druzes in the 1920s.

On 24 July a British force of cavalry, infantry and artillery led by Brigadier Dunn rode and marched into the Druze capital Suweida. It consisted of the Yorkshire Dragoons, the First Battalion the Essex Regiment and representatives of the Greys. A squadron of the Greys took the surrender of Salkhad. Despite Free French objections, two squadrons of the Druze Legion accompanied the force which occupied Suweida. It was a colourful and historic occasion. We rode up from the plain to Suweida a long column of cavalry and infantry, the horses sleek English hunters and small tough Druze mounts. We lined up alongside the heavily wired fortress. It had been bombed but was intact and the fortress guns appeared operational. The garrison was within. By the terms of the Agreement which had been signed in Acre on (appropriately or otherwise) 14 July, the garrison was to march out with full honours of war, that is to say with their personal weapons, eight rounds of ammunition to each man, their colours flying and their band playing. At 3 o'clock we were in position. The gate of the fort opened. Two squadrons of RAF bombers roared overhead. A band consisting of drums, bugles and fifes emerged followed by troops of the Foreign Legion and African contingents. We sat our horses. Salutes were exchanged and the

French marched through a silent Suweida in the direction of the Damascus road. A mile beyond the town they halted. Trucks were waiting for them and they were escorted to Ezraa where they were to entrain for Beirut. Here they refused to surrender their small arms, and moreover they were found to have some field pieces in their possession. It was an act symptomatic of the type of incident and of the sort of friction that was to mark our relations not only with the Vichy French but even more with the Free French in the weeks to come. On Brigadier Dunn's orders the recalcitrant troops were surrounded and presented with an ultimatum. They thereupon complied with the terms of their surrender and departed.*

Later that evening I went into the fort. The guns had been left undamaged, but the barrack rooms and buildings had been vandalised. The place was in a shambles and filthy, and thousands of contraceptives lay scattered over the floors. The garrison brothel stood just outside the barbed wire defences, half way between the fort and the *Etat-Major* offices. It too had been wrecked. A number of formidable looking ladies of various nationalities were, it seemed, ready to occupy their damaged quarters, but their clients had departed.

The Union Jack had been hoisted over the Vichy French Governor's Residence, and the Brigadier, Eddy Calvert the Brigade Major (a regular cavalryman who had been at Winchester with me) and I moved in, to find a Frenchman in occupation. He protested, the position was explained to him and he hastened away to Damascus. Within twenty-four hours the circumstances of our entry into Suweida and our occupation of the Governor's Residence had drawn a sharp protest from Free French Headquarters in Damascus. It was a further taste of the many problems of *amour propre* that were to arise between our allies and ourselves. For the moment a compromise was achieved when on the following day a Free French liaison officer, Major de Kersauson de Pennendref, moved in and joined us in the Residence. He was tall and elegant and had taken part in the Military Tournament at Olympia some years before in command of a troop of Spahis. He was less prickly and sensitive than some of his countrymen and we liked him. For a few days too we had with us the

* Just over two months before, at Amba Alagi in Abyssinia, the Duke of Aosta was similarly permitted by the terms of a surrender agreement to march out of his stronghold in military formation to a British guard of honour, and to hand over his arms a couple of miles away. Earlier, in 1914, the Turkish garrison of Hafuf had surrendered to Ibn Sa'ud and had been allowed to march out of the fortress with the honours of war. But apart from these two occasions the surrender of Suweida provided a spectacle the like of which had not occurred for many years, and will surely never be seen again.

young French Cavalry officer who had commanded the *Groupement Druze*. He was a professional soldier and spoke fluent Arabic, a rare enough combination. He had been devoted to and had had great pride in his command. For him it now lay in ruins, subverted by British intrigue and money, and commanded by amateurs. He came to discuss his future, whether to join the Free French or to return to Vichy France. He asked for the restoration of his command. He was concerned to carry on a service and a tradition to which he had been trained and to which he had pledged his loyalty. The Armistice Convention as signed on 14 July had stipulated that all locally recruited *troupes spéciales*, which included the *Groupement Druze*, were to be under British and not Free French command. We urged him to join the Free French in some other capacity. In tears he refused. His was a cruel dilemma, and a bitter conflict of loyalties. Nor did we know what personal considerations may have added to the complications of his problem. He left us and returned to France. He was a fine type and we felt sad for him.

At the meeting of the 14 July Armistice Convention General Catroux, although representing the Free French, was present but he was not a signatory. The terms of this agreement as set out led to great confusion and misunderstanding, and to particular fury on the part of General de Gaulle who was convinced that Catroux had accepted the surrender of vital French interests. As a result therefore a further document was drawn up on 24 July, interpreting with greater clarity the terms which had been agreed ten days earlier and making concessions to a number of Free French objections. The clause in this second document which particularly concerned me in my political advisory capacity was Article 8. This read: *'In view of the great importance of military operations which attaches to the maintenance of order in the Jebel Druze it is agreed that the French Delegate General will consult with the British Commander-in-Chief on all important measures concerning the maintenance of order in the area.'* This was running pretty close to precisely what the Druzes in assisting us had been determined at all costs to avoid; namely an exchange of Vichy French for Free French control. Moreover it conceded that the previous understanding whereby the *troupes spéciales* were to be placed under British and not Free French command should be reversed and that they would be incorporated into the Free French forces. To give effect to this revised agreement, the men of the Druze Legion were given the choice of joining a British Druze Regiment or attaching themselves to a Free French unit. The majority opted for the former, and in due course the regiment moved out of the Jebel and into northern Palestine. Here it gave constant trouble and was finally disbanded. Its usefulness had been peripheral and short-lived.

Furthermore, as a result of this second agreement of 24 July and of the consequential concessions made to the Free French, a French officer Colonel Olivier Roget, who had previously served in the Jebel, moved into the Residency. The Union Jack was replaced by the Tricolor and Brigade Headquarters betook itself to billets in the town.

As Political Adviser to the Commander of the 5th Cavalry Brigade which now occupied the whole of the Jebel Druze area, I found myself attached to the Spears Liaison Mission under Major-General E.L. Spears.* This organisation, which was responsible for the now thoroughly difficult and unhappy task of carrying out the terms of the Armistice Convention, established itself at Aley in Lebanon. A great deal of acrimony, rancour, misunderstanding, suspicion and intrigue continued to mark our relations with our Free French allies. In the circumstances of France's humiliation and de Gaulle's burning determination to efface it by re-establishing as a first step France's overseas empire, it was understandable that there should be friction. There were plenty of clashes of personality, but in the particular circumstances of Syria and Lebanon, it was not surprising that Free French suspicions that the British had every intention of depriving them of their right and indeed their duty to continue for the time being in full administrative control were both deep and acute. This suspicion was particularly active when it involved anyone holding the appointment of a Political Officer; in this role I must surely have appeared sinister and malevolent. I spoke Arabic; I had lately been serving with the Druze Legion; I was known to have been an administrative officer in Palestine and was friendly with the Emir Hassan Al Atrash, Sultan Pasha Al Atrash and other Druze leaders.

Leaving aside my relations with the Druzes and the French I found no difficulty in working in the closest accord and friendliness with Brigadier Keith Dunn and his staff. He had been a Gunner, but had the air and the interests of a Cavalry officer. He was tall, slim and good looking, and had great charm. He wore an eyeglass, his field boots (of which had several pairs) shone with a deep mahogany glow, and his breeches were of perfect cut. Whenever he crossed his legs he would place a silk handkerchief over the knee upon which the opposite boot was to rest lest a touch of polish mark his breeches. By a curious turn of fate he had taken part in the advance on Damascus in 1918 and had charged the Turks in the plain that lay just west of the Jebel Druze. Keith Dunn was also a cultured, sensitive man and

* Major-General Sir Edward Louis Spears, Bt., KBE, CB, MC, *b.* 1886, *d.* 1974.

showed a deep interest in the people of the Jebel, their history and their way of life. He was much admired.

Major-General Spears, who had started his career as a Cavalry officer in the 1914–18 war, was very different. He was gifted with great ability and energy, and held strong and at times inflexible views. He was very close to the Prime Minister. He did not see eye to eye with General Wavell, and had little time for General 'Jumbo' Wilson or, for that matter, a good many others. He was liable to sharp attacks of irritability, a state of affairs in no way improved by his suffering constantly from dysentery and a painful and persistent skin disease. I found myself obliged to visit him in Aley on a number of occasions, but I soon concluded that the more I was able to avoid bothering him and his organisation the better. And although the Jebel Druze was a particular point of friction between our allies and ourselves it was fortunately far from Aley and Beirut, and it was evident that the more we could settle our problems locally the happier we would all be. I thus confined myself, as far as I was able, to getting on with the Free French representative Colonel Olivier Roget, a dour suspicious man, his liaison officer who was debonair and anxious to be friendly, the Emir Hassan Al Atrash and the officers of the Headquarters of the 5th Cavalry Brigade.

The Emir Hassan was not a typical Druze, either in appearance or manner. The majority of his compatriots were lean fierce-looking men with large moustaches and burning eyes. They were habitually girt about with weapons of every kind. Their swash-buckling manner matched their picturesque flamboyance of appearance and dress. Hassan by contrast inclined to a soft plumpness, he normally wore a European suit and his manner was mild and courteous. Before and during the campaign he had maintained, together with his ex-wife Ismahan or, as she now called herself, Emily, the traditional Druze practice of keeping a foot craftily and firmly in both camps. He showed no hesitation in co-operating closely with the British and at the same time avoiding open disagreement with the Free French. When problems arose he was helpful. I saw a lot of him in his modest but comfortably furnished villa in Suweida which, although no doubt adequate for his essential needs, was one degree down the scale compared with the former house of the French Resident, now occupied by the Free French *Délégué*, Colonel Roget. I would call on the Emir Hassan when I had difficulties which I believed he could help me to solve, and sometimes he would ask me to visit him. On these occasions he would often unburden himself on the subject of Ismahan to whom he was deeply attached, whom he had divorced some years before and whom he now wished to remarry. She had been his second wife, and he had recently divorced his eighth. Marriage with a previously divorced wife is forbidden by the Druze religion unless the priesthood can be persuaded to make an exception. Persuaded the priesthood were and for a short spell the Princess returned to Suweida and entertained with grace and charm until more exciting prospects drew her back to Beirut, and Hassan was left to languish.

I lived in the Brigade Mess with a group of light-hearted British officers. Most of them were countrymen and before the war they had hunted. Some had brought their own horses with them and as batmen they had their peacetime grooms. Conversation was mainly of well remembered fox-hunting runs. Each morning we rose early and rode. The more thrusting spirits would set off on what was known as a 'Tantivy', a cross-country scurry to include as many jumps as possible. A point-to-point was held. This was exactly how Wellington's young officers spent their spells of winter inactivity in the Peninsula.

As time passed Article 8 of the revised Agreement came to be interpreted with increasing generosity in relation to French interests and prestige in the Jebel, and during the latter part of August a number of Free French troops moved into Suweida. Throughout the month a French contractor had been busily at work on the building that stood half way between the fort and the *Etat-Major*, and which had been so tactlessly damaged by the RAF. No time was lost and on the 30 August the French Military Authority was able to issue a *Note de la Place* which ran as follows:

NOTE DE LA PLACE

La maison de tolérance à Souedia qui avait cessé de fonctionner pour les raisons indépendantes de la volonté des tenanciers reprendra toute son activité le lundi 1° Septembre, 1941, dans les conditions suivantes:

I. REPARTITION DES L'OUVERTURE

Mardi et Vendredi		*Troupes Britanniques*
Lundi *Mercredi* *Jeudi* *Samedi* *Dimanche*	*de 21 h. à 23 h.*	*S/s Officiers E* *BM 3 et Légion, Cadres Français, Escadrons Druzes, Services divers*
Lundi *Jeudi*	*de 18 h. à 21 h.*	*Légionnaires et hommes de Troupe français ou assimilés d'origines diverses (Planton résidence etc.)*

Mercredi *Samedi* *Dimanche*	*de 18 h. à 21 h.*	*Tirailleurs et grades indigènes du BM 3. Militaires français Autochtones (Escadrons réguliers S S etc.)*

II. TARIFS

Sous-Officiers Européens	*40 Francs*
Légionnaires *Tirailleurs et Grades Indigènes* *Autochtones français*	*20 Francs*

N.B. *Il est rappelé qu'aucun Militaire, quel que soit son grade ou sa nationalité, ne peut se reserver l'exculsivité d'une quelconque des personnes qui sont appelées à exercer leurs talents et que celles-ci doivent rester à la disposition de tous.*

Cette note sera lue à deux rapports consécutifs dans les unités français.

Despite the thoughtfulness of our ally in setting aside special times for the accommodation of British troops, it was done without previous reference and was not officially recognised.

The late summer turned to autumn. The mornings were misty as we rode back to breakfast of bacon and eggs and fried bread in the Mess. In expectation of a German breakthrough from Stalingrad and an advance through the Caucasus, defensive positions were being reconnoitred and prepared throughout Syria. In the Western Desert the other arm of the great Axis pincer movement had already reached to within a hundred miles of Cairo. It was a time of great peril. In the Jebel they were unconcernedly gathering in the harvest around the black basalt villages among the hills. When the winter came the north winds would sweep down from Anatolia bringing snow. Then the Druzes would spend the greater part of the short days crouched in their sheepskin coats over their coffee hearths, while their herds grazed in the warmer lowlands of Trans-Jordan.

As the autumn gave way to winter, it became clear to me that the Sudan Government, despite my pleadings and those of Glubb and others, were not going to allow me to remain in the Army. I was summoned back to Khartoum. I left, but determined to do all I could to get back to a part of the world which seemed likely to become very shortly the centre of further activity and excitement. I was succeeded by an old friend, Walter Milner-Barry of the Trans-Jordan Frontier Force.*

* W.L. Milner-Barry, OBE, Greek Military Cross, *b.* 1904, *d.* 1982. Shell Co. 1928–40, C. Tennant & Sons 1953–72.

7

THE ARAB LEGION

(1942–1944)

The Sudan Government had insisted on my return and there was nothing for it but to go. It was December 1941 and the likelihood that the Germans would push through the Caucasus and thence into Syria and Iraq and south to the Canal became increasingly real. The Abyssinian campaign was drawing to a successful conclusion and the Sudan was safe. I had been somewhat comforted by a letter from Douglas Newbold in the early autumn telling me that I would probably be wanted as Private Secretary to the Governor-General, Lieut.-General Sir Hubert Huddlestone, but I had subsequently heard that the post had gone to W.H.T. Luce.* Bill Luce, for whom the future held an outstanding career, including the Governorship of Aden and the Residency of the Gulf, was a year or two senior to me and far better qualified. But I was disappointed, and my mood of grumpy frustration was in no way relieved when I reached Khartoum. I was to go as assistant to Geoffrey Hancock who was in charge of the Fung District of the Blue Nile Province.† I had a total of ten years' service and was therefore already due for automatic promotion to full District Commissioner. I had looked after Southern Palestine on my own for the greater part of a year. I had had the experience of the Druze Regiment and of serving as Political Officer with the 5th Cavalry Brigade. Now I saw myself being posted to a backwater. The Fung was a District very similar to the Nuba Mountains which I had left five years before. I am afraid that I made little secret of my gloom to Geoffrey Hancock who, after an adventurous spell with the Sudan Defence Force, with his wife in England and no doubt equally restless, bore my moodiness and self-pity with great patience and sympathy.

Singa on the Blue Nile was our headquarters. Geoffrey Hancock had a boat and in the afternoons taught me to sail. He sent me off on a number of what in peacetime would have been interesting and worthwhile tours. The countryside was green and broken and picturesque. I went up to the Abyssinian frontier. But I fretted, and wrote to Glubb and others asking them to try and engineer my

* Sir William Luce, GBE, KCMG, *b.* 1907, *d.* 1977. Sudan Political Service 1930–53.

† G.M. Hancock, OBE, *b.* 1901. Joined Sudan Political Service 1925. Retired as Governor Kassala Province 1950. Subsequently Adviser to the Ruler of Qatar.

return. They promised to do all they could and Hancock, with great understanding, said that he personally would put nothing in my way should an offer be made. But my release would rest with the Governor-General and by a fortunate chance he came on tour to Singa shortly after the New Year of 1942. I asked to be allowed to put my case. He listened, and said that he would think about it should Glubb or anyone else put in a convincing claim. And then, in early April, Glubb's request for me to come to the Legion was accepted. Malta was within an ace of falling, and the very real possibility of a German advance from the north, which would certainly mean the Legion's involvement, helped me. I packed my few possessions into three tin trunks, spent two nights in Khartoum and was back in Amman within a week, feeling decidedly cheerful.

I was given the Emir Abdulla's Commission and the rank of *Qaimaqam* or full Colonel, which carried with it the title of *Bey*. I found both embarrassingly elevated. But having served with the Druzes the previous summer, and having worked closely throughout my time in Beersheba with the Desert Patrol, out of which the fighting units of the Legion were now developing, I was on familiar ground and, more important, was among friends and acquaintances. Glubb took me to his house on the day after my arrival in Amman and we talked. He wanted me first to get to know the people and the countryside of Jordan and the desert tribes, the Beni Sukhr and the Howeitat; and then the more extensive areas of Syria, Iraq and later Saudi Arabia. Increasing numbers of Bedouin volunteers were coming in from all three. I was to begin by spending a couple of months or more travelling as widely as possible.

I started by putting in several weeks in the Syrian desert with Norman Lash, now commanding the First Mechanised Regiment. The Regiment had open Humber and Ford trucks and a few thin-skinned armoured cars made in Tel Aviv, carrying a Lewis gun mounted in the turret. The troops were armed with .303 short magazine Lee Enfield rifles and a few Hotchkiss guns dating from 1900 which the Household Cavalry had bequeathed to the Legion after the Iraq campaign. These Boer War veterans were fed by a metal strip and were constantly jamming. For weapon training targets, empty petrol tins were set out in the desert, and the range of this musketry practice was limited to two hundred yards. For all that they were accustomed to carrying weapons, few of the Bedu were natural marksmen. The men still wore the long khaki ankle-length dress, with a red cummerbund, a dagger and crossed and highly decorated bandoliers — the traditional uniform of the Desert Patrol. It was some while before we were issued with standard battle-dress and webbing equipment; and when they were first obliged to make the change from their tribal dress, the men found this European type of uniform irritatingly uncomfortable. They were used to wearing open sandals which meant that their feet were unusually wide. British Army boots were often an agony to them. So with their daggers they cut off the toe caps and made holes in the sides to let in the air. They found it difficult to understand why this was frowned on. It took weeks to get them to turn out in this new kit with their equipment properly and neatly in place.

Glubb also wanted me to become familiar with the work of the internal security forces of Trans-Jordan, for the Legion was a police force with men enlisted from the villages as well as an embryo army drawn almost exclusively from the desert tribes, and to this end I did a number of patrols with the *Darak*, the mounted section of the police responsible for the rural areas west of the Hejaz railway. I spent a week riding along the Druze frontier and down the Yarmuk valley with a Sergeant and half a dozen men from the Police post at Irbid. We slept and fed in the villages, occupying the *Mukhtar*'s or Mayor's guest chamber at night, stretched out on blankets and rugs alongside the walls. The smell of sweaty shirts and socks as the men pulled off their boots and settled down made sleep difficult at times, and the snoring of my companions was monumental in volume. The hillsides and valleys were green and fruitful. The Yarmuk river tumbled and foamed down its steep sided gorge.

One of the minor rigours of life at that time revolved around the problem of dealing with the major calls of nature. Among the Bedu, where the tents were set on the open gravel plains, and the visibility was seldom less than fifteen miles, it was simply necessary to walk off purposefully in any direction and one's hosts knew the reason at once and politely occupied themselves elsewhere. In the villages the situation was far less simple and less agreeable. Soon after one's arrival the host would furtively draw attention to the whereabouts of the family convenience. He avoided the embarrassment of approaching too close to what sooner or later would prove to be a place of such appalling squalor that the chances of achieving any success there except in extreme emergencies were small. Yet there was nowhere else to go. When one spent the night in a Legion fort the position was again different. As matter-of-factly as possible, one would tell the Sergeant in command of one's requirement. In every post there would be four or five short-term convicts employed on various domestic tasks. Immediately the Sergeant would call to the Corporal to prepare the latrine. The Corporal with great ferocity would order the convicts to bring water, buckets and brooms. There would be much shouting, sluicing and hurrying to and fro. One would wait with as much show of nonchalance as possible. Eventually the Corporal would report that all was in order. The Sergeant would click his heels and salute and one would be ushered in. By then the urge had probably disappeared.

After a couple of months of this spell of pleasant and varied familiarisation, I moved into Legion Headquarters in Amman and established myself in a small mess which consisted of Hugh Foot,* who was deputy to Alec Kirkbride, now back from Galilee as a Resident Trans-Jordan; Tadros Altounyian who had come to us from the Libyan Arab Force; and Marcus MacKenzie, a banker. A succession of guests came and went: Wilfred Thesiger, Stewart Perowne,† Mark Pilkington from the Household Cavalry who was attached to the Legion for a spell after an adventurous year in the Abyssinian war and was soon to be killed in the Western Desert, and a dozen others. In his autobiography *A Start in Freedom*, Hugh Foot has described how we became Arab enthusiasts and vied with one another in our study of the language and our pursuit of the Arab way of life. We carried at all times, as Glubb and most others did, our string of beads and we certainly worked hard at Arabic, but I am not sure that we were all non-smokers and entirely teetotal as Hugh suggests.

Although Islam forbids the use of alcohol there were Arab officers in the Legion who liked a drink from time to time, and among them was the Deputy Commander Abdel Gadir Pasha Al Jundi, a splendid old warrior who had served in the Turkish Army in the 1914–18 war, and had many tales to tell of those times and the early days of the Legion. His bearing was magnificent, his greying hair and upturned virile moustache were meticulously dyed jet black, and with his tall lambskin headdress and high-collared tunic, that by convention only the Emir Abdulla and Abdel Gadir wore when in uniform, he was the very model of an almost theatrical military type of eighty years ago. He was approachable and friendly, but a great upholder of the outward forms of discipline and not to be trifled with or taken lightly.

He enjoyed, as I have said, a drink now and again, and was especially fond of a particular type of arak obtainable only in Damascus. When occasionally duty took those of us who were privileged with his friendship to Syria, we never failed discreetly to bring two or three bottles back as a gift for our Commanding Officer's deputy, and in return he would invite us to dine, and dinner would go on until a late hour. The trouble about drinking arak at

* Lord Caradon, PC, GCMG, KCVO, OBE, *b.* 1907. Joined the Colonial Service 1929. Governor Jamaica 1951–7 and Cyprus 1957–60. Permanent UK Representative at the UN 1964–70.

† S.H. Perowne, OBE, *b.* 1901. Orientalist and historian.

night is that its effects are reactivated by one's first cup of tea or one's breakfast coffee. Those mornings could be a little confusing and one had to be careful. Abdel Gadir Pasha had a strong head and a stout constitution.

I have told of my first meeting with Glubb at the time when I was serving in Beersheba. As I came to work with him in the Legion I grew increasingly to appreciate the tireless dedication of this remarkable and sensitive man. He had little patience with anyone, and British officers in particular, who sought the lighter and possibly at times the rather less reputable forms of relaxation. He found it hard to understand why anyone ever wanted leave. He never took any himself. He found it difficult to make allowances for those whose standards of enthusiasm and conduct fell even marginally below his own. But where Arabs were concerned he was ready to be less demanding. His position in Jordan was unique and unchallenged and quite rightly so in the atmosphere and circumstances of the time. The conception of a British deputy and possible successor was something that naturally exercised him, but where could anyone with his unique qualities and experience be found? Had he been killed, or more likely assassinated, no one could adequately have taken his place. He alone held the confidence of the Emir Abdulla, the Government and, above all, of the Bedu. Glubb was the last of that small number of extraordinary Britons who, during the previous hundred years and in widely differing circumstances, had made a name in the service of Arab rulers: Thomas Keith of the 78th (Ibrahim Agha), Qaid Maclean, Russell Pasha and a few others. He was to be the last and the greatest of the British Pashas. I travelled often with him throughout 1942 and 1943 on exercises and inspections and nearly every evening when we were together in Amman I would go up to his house with a box-full of papers to work through and discuss. By eight o'clock we would have finished and we would then drink a glass of sherry. As I left the house I would pass a dozen or more Bedu waiting to see 'the Pasha'. For him this would mean another two hours' work. Not a Sunday passed, when he was in Amman, but he would be in church. He was the most dedicated and single-minded man, and one of the most devout, whom I have ever known.

In 1917 T.E. Lawrence wrote what was described as the *Twenty Seven Articles* or, as he put it, 'stalking horses for beginners in the Arab armies'. They were designed as a code of conduct for those who found themselves involved with the Bedu tribesmen who formed the Sherif's army. They contain much wisdom, and the final article sums up the essentials. 'The beginning and ending of the secret of handling Arabs', it runs, 'is unremitting study of them.

Keep always on your guard; never say an unconsidered thing; watch yourself and your companions all the time; hear all that passes, search out what is going on beneath the surface, read their characters, discover their tastes and their weaknesses, and keep everything you find out to yourself. Bury yourself in Arab circles, have no interests and no ideas except the work in hand so that your brain shall be saturated with one thing only, and you realise your part deeply enough to avoid the little slips that would undo the work of weeks. Your success will be just proportioned to the amount of mental effort you devote to it.'* And this is what Glubb did. We would all have done well had we too been able to follow these precepts and impress them on those British officers who joined us with no previous experience of work in the Arab world. Some, but by no means all, had an instinct for this sort of approach to the problem of making modern soldiers out of illiterate but proud tribesmen.

At this point I must jump forward to an incident many years later, in 1963. I was travelling in a taxi from Damascus to Amman. I had the seat beside the driver and in the back were two Syrians. One was a man of twenty-five or so, an Arab Legionnaire returning from leave; the other was a little younger, a schoolmaster from near Deraa in the Hauran. As we approached the Jordan frontier the talk between the two turned to the Arab Legion, now the Jordan Army. The schoolmaster brought up the dismissal of Glubb in 1956. 'What a fortune that man must have made,' he said, 'Commander of the Army for the best part of twenty years. Think of it; the stores, the arms, the ammunition — everything. He must have taken a very nice "rake-off" throughout all that time.' 'My dear fellow', the Legionnaire said, 'you've got it wrong. I personally never saw Glubb, but a lot of us in the Army knew him and talk of him, and I can tell you from what they've told me that so far from making a piastre out of the Army, Glubb constantly helped men in need from his own pay, and used to send to hospitals in Lebanon, at his own expense, fellows suffering from tuberculosis.' 'Are you sure?' queried the schoolmaster. 'I'm convinced,' answered the Legionnaire. 'I'll take your word for it,' said his companion after a long pause, 'although it sounds very extraordinary. I never thought he was that sort of man.' I remained silent throughout this conversation, but as we drove in to the frontier post I felt happy that justice had been done in however small a way.

I was taken to call on the Emir Abdulla within a week of my arrival and thereafter I attended, whenever I was in Amman, the

* Quoted by John E. Mack in *A Prince of Our Disorder* (London: Weidenfeld and Nicolson, 1976).

Friday *Diwan* which he held for all officers above the rank of Major, and which followed his morning visit to the mosque. The Emir was a short but impressive figure in a perfectly tailored plain light-grey gown that matched his neatly trimmed grey beard. He wore a white close-fitting Mecca turban and a curved gold dagger at his belt. With the Emir at his desk we sat on small wooden chairs in a semi-circle facing him, Glubb on the left, Abdel Gadir Pasha next and then by rank to the most junior officer on the right. Few ventured to cross so much as their ankles. We sat bolt upright. The Emir would address a few questions to Glubb, a few to Abdel Gadir, and then at random to three or four officers of lower rank. It was all very formal. After half an hour or so coffee would be served and the Emir would indicate that the audience was at an end. We saluted and withdrew.

In the following three years I lunched or dined fairly frequently at the Palace — often these were small intimate occasions. I accompanied him on exercises, and he was a regular visitor to the Mechanised Brigade and to the 3rd Mechanised Regiment when I came to command it. He enjoyed few things more — as does his remarkable grandson the present King Hussein — than being with his Bedouin troops. He had the gift for combining familiarity with a measure of royal reserve. But for all that I saw much of the Emir I never came very near to him. There was no reason why I should; his close contacts were with Glubb and Kirkbride, whom he had known for many years. This triumvirate, together with the Prime Minister, ruled Trans-Jordan.

An atmosphere reminiscent of the Arabian Nights, whereby a man might find himself faced either with sudden good fortune or with the reverse, was liable to be a feature of the Emir's court. On 3 November 1942 he happened to be at Azraq where the 1st and 2nd Regiments were training and where the nucleus of the 3rd Regiment was being formed. Glubb was there as were the Commanders of the three regiments, half a dozen Arab officers and some NCOs. We sat in a tent waiting for dinner, drinking tea and talking. The battle of El Alamein had started on 23 October. It had reached a point of crisis two days later, and in the following week there was much hard fighting. The real turning point came early on 2 November when Montgomery threw in the last two brigades of his infantry reserve. By dawn the following day the armoured cars broke through. It was while we were thus sitting that our Arab Signals officer came to the entrance of the tent, saluted and whispered to Glubb. Glubb smiled and nodded and turned to the Emir. 'Your Highness, the battle of El Alamein has been won,' he said. 'Our Brigade wireless operator has been listening to the news.' The Emir gave no obvious sign of relief or satisfaction but after a moment's pause he said, 'That wireless operator, I would like him promoted to the rank of Corporal, let his Corporal be made a Sergeant, and I would like the Lieutenant who has just brought us this good news to become a Captain.' 'I will see that your order is obeyed, Sir,' Glubb answered.

The Emir was a great purist in the matter of the Arabic language, and he much disliked sloppy or, as he saw it, inaccurate translations of technical military terms, or the use of foreign words for which Arabic provided no immediate equivalent. We had adopted the word 'mortar' for both the two- and three-inch mortars with which we had recently been equipped. This word, he ruled, should no longer be used, and he coined his own translation '*madfa' gausi*' — i.e. a cannon that throws its projectile in an arch. He objected to the anglicised 'telephone', and it became '*hatif*', which indeed means 'an invisible caller'; and hearing a young wireless operator using the second form of the verb for 'reply' he instructed him to use in future the purer and more classical fourth form. The Bedu soldiers, who probably spoke a purer form of Arabic than was used anywhere else in the Arab world, approved of these edicts.

The Emir was also an enthusiastic rifle shot, and in combining unorthodoxy of style with astonishing accuracy, he was in a class by himself. In the early spring of 1944 he came down to the Jordan valley to spend a day with my Regiment. Knowing that he enjoyed exercising his skill as a marksman, we had selected a first-class rifle and had set up, and filled with sand, half a dozen four-gallon petrol tins about two hundred yards out on a hillside beyond the Mess tent. During the morning the Emir watched various exercises and then he lunched with the officers and NCOs of one of the armoured car squadrons. When the meal was over I suggested that he might like to try his hand with a rifle. He readily agreed. I pointed out the targets and handed him the weapon we had chosen for him. He felt its weight and its balance, and then he turned to two of his colourfully armed negro bodyguard. Each carried a rifle, a revolver, two crossed bandoliers and a silver dagger in his belt. 'Go up,' he said to them, 'and sit beside those tins, one on the right and the other on the left, and signal to me after each shot whether I have hit the target.' I was not at all happy with this perilous arrangement, but obviously there was nothing I could say. The two men plodded off apparently unmoved, climbed the slope and sat down half a dozen yards on either side of the line of tins. 'Nearer', shouted the Emir, waving to them. They moved closer in until little more than a few feet separated them from the targets. The Emir loaded and stood, leaning his left shoulder against the tent pole. His left hand grasped the rifle just behind the magazine. His feet were close together. It was an extraordinary position and not at all in accordance with the drill book, or with anything I had ever seen at Bisley, or with what we had been teaching the soldiers.* I watched the muzzle. It seemed to be waving around a good deal as the Emir took aim and fired. Could he possibly hit the target with this remarkable stance? A little spurt of dust showed itself somewhere — it was difficult to tell exactly where — but somewhere near the right hand target. The marker got up, leant over the tin for a moment and then waved his red and white headcloth in triumph. 'A hit', he shouted. The Emir then took the second tin and the third and so on. On each occasion there was a spurt of dust, and on each occasion the marker moved to examine the target and to signal success. Having apparently hit all six tins starting on the right, the Emir repeated the performance starting on the left. Satisfied, he handed me the rifle, sat down and accepted a cup of coffee. The bodyguards came clattering down the hillside with the six tins and brought them to their master, beaming with triumph. The Emir smiled modestly as we congratulated him. I glanced at the tins. Each showed two neat holes on both sides. Can there be any doubt that the Emir achieved these twelve hits? With a thrust and a twist of their daggers, either of the two bodyguards could discreetly have simulated a bullet hole, but I believe that the Emir's marksmanship was as accurate as it appeared to be.

The crisis of the summer of 1942 in the Western Desert and the Allied withdrawal to El Alamein came and passed, inspiring an unknown wit to write:

From East from West throughout the desert heat
There sounds the tramping of a million feet,
From GHQ the answering murmur comes,
The solemn shifting of a thousand bums.

I had been detailed to take over command of the 2nd Mechanised Regiment that autumn, and in order to become familiar with the Fords and Humbers with which the Legion was equipped; I went to Sarafand in Palestine and attended a motor transport course. I spent July on a prolonged reconnaissance of Southern Palestine, Sinai and southern Trans-Jordan, mapping those stretches of desert that

* The Emir's curious stance may well have been instinctively right, and we completely wrong. In *A History of Marksmanship* (Longman 1972), Charles Chenevix-Trench, with whom I used to shoot at Bisley, examines the stances recently used by international rifle shots when in the standing position: 'The Russians, unhampered by tradition, re-examined the standing position *ab initio* and developed one in which the feet are close together, the body bent back so as to make the rifle's centre of gravity coincide with that of the body and minimize the muscular effort and tension. It looks awkward . . . but for target shooting it has been proved over and over again to be far superior to the orthodox shooting position as taught by, say, the British Army Small Arms School.' A photograph in the book shows this modern Russian stance with the competitor's left hand holding the rifle precisely as the Emir did, i.e.

would be negotiable or otherwise by motor vehicles, and identifying areas which might be used as centres of resistance if the Germans crossed the Canal. Had they come south through the Caucasus and Iran, the Legion's role would have been to operate in the deserts of Syria and Iraq as a long-range desert force. Our training was geared to these roles.

I followed this reconnaissance with an interesting three weeks with a small detachment of 1st Mechanised Regiment in the desert south of Ma'an and along the Saudi frontier in a search for the murderers of five Saudi merchants at Ashadir, a remote area just inside Trans-Jordan. They had been on their way north from the Hijaz and had camped in the sand dunes. A party believed to be Trans-Jordanian tribesmen had surrounded them and shot all five as they sat round their fire. We found their remains. Our search and our enquiries took us into Saudi Arabia to meet and discuss the case with the Emir Abdul Aziz Al Sudairi, Governor of the Frontiers. We rounded up hundreds of camels from those sections of the Howeitat which we suspected of being implicated, and impounded them in and around Ma'an. But in spite of this form of communal pressure which was normally employed in circumstances of this sort, and our close working relations with the Saudi authorities, the murderers remained undetected, and eventually the camels had to be released.

Meanwhile my Headquarters work in Amman came to include responsibility for overseeing the Pay and Records Department. An enterprising Chief Clerk had recently enlisted his son at birth, opened a file and a salary sheet in his name, promoted him after six months to Corporal and drawn his pay and allowances for nearly a year before being discovered. I ran the promotion examinations and practical tests for the rural police. I worked in close association with Omer Bey Al Omeri, a Syrian of great polish and charm who was the Legion Quartermaster, and with Ahmed Bey Jundi the Commandant of the Training Depot, who had also served in the Turkish Army as a young man. He matched Abdel Gadir Pasha in the formality of his outward manner and bearing, but 'off parade' he

---

behind the magazine, and with the left elbow tucked in against the left hip.

Chenevix-Trench records another story which shows that the Emir was not alone in relying on the accuracy of his marksmanship to justify an unusual method of signalling his shots. 'It concerns the 2nd Battalion, Rifle Brigade,' he writes, 'whose Commanding Officer in 1805 was Lieutenant-Colonel Wade, an excellent rifle shot. He and two private soldiers named Smeaton and Spurry used to hold targets for each other up to 150 or even 200 yards. When the Earl of Chatham, inspecting the battalion, remarked on the danger of this practice, Wade protested that there was no danger, and, bidding a rifleman hold a target for him, aimed and hit it. Lord Chatham was horrified, but Wade nonchalantly informed him, "Oh, we all do it." He then held a target for the rifleman's fire.'

was warm-hearted and amusing. Finally my Headquarters work brought me the co-operative friendship of *Miralai* (Brigadier) R.J.C. Broadhurst Bey. Ronnie Broadhurst had come to the Legion from the Palestine Police several years before and was a constant source of information and advice. He spoke and wrote fluent Arabic and he was a particular favourite with the Emir Abdulla with whom he had established a social relationship denied to other British officers with the exception of Glubb.

The latter part of September 1942 took me off to a training course that appealed to my taste and sense of romanticism. This went under the code name ME 104 and involved a fortnight spent on the top of Mount Carmel with half a dozen officers drawn from various units in the Middle East. Here we learnt about sabotage and explosions and made ourselves familiar with the use of German and Italian small arms. We were taught unarmed combat and set to swim across Haifa harbour carrying limpet mines. We lived in some comfort in huts among the pine trees and carobs and oleanders, and we enjoyed a magnificent view over Haifa Bay. The school was supposed to be especially security-conscious and was surrounded by barbed wire, though some weeks after I had completed the course a small party of Jews broke into the armoury at night and made off with all the weapons and ammunition. Not surprisingly this cost the Commandant his job.

While I was at ME 104 a Colonel Keble came from GHQ Cairo and lectured us on what was being done in the Western Desert by way of infiltration, sabotage and suchlike. I had already volunteered — with much doubt and misgiving — for a parachute course and I asked him to get me into an organisation that would enable me not only to take part in activities of this sort, but also if necessary to pass myself off as an Arab. This was a conceited idea but I believed that among the Senussi I might have been able to pose as a Druze or as a villager from somewhere in Lebanon. The Arabic spoken in the Levant and North Africa was, I thought, sufficiently dissimilar to make a deception of this sort possible. I was far from being a fire eater, but it irked me that I seemed always to be on the fringe and never directly involved in the adventures that most of my friends were suffering or enjoying. No doubt it was a crazy notion, and although the Colonel seemed enthusiastic, I heard no more. I went back to Trans-Jordan and spent an enjoyable three weeks teaching the Mechanised Brigade at Al Azrak all I had learned on Mount Carmel. I have never had such enthusiastic pupils for any form of instruction.

Thus the autumn of 1942 passed into a winter in which snow fell heavily throughout Trans-Jordan and a number of tribesmen and their families died of cold. With the spring I was able to get away to Syria and Iraq where the 1st and 2nd Mechanised Regiments were exercising. The German threat to the Middle East was beginning to recede. The tide was turning in Russia.

In May I was sent to Cyrenaica with a training team consisting of an Arab officer and two NCOs, to help in the creation of a Libyan Gendarmerie Force to be responsible for policing the desert areas. We went up through the debris of the fighting and the Axis withdrawal to Agedabia, where I left my Arab Legion party. On our way through Cairo I had called on the Emir Idris, the Senussi leader in exile, and had handed him a letter from the Emir Abdulla, and on my way back I called again to collect his reply. With his quiet voice and manner, scholarly appearance and thick spectacles, he seemed to me to lack the colour and dynamism required for a national leader in exile. The Emir Abdulla evidently felt likewise for on my return, when I spoke respectfully of the Emir Idris, he merely pinched his forefinger and thumb together, waved his hand in the air, made a buzzing sound and uttered the one word 'Mosquito'. I could do no more than smile politely.

Despite all these interesting and at times challenging activities, I began by the early summer of 1943 to grow restless. A year earlier I had been denied the six weeks' attachment to a British Armoured Car Unit in the Western Desert that Glubb with the support of 9th Army had done his best to acquire for me. It was to have been a preliminary to my taking over command of 2nd Mechanised Regiment which was then forming, or alternatively 3rd Mechanised Regiment which was, at that time of crisis in the Desert, about to be formed. The opposition had come from MacMichael. I suppose he had seen me as potentially of greater use as an officer in a political role than as a unit commander. As High Commissioner for Trans-Jordan as well as Palestine he was, unfortunately for me, in a position to influence the decision. He had helped me a great deal in the past, and perhaps it was ungracious of me to feel as I did, but I was disappointed to have missed this chance of an experience of action in the Western Desert. Still, Glubb continued to do what he could to widen my military training. He had already sent me on a number of desert exercises and given me responsibility for helping to train and for inspecting our growing number of infantry companies. These, recruited from the rural areas of Trans-Jordan, Palestine and elsewhere, were designed to fill — and were already filling — the role of static guard and lines of communication troops within the Middle East. What we now hoped was that the Mechanised Brigade would be required to operate in a combat role outside the Middle East. Nonetheless towards the end of June 1943 I felt unusually low and depressed, and momentarily drained of energy and enthusiasm. I had had no leave; I had been working long hours with very little let-up; I had had sandfly fever; I had twice been involved in near escapes in the air. In the first of these I had been flying to Iraq in an open aeroplane when the engine caught fire and the RAF pilot, an American, was lucky to bring us down safely in the desert. The second involved an aeroplane of some interest, Puss Moth GA ABBS, which had originally belonged to King Edward VIII when he was Prince of Wales. In the early 1930s he had sold it to Sir Francis Humphrys, the last High Commissioner and the first British Ambassador to Iraq. Sir Francis had been a 1914–18 war pilot and he flew the plane himself during the time in which he was serving in Iraq. The Legion had no Air Force, and although we were generally able to call on the RAF to provide a taxi service when necessary, we felt the need for, at least, a symbol. Lord Apsley was attached to the Legion and he was a pilot;* he found GA ABBS in Iraq and because the Trans-Jordan Government had no funds to purchase an aeroplane for the Legion, half a dozen of us decided to buy it privately. Apsley went to Iraq and brought the plane back to Amman. For several weeks it operated flying Glubb and others to various destinations throughout the Middle East with Apsley at the controls.

I had been in Palestine and Apsley was to pick me up at Kalandia, the nearest airfield to Jerusalem, and fly me to Amman. Kalandia was no more than a somewhat hazardous airstrip at the best of times; it was narrow, hedged in by hills and with a main road running along one side of it, and was subject to sudden gusts of wind. We were due to leave early and we met at the airfield before breakfast. The plane was ready and we climbed in. No sooner were we clear of the ground than there appeared on the main road and directly in our flight path, a country bus crowded with passengers and with its roof piled high with luggage. Allen Apsley's avoiding manoeuvre took us straight at the stone wall which bordered the far side of the motor road. We hit the top, the undercarriage was swept away and we careered on into the field beyond and after several alarming seconds came to rest, the nose in the earth and the tail in the air. We emerged shaken but unharmed. The plane was a write-off, but I like to think that despite its ignominious end, GA ABBS was the original parent of the Royal Jordanian Air Force.

In my state of malaise I went to see our Medical Officer. 'There is nothing wrong with you,' he said, 'that a fortnight of change of scene and activity won't put right. Go away somewhere.' I decided

* Lord Apsley, DSO, MC, MP, *b.* 1895, *d.* 1942. Ironically he was killed on his way to England in an RAF plane which crashed in Malta some weeks later.

that the best antidote to the desert and my desk must surely be the sea or the mountains, preferably the sea. I thought that it might be interesting to find a Lebanese family that would lodge me, and to explore the coastal villages. So I went to Haifa with the intention of simply spending a night there and then hitching a lift up the coast to Tyre, or Sidon or Byblos. Haifa was full of Allied troops of every sort: Australians, New Zealanders, Poles, Yugoslavs, Indians and Africans. I found a room in the Officers' Club and before dinner I made my way to the bar. Ordering a drink I looked around at the great variety of services represented. The Navy seemed to predominate and beside me there stood a breezy swashbuckling Naval type with a wavy gold band on the shoulder tabs of his white uniform shirt, and a large fair beard. He had a loud but friendly fog-horn voice, a fund of bonhomie and a large glass of gin in his hand. We started talking and I told him that I had a fortnight to spare and was looking for something to do, something out of the ordinary if possible. He led me to a quiet corner. 'Why not join me?' he said. 'I've got a *caique*, a Greek coastal vessel, she's an 80-ton schooner and I'm short of a hand. We're sailing at dawn, and barring mishaps, I'll guarantee to get you back here in ten days' time. But keep it to yourself and no word, please, to your people in Amman. I'll tell you more when you come aboard. You'll find us easily enough, HMS *Siesta*.' This seemed a remarkably fortunate chance and I accepted immediately. Shortly before sunrise next morning I made my way to *Siesta*'s berth among the small vessels lying in Haifa harbour.

The vessel in which we picked our way through the crowded harbour was indeed to all appearances a *caique*. She had a mainsail and a jib, was thirty feet in length, and was equipped with an auxiliary motor. As she was intended to give to enemy agents, aircraft and possibly submarines the appearance of a vessel engaged in carrying commercial cargoes between the Levant coast and the Eastern Mediterranean islands, she was gaily painted a customary red, blue and yellow. HMS *Siesta* formed one of a number of small vessels known, for cover purposes, as the Levant Fishing Patrol. Late in 1942 the Army had established an organisation known as M04 which operated a fleet of small *caiques* engaged on clandestine operations in the Aegean. They carried men and weapons to enemy-occupied territory in the Dodecanese and Greek islands, and sometimes to the Greek mainland. Control of these operations was shared between the Navy, which operated a number of their own vessels known as the Levant Schooner Flotilla or Special Boat Service, and M04 which controlled eight *caiques*, all based on Haifa. Later they all came under the code designation of Force 133.

On this present occasion *Siesta* was carrying rifles, light automatics, ammunition and grenades, together with two British NCO armourers, for possible trans-shipment in Cyprus to a vessel which would take our cargo on to a further destination where it would be handed over to resistance groups. There were six of us aboard. A British Major, the two NCOs, an Arab cabin boy, myself and the Captain, Sub-Lieutenant R.M. ('Chips') Beardson, RNVR, my chance acquaintance of the previous night. In appearance he would have made a formidable pirate: sunburnt and generously tattooed, and wearing only a pair of grubby shorts and a green ski-ing cap.

The sun shone, the sea was calm and Mount Carmel and the mountains of Lebanon slowly slipped away behind us. We sat on the open deck. Below was a small cabin with six bunks set in tiers of three, port and starboard of the mess table. Forward of this there was a small galley. With the reinforcement of the auxiliary motor and a light wind filling the sails, we made our way steadily westward. Although the Germans and Italians had long since been driven out of North Africa, enemy submarines were still active in the Mediterranean, and were operating between Cyprus and the Levant coast. It was in this month, June 1943, that Caique No. LS4 working out of Beirut was lost without trace of her way back from Cyprus. We therefore kept an alert watch for both aircraft and submarines.

However, we sailed on unmolested. The sun set, it grew suddenly cold, and leaving the helmsman on deck the rest of us went below for strong gins and water and a bully beef stew prepared by the Arab cabin boy. Beardson had a powerful baritone voice and a vast repertoire of unprintable versions of sea-shanties. We sang till well after midnight. Already I was beginning to feel a lot better. We slept, taking turns at the watch every two hours. Just before dawn, a low line of grey blue mountains rose up to the west. It was Cyprus, and by mid-afternoon we were moored in Famagusta harbour. We waited to learn whether we were to hand over or sail on with our cargo. The following night the cargo was unloaded and transferred to two smaller and possibly more innocent-looking *caiques* that moored themselves alongside us. It was disappointing that our share in this particular exploit, small and uneventful as it was, had ended. The more fortunate armourers disappeared and after a further day in Famagusta we sailed in the evening for Haifa. The wind got up, the auxiliary engine broke down constantly, and the voyage back was a rough one and took twice as long as our easy passage out. But the foul weather had blown away the last traces of my malaise and I returned to Amman completely recovered.

Within a month or so of my return I was at last given command of 3rd Mechanised Regiment, or rather the task of completing the initial formation of the Regiment; and as a preliminary to this I went off to attend a three-week unit commanders' course in a camp among the sand dunes at Deir Suneid near Gaza. There were twenty or more of us, Majors and Lieutenant-Colonels, including several officers from Allied forces. Among the latter was Prince Peter of Greece who showed extraordinary skill in catching the crabs that abound on the sandy beaches of Palestine (having caught the crabs, he ate them raw).

All these officers had not only seen a lot of action in the Western Desert or elsewhere, but had received a great deal more basic training than I had. I was not an outstanding student, but I probably absorbed a lot that was to be useful in the year to come, and the course gave me a confidence I needed for this new venture. I went out to Azraq in a state of enthusiasm to join the rest of the Mechanised Brigade, and start building up the 3rd Regiment.

The Legion had done magnificently in both the Iraq and the Syrian campaigns of 1941. The men had shown initiative, and steadiness and courage. But they had been fighting on their own ground and in a style that came naturally to them — the traditional tactics of the tribal raid. Their weapons and their equipment were simple and familiar. In numbers they had been no more than two hundred and fifty, and nearly all of them were men of several years' service with the Desert Patrol. Both campaigns had been short and had ended in success. Above all the men had fought under the direct command of Glubb, whom they had known, admired and trusted completely, for over ten years, and under Norman Lash, who during the previous two years or more as the Officer in Charge of the Desert Area of Trans-Jordan they knew and liked. Lash spoke fluent and accurate Arabic, and both he and Glubb knew every man under their command.

It was on the foundation of that record of success, and with a steady stream of volunteers from throughout the deserts of Arabia that during the latter part of 1941 and into 1942 and 1943 we were endeavouring to build a force many times as large in manpower, with new weapons and equipment, and to bring it up to the standards in tactical training, administration, communications, maintenance, hygiene and discipline of other Allied forces in the Middle East. If we were to be given an operational role — and by the end of 1943 that role would have to be overseas, in Italy or the Balkans — we needed to match and indeed surpass those standards. Our two greatest assets were Glubb's dedication combined with the loyalty of the Legion to the Emir Abdulla, and the natural enthusiasm and courage of these tribesmen. Our difficulties sprang from various circumstances. We were expanding perhaps tenfold. Of Arab officers and senior NCOs we had the veterans of the summer of 1941, some of them men with five years' service or more, but with very few exceptions all were illiterate. The principles of tactics and the use of new weapons and vehicles came comparatively easily to both trained men and recruits, but they all found it less easy to appreciate the importance of constant and careful maintenance; in particular written orders meant nothing and instructions other than verbal ones posed a host of problems. Illiteracy and no knowledge of English meant that there was no way for even the otherwise brightest officers and men to benefit from the many instructional courses the British Army was running throughout the Middle East. The half-dozen non-Bedouin officers we had in the Brigade were more technically efficeint and professionally qualified than their tribal brother-officers, but basically they were men of different material with a different scale of values.

Such a high percentage of illiterate men meant too that in signalling, stores and other services we had to bring in educated young villagers. This led to jealousies. Moreover there was always an element of tribal feeling among the Bedu themselves which was liable to create friction.

In all the three Mechanised Regiments, each of which consisted of two Armoured Car Squadrons, two Squadrons of Lorried Infantry and a Headquarters Squadron, together with our 25-pounder artillery unit and our Brigade Signals, the Squadron Commanders and the Adjutants were Arabs. Norman Lash now commanded the Brigade, and the Commanders and the Seconds-in-Command of the three regiments were British. In addition we had two or three British officers attached to each regiment as instructors. Of these dozen or so British officers, some of whom had already seen a good deal of action, only very few were what one might call Arabists. The rest, after some months with us, had only a fragmentary knowledge of the language, nor were they all temperamentally suited to subscribe to Lawrence's twenty-seven articles. And so sometimes it was an uphill struggle to build a harmonious and effective organisation out of elements that held different standards and priorities and sympathies.

Camp hygiene was a constant headache. The Bedu just hated using a latrine. Being extremely modest in these things they wanted privacy, the privacy of a fold in the ground or the shelter of a bush. Once we had moved from the wide spaces of the desert where all three regiments did all their initial training, first to Jericho in the Jordan valley, and then to the hutted camps along the coast of Palestine south of Gaza, this became a real problem involving constant and at times self-defeating disciplinary action. The matter of rations created problems too. The Bedu had come to accept and indeed to like bully beef, but for fresh meat we could no longer buy sheep once we had moved away from Azraq. We had therefore to rely on British Army supplies, which meant accepting frozen mutton from Australia and New Zealand. There was no knowing whether it had been slaughtered in accordance with Muslim practice, but this was not the real worry to the men, which was whether it was sheep at all. It might, they suggested, be dog. There was that little tail on the carcass that looked more than suspiciously like a dog's tail. And then the head was missing from the carcass. Why? A lot of the men refused to eat it until we took a party of Squadron Commanders and NCOs to the RASC cold stores in Jerusalem to examine the carcasses in detail, to talk with the British officer in charge who, with Indian and other non-Christian units to serve, had a wide and sympathetic experience of these problems. He reassured us. The regimental *Imam* added his own conviction that the meat was genuinely sheep and nothing sinister, and finally all was well.

Every morning we began with forty minutes' physical training. This was an activity which the Bedu found difficult to appreciate. They were hard fit men in any case, their lives had been spent in the open air, they were used to an active existence; why then was it necessary to subject them to the absurdities of jumping up and down, bending and twisting their arms around? There were two exercises in particular of which they found the propriety doubtful to say the least. Press-ups they were prepared to do under some protest and with a good deal of embarrassment. Was it necessary, with all its apparently male associations, to do something quite so crude? As for the companion exercise that involved lying on one's back and making circular movements with one's legs in the air, no: this was an utterly unseemly activity for men. We abandoned it. But when it came to things like going through an assault course which called for the sort of muscles and the agility we had hoped to develop through these PT parades, they were all enthusiasm.

Despite all these problems, some of them wearing and some of them humorous, we made steady progress and by the early summer of 1944 we were beginning to do rather well on exercises and to look rather good. Our Tel Aviv-manufactured armoured cars made of mild steel sheets and three-ply wood had been replaced by Marmon Harringtons from South Africa, armed with a two-pounder and a Browning in the turret. This was more like it.

But by the late autumn of 1944 the Middle East was no longer an operational area, and it had become disappointingly clear that the Legion was not going to be employed in Greece or the Balkans. The prospect therefore was of garrison duties in Palestine, Syria, Jordan and Iraq, and the continuation of training. The Sudan Government was pressing for my return and now, in contrast to 1941, there seemed every reason to suppose that I would be more usefully employed there than with the Legion. I told Glubb that I thought I ought to go and he agreed. I had had no leave apart from a few days now and again since the early summer of 1938. As part of the arrangement for my return to the Sudan, I asked for and was given two months to be spent in England. It was early November, and 3rd Mechanised Regiment was camped in the Jordan valley. Our standard of training and general efficiency had become fully equal to that of the two other regiments in the Brigade, and they had been formed well before we had. We had recently moved over from the coast to hunt for a small band of German and Arab parachutists who had been dropped near the northern end of the Dead Sea. They were brave men, but theirs was a hopeless operation and they were soon found and captured.

The time came for my departure and I held a short parade to say good-bye. I found it a moving occasion. Although we had not taken part in any combat, these 650 men and I had worked together closely for a year in our endeavour to create an efficient and modern fighting unit. We were none of us professional soldiers; a few had seen brief spells of action in Iraq and Syria but that was all. We were comrades in arms, if not comrades in combat. Of the five Squadron Commanders who served with me during my time in 3rd Mechanised Regiment all were able and enthusiastic officers, but today, after more than thirty-five years, it is perhaps Lieutenant Ghazi Al Harbi whom I remember most clearly. Ghazi came from the Hijaz, from the Beni Harb, and he joined the Desert Patrol in the early 1930s. He had shown great courage in the Iraq and Syrian campaigns and had been decorated and commissioned. He was thickset, a little below average height and more heavily bearded than most Bedu. For all his courage in war and his enthusiasm for soldiering Ghazi was soft-hearted, sentimental and easily moved both to tears and to laughter. And he was exceptionally frank and outspoken, but never other than gently so. He had recently married a young wife to whom he was greatly devoted. He had installed her near Damascus, and in consequence he frequently asked for compassionate leave. Eventually I remonstrated with him: he had already had much more than his due share; what about others? 'You don't understand,' he said, 'you are not married. Just you wait until you are, and then you'll know how I feel. And besides,' he added, 'you are too lean and you eat too little. When you marry, your wife will certainly urge you to eat more. "Have this little bit extra — for my sake" she will say. And you will eat that little bit extra and then you will become less thin and less inflexible, and you will understand more of human nature.' I asked him whether, when he was on leave, he talked to his wife about the regiment, and our life and what we did. 'Of course not,' he said, 'these are military secrets.' 'Well then', I replied, 'what do you talk to her about?' He looked at me with a sly twinkle. 'I say to her, "how sweet you are." ' He was the only one of the five Squadron Commanders who gently and humorously pulled my leg.

Ghazi served with outstanding bravery in the battle for Jerusalem during the first Arab-Israeli war and then he left the Legion. He joined the Royal Guard in Saudi Arabia and eventually retired as a Brigadier. In 1976 when I was in Riyadh I managed to track him down and went to call on him. He was an old man now but his memory of those days and of our shared friends was very clear. We were glad to see each other.

The day after this farewell parade I went to Amman to attend a party given for me by all the senior Arab officers of the Legion. I made a speech. I had taken a lot of trouble to get the sentiments and thoughts I wanted to express properly phrased in Arabic. I was touched by the emotional response that showed itself; but these were a people who instinctively take a delight in and are moved by words. Indeed I have often thought that Arabic by its very range and richness may perhaps be a handicap to the Arab people in taking their place in the modern world. It possesses, and lends itself to the repetition of, pious sentiments which sound magnificent but often lead only a little way beyond their utterance, and it tends to favour the striking of attitudes that remain only a noble pose. It so often forms a refuge for those whose intentions at the moment they are expressed are genuine enough, but which fall short in the execution. *Inshallah* — 'God Willing' — can be interpreted, in so far as effective action is concerned, in more than one way. The West and its languages are more pragmatic. Arabic sometimes gets itself lost through the very wealth with which it expresses itself.

Thirty-two years were to pass before I saw the Regiment again. Ma'an Pasha Abu Nuwar, who had been gazetted a Second-Lieutenant in the Legion shortly before I left, had in due course come to London as Jordan's Ambassador. In 1976 he gave me an invitation from the Chief of Staff of the Jordan Armed Forces to spend ten days in the country as the guest of the Army. My wife, Silvia, was included in the invitation. We accepted this very generous gesture with delight and were treated with overwhelming hospitality and kindness throughout our time in Jordan. We were provided with an air-conditioned Mercedes with a dashing military driver; a charming young officer, Qasim Bey Al Khasawne, accompanied us as guide and companion, and we were taken all over the country. The Legion had come of age and was now a battle-tested army. The men looked as tough as their fathers in 1944, but to this was added a level of education and technical skills that had been absent before. And Bedu and townsmen were serving together apparently without any of the jealousy and suspicion with which we had had to contend.

Two days before the end of this unforgettable visit I went and lunched with the Regiment, now named Princess Basma's Regiment. They were camped on the Syrian frontier close to where we had ridden into the Jebel Druze in 1941. 'You must come back and visit us again the day after tomorrow,' the Colonel Audi Bey Abdel Nebi said as I was about to leave. 'It's our Regimental Day, Princess Basma's birthday.' We were due to fly back to London the next morning but this was an occasion I couldn't possibly miss. I accepted. 'Good', the Colonel said, 'be with us at eight.' Two days later I drove back to Mafrak. The outline of the Druze mountains with all its associations showed dimly to the north. I had expected a dinner, a hundred or so guests perhaps, possibly an hour or two of dances and songs, but I found a vast concourse of two thousand or more gathered about the Regiment's camp. There was the Divisional Commander Khalid Bey Abdel Nebi, the Brigadier Saleh Bey Melkawi, notables from the neighbouring towns and villages, soldiers' relatives and friends, and the Regiment's veterans. We dined traditionally and then the party began. There were songs and sketches and dances. At intervals the Regiment's *Imam* addressed us. From time to time the band played the Jordanian National Anthem. Belief in God, Loyalty to the King, the memory of dead comrades, pride in the Army and the Regiment: these were the lessons that were repeated time and again that evening and they were absorbed with enthusiasm. I found it all very moving and I wondered whether we in Britain had not ourselves fallen short of some of the standards we had tried to teach to these and other people of alien cultures in the past. I wondered whether our present priorities were right. What virtues did we now value?

But the most moving moment for me came shortly after midnight. I was sitting beside the Divisional Commander. As the events on the programme drew towards their end a party of soldiers placed a large table in front of him. On it was a collection of silver cups. He explained that these were the Regimental prizes which were competed for and awarded annually; the best rifle shot, the best driver, the best recruit and so on. 'I shall present them to the winners,' he said, 'as soon as the party ends.' The last item was a reading from the *Quran*. Then for the third time that evening the band played the Anthem. As we sat down, the floodlights were switched on, and the prize winners were fallen in. The General turned to me again. 'No, I would like you,' he said, 'to present these cups on my behalf. You formed this Regiment. We owe you at least this small symbol of gratitude.' He stood up and made a short speech. 'Sitting beside me', he said, 'is the man to whom this Regiment owes its inception thirty-three years ago. We are happy to have him with us this evening; and to show him that we value the foundation that he laid, it is right that he and not I should present these cups which signify the Regiment's skills and standards.' There was applause. I was too moved to speak. I presented the cups. The band played the Anthem once again. I was led to my car and driven back to Amman under the stars. It was two in the morning when I reached the Embassy Residence where we were staying and nearly dawn before my thoughts allowed me to sleep.

But now back to the early winter of 1944, with the Allied armies deep into France, it was time to say good-bye to the Emir Abdulla and Glubb, and that done I drove down to Cairo. The Sudan Government had arranged for me a passage home in a troopship, and we sailed in a convoy of thirty or more vessels impressively accompanied by half a dozen naval escorts. It was not a comfortable voyage by any standards. We slept twenty together, in a series of three-tiered bunks, in cabins designed to hold four. We were greatly bothered by bed bugs. We washed and ate in relays. Wherever we were, we carried our lifejackets and a small bag of essentials in case we were obliged to leave the ship in a hurry. We paraded for boat drill and PT every morning. Deck-space was limited to a few square feet. At times it was rough, but we played housey-housey and there were concerts, quizzes, discussion groups and church parades. The voyage lasted three weeks and took us through the Straits of Gibraltar far out into the Atlantic before we turned north-east to Scotland. In a cold wet grey December dawn we landed at Glasgow and I phoned my parents who, despite the Blitz, had courageously remained at Oxshott. By the next morning I was home. My father had aged and looked frail and tired. My mother, brisk and efficient, overjoyed in my return, seemed scarcely altered. I had brought them what little I could to supplement their austere civilian rations: some rice, sugar, dried milk, chocolate and dates. The period of flying bomb attacks on London and the southern counties had passed its peak but was still not ended. England was cold and dark, and men and women were desperately tired, but among people of every sort there was a spirit I had never previously experienced nor, sadly, have I known it since.

PLATES

1

2 4
3 5

6 8
7 9

10 12
11 13

14
15

Part II
'SHADOWS ON THE SAND'

8
BACK TO THE SUDAN
(1945–1949)

Silvia Cornwell-Clyne and I first met in August 1937 as lunch guests of Martin Parr at the Oriental Club in Hanover Square. She was his cousin. The next day my leave came to an end and I returned to the Sudan. When I got back to El Obeid I wrote to her. After an interval she replied. And thus there began a correspondence that lasted for over six years. To start with there had been a letter every two or three months, but it had progressed by the time I was in Beersheba and the war began to one a month. By 1942 we were writing once a week and continued to do so. It was an unusually long-range courtship, during which we never met and never exchanged other than written words. But it laid a foundation of singular depth, and we both came increasingly to feel, as these years passed, that we were growing extraordinarily close. Even so, we both knew well enough that although our next meeting might possibly mean a great deal, it could equally mean that we had simply been building on nothing more than a romantic vision.

Within two days of my return to England in that last December of the war we once again lunched together in London. As we talked it began to seem as if our long association on paper might come to mean more than a mirage. She was busy all day as a forewoman in a Government-controlled photographic unit engaged in work for the Forces. On certain nights she served as a fire-watcher on the roof of the Milk Marketing Board at Thames Ditton, for the flying bombs were still coming over. Fortunately our parents' homes in Surrey were not far apart, but although our opportunities for meeting were limited and my leave was short, within little more than a fortnight our minds were clear. We were equally clear that we were taking a risk. But there is no marriage without an element of risk, and marriage brings its own stability.

We were married on 22 January 1945 in Winchester College Chapel by my old housemaster, 'Ping' David. Jack Parr was my best man. With war-time austerity and restrictions everything was very simple. Silvia had no bridesmaids, but friends gave her their precious clothing coupons to enable her to buy enough material for a wedding dress. Our parents and a dozen friends managed to make the journey to Winchester and from there we went off by train for a short but supremely happy honeymoon at Chagford in Somerset. It was January and very cold. The taxi we had ordered was unable to get through the snow to the station, and we had to trudge knee-deep carrying our suitcases. But we were given a warm welcome at the Millend Hotel and had a wood fire in our room. Our happiness, great as it was then, has grown unclouded ever since. Silvia was twenty-five, I was just thirty-six.

Within a month we were both on our way to the Sudan. For Silvia, who had never seen Africa or the Middle East, it was all an immensely courageous step. For her parents, now alone since their only son Christopher had been killed in 1942 serving as a pilot in the RAF, it was an even harder moment than it had been for mine when I first set off for the Sudan in 1931.

We sailed from Liverpool. It was March 1945. The Western Allies were across the Rhine and the Russians were on the Oder. Although the end was in sight Germany was not yet beaten, and German submarines were still active. Our convoy, impressively escorted by naval vessels and barrage balloons, made its wide detour into the Atlantic before turning back to Gibraltar and the Mediterranean. The conditions of travel were no more comfortable than they had been the previous December. I was in a starboard cabin with twenty-four other men. Silvia was in a port cabin with twenty other women, all Copts, Greeks and Cypriots from Alexandria and a boy alleged to be too young to sleep in a cabin allotted to men. Whatever his true age, he had certainly gone beyond a point in years, inclinations and above all curiosity to justify his special status. He was a great feigner of sleep, and Silvia soon had to learn to dress and undress under the bedclothes.

Once past Gibraltar most of the escorting vessels disappeared and the convey made its way unmolested through the calm spring Mediterranean weather to Alexandria. The Egyptian Customs were as chaotic and inconsequent as only Egyptian organisations at that time could be. We had with us two trunks, which contained our few war-time wedding presents. These we declared. Among them, packed between towels and sheets, were half a dozen gramophone records. What were these records? we were asked. We told them that they were of well-known classical pieces. Had we a gramophone with us? No. Why then were we importing records? Because we had a gramophone in the Sudan whither we were bound. Perhaps, but it would be necessary for the Customs authorities to play the records. It was a precaution; records could contain subversive matter, especially in wartime. So it went on. It was all quite amicable but the Customs officers were inflexible; then suddenly and inexplicably the whole thing was dropped, perhaps because the Cairo train was due to leave and the Customs offices to close — anyway it was lunch time. We passed through without further difficulty. It was characteristic of Egyptian illogicality, with which I was later to become far more familiar.

After three days in Cairo we were on our way south: to Aswan by train, by river paddle-steamer to Wadi Halfa and thence, again by train, to Khartoum. Douglas Newbold, now Civil Secretary, had written asking us to stay with him. At Wadi Halfa we learnt that he had had a fall from his horse and was seriously ill. Before we reached Khartoum he was dead. His death was a tragic loss to the Sudan and to his friends. His successor was James Robertson.* We had been neighbours ten years earlier when he was District Commissioner Western Kordofan and I was in Talodi, and from now on we were to become increasingly associated, and our admiration for 'John Willie' and his wife Nancy grew progressively.

Not surprisingly the Sudan in 1945, after five and a half years of war, was a different place from what it had been in 1938. The change was not immediately or distinctly apparent but it could be felt, particularly in the towns. There was no unfriendliness, but there was a new atmosphere of independence, self-confidence and sometimes self-assertiveness. Thousands of townsmen and many more from tribal areas, men who had had some form of education and men who were illiterate, had volunteered and joined the Sudan Defence Force. They had served in half a dozen countries and had mastered the use of machines and weapons. They had seen Europeans kill one another and had themselves killed Europeans. These men were now returning home. The politically conscious could see clearly that without the help of the Sudan, Britain would scarcely have been able to hold the Middle East in 1941 and 1942. They had perhaps set aside the thought that without British and Indian aid the Sudan would have been over-run by the Italians, and that their lot might have been hard in consequence. The Atlantic Charter had given encouragement to those who hoped for rapid constitutional change. A revision of relations between Britain and Egypt, especially with regard to the Sudan's future, seemed inevitable. There was now a Press of some consequence. In the larger towns and in the Provinces local govern-

* Sir James Wilson Robertson, KT, GCMG, GCVO, KBE, *b.* 1899, *d.* 1983. Sudan Political Service 1922–53. Governor-General Nigeria 1955–60.

ment, which developed steadily during the war years, had afforded many Sudanese a share in managing their own affairs in town, Province and rural Councils. Early in 1944 an Advisory Council had been established for the Northern Sudan, and although this was only a consultative body, and was criticised by the intelligentsia as having no executive power and not representing the South, it was a first step towards a democratic system of government at the centre. Before long it was to be replaced by an elected Legislative Assembly and an Executive Council.

Sudanese nationalism had grown slowly. It had shown itself momentarily in the early 1920s, inspired by a very small minority and in conjunction with an Egyptian movement aimed at uniting Egypt and the Sudan under the Egyptian Crown. The manoeuvre ended in failure in 1924, and for the next ten years or so it remained inert. In 1936, under the shadow of Mussolini's invasion of Abyssinia, Britain and Egypt signed a treaty of alliance. The treaty had reference to the Sudan, and the small but increasing number of educated Sudanese had resented the fact that they had not been consulted. Meanwhile Egypt pursued her claim, consistently maintained since 1899, that the Sudan was an integral part of Egypt, over which she exercised *de jure* if not at present *de facto* sovereignty.

Early in 1938 a group of educated Sudanese elected from among themselves a body designed to represent their country's national aspirations and styled it the 'Graduates' Congress'. It marked the first important milestone on the road to the political development of the Sudan and at the same time the first and inevitable manifestation of that demand for self-determination which, however premature it may seem to the tutelary power, is the natural and inescapable consequence of the tasks which that power takes upon itself in developing and educating a country under its guardianship. The Congress addressed a letter to the Government asking that in future it should be consulted, as a body, on matters of public interest. The flaw lay in the fact that although the Congress represented a proportion, perhaps a quarter, of the five thousand or so Sudanese who had progressed educationally beyond elementary level, most of them Government officials, its representation ended there. It could not speak for the rest of the country. It could not indeed speak, as it claimed, for all educated Sudanese. The Government was not to be drawn, and its reply came as a disappointment to the Congress and, in particular, to its Secretary Ismail El Azhari, a schoolmaster of whom a great deal more was to be heard in the next twenty years.

After the outbreak of war the Congress became increasingly active, and involved itself directly with leading Egyptian politicians. By 1942 it was seriously in conflict with the Sudan Government. The moderate elements in the Congress lost control of its policies, and by the time the war ended it had become an extreme pro-Egyptian political party. As this conflict between the more active of these local politicians — now led by El Azhari — and the Sudan Government gathered momentum, a further influence made itself felt. This was a resurgence of the old and bitter rivalry between the two great Northern religious sects, the *Ansar* — the followers of Sayyed Abdelrahman Al Mahdi — and the *Khatmia*, the adherents of Sayyed Ali Al Mirghani. Each, with around two million adherents, represented a large proportion of the Muslim population of the Northern Sudan. The two and a half million Southerners remained politically unaware and inactive. This growing hostility between the *Ansar* and the *Khatmia* now gave the Egyptians an opportunity they had long sought and which they were not slow to make use of.

Within the coming nine years things were to move much faster than any of us had foreseen. Perhaps we could have been more imaginative, more flexible, even more opportunist. But however much we might appreciate the potential strength of the politically conscious few, however much we might sympathise with their aspirations, we were bound, as we saw it, by the restraints of three principal factors. We felt obliged to consider the attitude of the tribal leaders on whose loyalty and co-operation we had relied for over forty years, who by tradition represented the vast majority of the population, and who were out of sympathy with the claims of the Graduates' Congress and their supporters in the towns. Secondly, there was the South to consider, still untouched by Northern politics, largely pagan and deeply suspicious of the Arab North, and with nearly a third of the total population of the country. And finally we felt bound to reject Egyptian claims to sovereignty over the Sudan which we did not believe (rightly, as events turned out) were acceptable to the vast majority of the Sudanese. Against this background of increasing political awareness I was posted as District Commissioner El Obeid. I was delighted to be going back to Kordofan and especially to El Obeid where I had many Sudanese friends. It was a good place to take a bride.

Work and life in El Obeid were much as they had been seven years before. It was mainly an urban job with much time given to the Town Council, to rationing the many essentials that were still in short supply, to demobilisation and to town planning and improvement. El Obeid was the railhead of the western line from Khartoum, and the Sudan's principal market for the trade in gum arabic. Its population had risen during the war years to over 60,000, and it was fast becoming the educational centre of the Western Sudan. But El Obeid District also included a rural area which involved a certain amount of welcome touring among the Bederia, a peaceful people who drew their livelihood from their flocks and herds, their agriculture, and gum picking in the thorny acacia forests that grew in the sandy plains and dunes of Central Kordofan. Twenty miles south of El Obeid lies the forest of Sheikan where in 1883 among the dense thorn trees a Mahdist army of 50,000 men overwhelmed and massacred a force of 10,000 Egyptians led by a British Colonel, William Hicks. More than sixty years later thousands of tiny white chips of bone lay scattered over the area of the battlefield.

There was never a lack of variety in the problems that came our way. In the early summer of 1947 it was an epidemic of smallpox, which started in the West African quarter of El Obeid, and was mainly confined there. How many hundreds of deaths it caused we never knew, for no sooner did people become ill then their relatives carried them out of the town by night and buried them up to their necks in the belief that the cool sand would relieve their sufferings and effect a cure. It seldom did. To begin with most of these West Africans refused to be vaccinated in the belief that it would cause sterility. The epidemic spread alarmingly, and we were finally obliged to cordon off the whole quarter with its ten thousand inhabitants and vaccinate everyone house by house. It took a week and called for tact and patience. The Police were firm and kindly, the Medical Department orderlies persuasive and gentle. There was no violent resistance and at the end of a month the epidemic ceased.

For recreation we rode, and there was polo twice a week. Silvia, who before the war had done a spell at the Royal Academy of Dramatic Art and the Regent's Park Open Air Theatre, organised a play-reading society and we met fortnightly with a dozen or so members, Sudanese and British. With the co-operation of the Town Council and the help of some gangs of prisoners I created a race course, and we held a series of flat and hurdle races which drew large and enthusiastic crowds. We lived in a simple but comfortable brick bungalow of four rooms and a bathroom, and we had a garden of shrubs and, in the rains, two large flower beds of blue and white petunias and pink periwinkles. We enjoyed the luxury of electric light, and for the first time in my Sudan service I had a refrigerator and a radio. In the evenings we sat out and dined on an open square cement platform in the garden, and at night we slept on the flat roof. About once a week we gave a small dinner party. Our Sudanese guests were always men: the ladies still kept to their homes, and a demand for girls' education was only just beginning to be made. Social life was simple and limited.

El Obeid, like Kassala and other large towns in the Sudan, had its corps of night watchmen under the control of the local authority.

Most were old soldiers. Each was armed with a stout staff and a whistle, and was responsible for a numbered section of the town. Every hour after sunset, to ensure that they were awake and alert, these 'Charlies' cried out their numbers in rotation, and lying awake in bed one would hear their prolonged siren call *wahid*, *ithnain*, *thalatha*, and so on. This weird sound often woke the dogs to a chorus of barking and made the donkeys bray.*

Throughout 1946 and 1947 the pace of political and constitutional development quickened. In 1945 the *Ansar* formed a political party, *Al Umma* ('the Nation'), in opposition to *Al Ashigga* ('the Brethren') which had already been established with the support of Sayyed Ali Al Mirghani and his adherents the *Khatmia*. The politics of the Northern Sudan had crystallised out of sectarianism: a sectarianism which had had its origins in the rise in the early 1880s of the Mahdi, the expulsion of the Egyptians, the rule of the Mahdi's successor the Khalifa, and the consequent harassment of the *Khatmia*. In the personal rivalry of the two Sayyeds there lay a deep and dangerous element of conflict. Each was anathema to the other, and the followers of both were fanatically loyal to their leaders. While the *Umma* party called for early independence through co-operation with the British and Sudan Governments, the *Ashigga* demanded immediate unity with Egypt, a claim which the Egyptians enthusiastically supported. Already Ismail El Azhari had claimed the right, as leader of the *Ashigga*, to speak for the Sudanese people as a whole, a claim scornfully rejected by his political opponents.

With the end of the war Britain and Egypt were both anxious to re-negotiate the 1936 Agreement. There were a number of problems to be considered but none so difficult as the future status of the Sudan; and this time the Sudanese were determined that in any discussions their views should be heard. An all-party Sudanese Delegation therefore went to Cairo early in 1946 to talk to the Egyptians, but it rapidly broke up over the question of sovereignty.

The British Government had already in March that year made it clear that no change should be made in the status of the Sudan arising out of any treaty revision until the Sudanese had been consulted through their own constitutional channels. Nonetheless negotiations between Sidqi Pasha the Egyptian Prime Minister and Mr Ernest Bevin the British Foreign Secretary were opened in London that summer.

In the course of these talks Mr Bevin allowed himself to be persuaded, contrary to the advice of the Governor-General Sir

* Their function was similar to that of the night watch established in London in 1640 by Charles I: hence the name.

Hubert Huddleston, to accept a provisional protocol on the Sudan which, although it spoke of the right of the Sudanese to choose their future status, also referred to unity between the Sudan and Egypt under the Crown of Egypt. In October 1946 news of this draft protocol was publicised by Sidqi Pasha and claimed not only as an acceptance by Britain of Egyptian sovereignty over the Sudan but also as rejection of the right of the Sudanese to a future status independent of Egypt.

The pro-independence parties in the Sudan were horrified and interpreted the protocol as a betrayal by Britain. There were demonstrations in many parts of the country, particularly in the Western Sudan including Kordofan, and anti-Egyptian feeling ran very high. We were faced with the possibility of a serious breakdown of public security. In consequence the Governor-General informed the British Government that unless it reaffirmed the right of the Sudanese to an independent choice on their future status he would resign. The re-affirmation was given, and in January 1947 Egypt withdrew from the negotiations.

The abortive Sidqi-Bevin protocol demonstrated three things: the inflexibility of Egypt on the sovereignty issue, the length to which the British Government was prepared to go in attempting to secure an agreement with Egypt, and finally the determination of the British authorities in the Sudan to stand firm, if necessary against the British Government, on the right of the Sudanese to choose their own future status. The Egyptians — and the Americans — could never understand why this should be so.

In the midst of all this, many of us, including thoughtful Sudanese — wondered how far it was right to introduce parliamentary democracy to peoples accustomed to traditional forms of administration and rule, to whom the principles and practices of Westminster were altogether foreign and often incomprehensible. But we had no choice; it was what the politically conscious in the Sudan and in many other dependent territories were demanding, and would continue to demand. Western democracy was the only form of government with which we — the British — were familiar and were therefore capable of framing. We were in no position to guide peoples for whom we had assumed responsibility in any other direction. It would be for them to demonstrate in due course, as almost all did, that it was an alien system that would not work.

As the three-year life of the Advisory Council for the Northern Sudan (see p. 166 above) drew to its conclusion, the Governor-General convened a conference to work on proposals for further constitutional advance. By July 1947 the conference's proposals for an elected Legislative Assembly and an Executive Council to include

Sudanese ministers were ready. The British Government accepted them but the Egyptian Government demanded far-reaching amendments and in particular insisted once again on acceptance of the principle of the Unity of the Nile Valley under the Egyptian Crown as a prerequisite to any agreement involving the Sudan. The negotiations between the Co-domini dragged on throughout late 1947 and into 1948 when, despite Egyptian objections, the Assembly and the Executive Council were established.

Half way through our third year in El Obeid, Ewen Campbell, the Governor,* asked me whether I would care to move to Western Kordofan District. I had already been asked whether I would like to consider a secondment to Libya where Duncan Cumming† was Chief Civil Affairs Officer, but Ewen Campbell's offer seemed something more of a challenge. Western Kordofan ranked high in the hierarchy of Districts. It provided much variety ranging from camel nomads in the north to sections of the pagan Nyork Dinka living on the Bahr Al Arab in the south. It was a little smaller in area than Greece, and had an estimated population of just under half a million. District Commissioner Western Kordofan had two British assistants, two *Mamurs* and a Sudanese Police officer to help administer this considerable bailiwick. There were no other British in the District, and only a handful of Greek merchants. The District Headquarters, Nahud, was a picturesque half-Arab half-African town of single-storeyed grey mud buildings, broad sandy streets and avenues of shady trees. But it was very remote and I wondered how far I would be justified in taking Silvia, our daughter Peta born in England in March 1946, and a European Nanny to a place where life would be fairly primitive. True the town had a Sudanese doctor, but the sandy airstrip was only fit for use in emergencies, and not always then. Six hours of driving over an appallingly rough and rutted sandy track separated Nahud from El Obeid. I would need to do a great deal of touring for long periods during which my little family would be on their own. Nahud's water supply was limited in both quantity and quality. There was no electricity. The District Commissioner's mud-walled thatched roof house consisted of a large sitting room with a small dining area leading off it, a bedroom and a small dressing-room attached. There was a single guest room in one corner of the dry sandy compound and an earth closet in the other. The wooden flap of the latter had been embellished by a previous owner with the neatly painted inscription 'A Present from

* E. Campbell, CMG, MBE, MC, *b.* 1897, *d.* 1975. Sudan Political Service 1921–47.

† Sir Duncan Cumming, KBE, CB, *b.* 1903, *d.* 1979. Sudan Political Service 1926–51. Chief Administrator Eritrea 1951–2.

Headquarters'. Alongside the bucket there lived a friendly hedgehog. The compound sheltered snakes.

It was not an easy decision to make. I asked Ewen Campbell to give me twenty-four hours to think it over. Silvia characteristically never hesitated; she said we should take it. She was right. It is seldom wise to reject the offer of an appointment whatever its apparent disadvantages may be.

And so we set off for Nahud shortly after Christmas 1947, taking with us Peta and her Nanny, our ponies, the grey West African parrot we had acquired and a magnificent white Persian cat which Silvia had been given by Guy Foley. For the next two years Western Kordofan gave us a very full and a busy life. There was much touring to be done, and I travelled mainly by truck over what were always rough and sometimes muddy and sometimes sandy tracks. Very occasionally Silvia was able to come with me.

It was in the course of one of the few tours which we were able to do together that we breakfasted early one morning with the Sheikh of Umm Bel. Umm Bel lay north of Nahud. Out of politeness and duty I have eaten many meals in Africa and Arabia which have been a test of stomach and stamina, but none more so than that breakfast at Umm Bel. There were only four of us: our host, his secretary and ourselves. The first course put us on immediate trial. It was a dish of raw onion and raw goat's liver, well seasoned with lemon juice and red pepper. There could be no question of concealing bits in one's handkerchief or slipping them under the table. We were sitting on the floor and were directly under the eye of our host who watched us closely, and constantly urged us to eat more for the greater honour of his house. We put up a very creditable performance but it called for fortitude. Then came chocolate blancmange. How his wife had managed it I don't know, but there it lay at the bottom of a large enamel bowl, dark and solid, and rather dusty. We dealt with that too and the worst was over, for all we had to contend with thereafter was a tin of Mackintosh's toffee and a bottle of Melotti beer which, as the label showed, had been brewed in Eritrea in 1940.

Paul Howell* looked after the Messeria, cattle-owning, semi-nomadic and greatly given to their own internal political intrigues and plots. He was also in charge of the Nyork Dinka in the southern half of the District. The Messeria enjoyed a steady summer rainfall, parts of their countryside were heavily wooded, and their grazing was lush. The Dinka lived on and around the rivers and pools of the

* P.P. Howell, CMG, OBE, *b.* 1917. Sudan Political Service 1938–54. Head Middle East Development Division Beirut 1961–9. Fellow and Director of Development Studies, Wolfson College, Cambridge 1971–.

Bahr Al Arab, fishing and hunting crocodiles. The Hamar, also semi-nomadic but camel breeders and gum pickers, occupied the north. Theirs was a country of sparse rainfall, scattered thorn trees and gently rolling sand dunes. Living in grass-hutted villages, they drew their water from deep wells or from storage in the hollowed trunks of tebeldi trees. The tebeldi, or baobab, is one of the most singular features of the semi-desert landscape of Central Africa north of the Sahara. Enormously broad at the base, its trunk, smooth and silver grey, rises to forty feet or more and then divides into a score of short thick branches that spread themselves like arms in supplication. For part of the year it is gaunt, leafless and monstrous, like a relic of an antediluvian age; then in its season it puts on a rich foliage, rising above the thorned and spindly acacias that so often surround it.

Aubrey Tennyson* was responsible for the Hamar. The two *Mamurs* did leave-relief duty with the tribes, and dealt with much of the heavy load of routine work at Headquarters. Nahud was a busy office, and because the Province Judge in El Obeid could seldom spare time to visit us, we all took our share of Court work. We averaged about one murder a month, for both the Messeria and the Hammar were prone to sudden violence, particularly over women and land. And although most of the day-to-day criminal work was dealt with by the tribal Courts, the more serious cases fell to the District Commissioner and his staff for enquiry and trial. We aimed whenever possible to take those cases in the area in which the crime had been committed rather than bringing witnesses into Nahud. Of the dozen or so of homicide cases that I tried as President of Major Courts during my two years in Western Kordofan, the most baffling and most brutal was the melon seed murder.

There lived in Nahud in January 1949 a young man of seventeen who had recently left school and had so far failed to settle to a career. His name was Mohammed Suleiman. His father Suleiman had died some years before, and the lad had been brought up by his uncle Ahmed the son of Hassan, a Police officer. Mohammed had urged his uncle to lend him £30, arguing that it would enable him to go to the south-west, to Dar Rizigat, buy melon seed, hire camels and bring the seed back to Nahud where he would sell it at a profit. It was not an unreasonable project, for melon seed was a lucrative crop in the Western Sudan and Nahud was one of the main centres of the trade. From there it was exported to Egypt where townspeople roasted it with salt and then nibbled it, eating the kernel and spitting

* A.D. Tennyson, *b.* 1920. Sudan Political Service 1945–55.

out the husks. Great quantities were consumed in the coffee shops and cinemas of Cairo.

Ahmed the uncle was eventually prevailed upon; he gave Mohammed his £30 and the boy set off for Dar Rizigat, going by way of the market town of Muglad where he fell in with one Ali Ismail. He too was bound for Dar Rizigat and offered to accompany Mohammed and furthermore to advise him on how to select the best seed. In due course the two reached their destination, a melon seed market where farmers and merchants from all over the Western Sudan congregated to buy and sell. Here Mohammed and his companion Ali attached themselves to a party of half a dozen other middlemen engaged in a similar enterprise. Among them was a man from Darfur, Adam Mahdi. The three, Mohammed, Ali and Adam, lodged and fed together and when the time came for the whole party — eight in all — to leave for the 150-mile ride to Nahud, the others noticed and subsequently recalled the kindly concern that the two older man showed towards their young friend.

The way from Dar Rizigat to Nahud lies through a country of thick thorn bush and, at that time of year, of tall dry grass. It was necessary therefore for the camels to move along the narrow track in single file. The weather was hot and the caravan travelled between dusk and dawn, resting by day while the animals grazed. On the night before they were due to reach Nahud the moon rose late and the track was exceptionally narrow and winding. Ali and Adam with some of the baggage camels had fallen to the rear of the column and had become a little separated from the rest. The caravan — the camels tied nose to tail — moved slowly and with difficulty between the thorn trees.

It was around midnight when those riding ahead heard the two men at the rear of the party call to Mohammed to give them a hand with one of his sacks which had slipped and needed adjustment. Mohammed rode back. A little later he rejoined the main group saying that several of the loads including his own had been ill-balanced and that one of the camels had been giving trouble. A while passed and Mohammed responded to a second call from his friends and rode back once again. That was the last the leading party saw of him. An hour later Ali and Adam caught the leaders up and told them that Mohammed had complained of feeling unwell, that he had therefore decided to take a short cut back to Nahud and had asked them to call at his uncle's house as soon as they arrived. The story sounded likely enough, and the party reached Nahud at dawn. That afternoon Ali and Adam told the others that they had been to see Mohammed, that he had fever, and that he had asked them to deal with his consignment. Once again there seemed no reason to suppose that this was not the truth.

The merchants sold their seed, and after resting their camels for a day they departed.

Two or three weeks passed and Mohammed's uncle became anxious. The boy should have been back by now. He began to make enquiries but they led him nowhere. Melon seed merchants were constantly arriving from the south, selling their seed and setting off again. No one apparently had seen or knew of Mohammed. There was nothing to support or to dispel the growing suspicion in Ahmed's mind that the delay in his nephew's return indicated something sinister.

And then there appeared a piece of evidence which convinced him that his nephew's continued absence must mean that he had been the victim of an attack. He had already alerted, among others, his contacts in the red light quarter of Nahud where, after their long journeys, merchants frequently sought recreation. A girl, who on occasions provided the Police with scraps of information, heard that a friend and neighbour of hers, who followed the same profession, had been given some weeks previously, and by a client whom she had not previously seen, a present of a leather purse. The client, whom she said she would certainly recognise again from a scar on his left shoulder, had told her that he had bought the purse from a man in Dar Rizigat. The purse was produced and shown to Ahmed. Although there was nothing particularly unusual about it he recognised it at once. It had an ink stain in one corner. It was without any doubt his nephew's. So here was one piece of evidence. But there was no body and no witness apart from the prostitute, and she knew nothing of her client except that he was not a local man and had a scar on his left shoulder. The breakthrough came a fortnight or so later. The girl reported that the man who had given her the purse was in Nahud and had arranged to come to her that night. He was arrested. His name, he said, was Ali Ismail; his home Muglad, his profession farmer and melon seed merchant. He admitted travelling from Dar Rizigat with a party of merchants including a lad named Mohammed Suleiman. Mohammed, he said, had complained of being unwell and had left them on the night before they reached Nahud. He gave the names of all those who had come with him to Nahud from Dar Rizigat. He was found to have several scars on both shoulders. He said he had previously visited the girl but denied all knowledge of the purse. Adam Mahdi, he said, had returned to Darfur.

The Police invited him to show them the track which the party had followed into Nahud and the place where, as he alleged, Mohammed had left them and ridden away on his own. Although he appeared eager to help and led the Police to several tracks which he said might well be those they had followed he could not, he claimed, be certain. The Police were none the wiser, but they kept their man under arrest. During the next ten days they combed the countryside and all the ways leading out of Nahud southwards in the direction of Dar Rizigat. And finally they found what they were looking for. At a point on one of these tracks, where the thorn was thick and the grass high, they came upon a place where the ground showed signs of disturbance. From here a narrow path led into deep bush and at the end of the path were the remains of a body, eaten by vultures and scattered by jackals. The head was intact but the skull had been fractured, and after a further search they came upon a blood-stained club. There was no doubt that these remains had once been Mohammed Suleiman.

Tracing the merchants who had travelled with Mohammed and Ali presented no problem. They gave their statements to the committing magistrate and they identified the club. The murderers would naturally have wished to avoid using a knife and risking blood-stains. Adam Mahdi was never found. Ali was tried and hanged. It was a singularly atypical Sudanese murder in its long and careful planning, in the nature of its motive and in the brutality of its execution.

No record of the Sudan and the Sudanese would be complete which failed to say something of the convicts for whom we as administrative officers were responsible. In Nahud there were normally a hundred and fifty or more. They had humour, a robust readiness to accept events as they came and a community spirit that sometimes showed itself in odd ways. Prison life, apart from the fact that it meant celibacy, was not all that harsh, and the food was probably better than most got at home. Once a week there would be an inspection by the District Commissioner who would be accompanied by the doctor, and the Prison Clerk with the roll of those present. The convicted prisoners would be paraded first and their names checked. Each man, as one walked down the line, would have the opportunity of raising a complaint or a problem, and not infrequently they did so. Complaints were rare, but problems, generally to do with home of family, were more common. Next came the remand prisoners, and the dates set for their trial would be confirmed. Finally there would be an inspection of the barbed wire compound, the barrack rooms in which most of the men slept, the kitchens and the latrines. Convicted men did eight hours outside work, in gangs of half a dozen, under an armed guard. These fatigues usually consisted of tasks such as grass cutting for the police horses, tree planting, and preparing material for the erection or repair of mud-brick or stone buildings, water carrying and so on. Often they sang in chorus as they worked. I cannot remember any occasion of serious trouble or indiscipline in District or Province prisons. Once an armed prison warder drank himself into a state of incapability while his gang was at work and finally collapsed insensible. The gang bore him back to the prison and handed him, his rifle and his five rounds of ammunition to the guard. There was a time when a flash flood in the middle of the night threatened the school and the market place. The prisoners were awakened and bearing oil lanterns, spades, picks and mattocks were hurried to the point where only an immediate diversion of the flood waters could save the threatened buildings. It was pouring with rain. The men, though soaked and cold, worked with a will. The waters gained on them. Only a supreme effort could avert a disaster. 'Now lads,' shouted a long-term recidivist, 'come on, put your backs into it — for the honour of the prison.' They worked till dawn and, their task successfully accomplished, they marched back to the prison shouting, laughing and leaping in triumph.

When a man had served a portion of his sentence and his conduct was satisfactory he become eligible for guarantee. If he could find a reliable guarantor he merely slept and fed in prison, and came and went and carried out, unescorted, whatever tasks might be allotted to him. A number worked as gardeners and odd job men about the houses of the more senior officials, or in the Police lines or around the offices. They quickly idenfified themselves with their particular household and became like members of the staff. We had one, a murderer, who took a delightfully proprietary interest in Peta when she was two; when others failed, he could immediately stem her tears whatever their cause. Neither understood a word of the other's language. Sometimes when I went on tour I would take a guaranteed man from the area I was visiting so that he could have a night with his family. I remember no case of anyone breaking guarantee.

There were many ghosts and tales of ghosts in the Sudan, and Western Kordofan had its share. One story must suffice. It happened in the 1930s to an Assistant District Commissioner who had been posted to Darfur. He was travelling by truck, with his police driver, his butler and his cook, up the road from the railhead at El Obeid. On the first day, after hours of churning through the sandy track that leads westwards, he came at sunset to Dam Gamad, a small sand-swept market town with very little to commend it. It was dusty and featureless, and all round it lay an open countryside of undulating sand dune and flat plain covered with thorn trees. The road, a wide meandering track, scarred by deep wheel ruts, stretched east and west. Settled into his night's lodging in the grass rest house on the edge of the town, this young administrative officer was called on by the Sheikh who was accompanied by a small boy bearing a tray. There was tea in a brightly painted teapot, and coffee in an earthenware long necked pot decorated with coloured beads. The Sheikh and his guest sat and sipped and talked for a while. Then the Sheikh withdrew. The servants lit a fire and the young man watched the shadows that came and went as the dry timber flared and glowed. His attention was attracted by an apologetic cough. He looked up and there just within the circle of light stood a man. He was well past middle age and his thin face was deeply lined; but for all that he seemed worn and frail, he held himself firm and erect. He was dressed in the remnants of army uniform; a tattered khaki jersey on which there were two campaign ribbons, frayed khaki shorts, and a pair of ancient puttees on his spindly legs. He was evidently an old soldier and he had the appearance of being the rest house guardian. He saluted and said that he had brought water and wood to the cook. He hoped that the rest house had been found in good order. 'Why yes,' the traveller said. 'Come and sit down.' They talked. This worn and fragile veteran described how after more than twenty years' service in the 9th Sudanese Battalion of the Egyptian Army he had retired with the rank of Corporal and a small pension. This was now supplemented by his salary as guardian of the rest house, an appointment in which he hoped he gave satisfaction. His name was Mohammed Khatir. He rose to go. 'I will be here to see you off in the morning,' he said. He saluted and withdrew into the darkness, and the sound of his footsteps in the sand quickly faded. The administrator ate his dinner and went to bed. The party was preparing to move off next morning after a dawn breakfast, and the truck was being loaded when the Sheikh of Dam Gamad arrived to say goodbye. 'After you left me last night I had a long talk with old Corporal Mohammed Khatir, the rest house guardian,' the Englishman said. 'He told me all about his Army service.' The Sheikh looked puzzled and then incredulous. 'There is no power and majesty save in God the Mighty,' he said, 'Mohammed of the 9th Sudanese certainly used to look after the rest house, but he died two years ago.'

Among the many projects and schemes that fell to the lot of a District Commissioner, one that I think we all found particularly rewarding was re-afforestation. For three or four miles around the big towns, and Nahud was no exception, the ever increasing herds of goats — evidence of rising prosperity among the less well-to-do — had denuded the land of every vestige of cover less than six feet in height. A goat standing on its hind legs can nibble anything below that level. Only the poisonous and evergreen but sinister looking 'Dead Sea apple' was immune, and even the dry leaves of these they consumed. In consequence the areas of wind and water erosion spread, the wood-gatherers were forced further and further afield, and thus the range of devastation was progressively enlarged. It was a great thing to have the authority to enclose these barren areas with a thorn fence and to plant them in the early rains with quick-maturing indigenous shrubs. Within two years you could see the beginnings of a result to your work. Your successor would find that by the end of his term of office the trees had grown to a respectable size, and within seven to eight years of the original sowing there would be a re-afforested area running up to the outskirts of the town in which controlled grazing and wood collection would be possible. It was all very satisfactory.

It was the same with anti-erosion work where the flash floods that so often swept into the towns could be first controlled and subsequently halted by a series of simple brushwood and stone barriers set up at intervals along the worst of the water courses. And then too there was an immense sense of achievement in the digging of simple reservoirs consisting of an earth ramp and channels from a catchment area, and an excavation of a metre or so in depth which, if the site was well chosen, would provide a village with water for its animals for many months after the rains had ended. In executing all these projects we generally had to use prison or voluntary labour — it was seldom that the District budget provided other than a minimum. But by tradition the Sudanese would usually co-operate in this sort of communal work. All that was needed was the suggestion, the tools and the encouragement.

We were wonderfully served throughout our time in the Sudan by our dignified, imperturbable and tireless domestic staff. They adapted themselves with amazing cheerfulness to our ways, to the food we ate, and to the hours we kept. They were equally reliable whether we were travelling or at home in the station. Travelling would inevitably mean long hours walking, riding or perched, hot and dusty, on the back of a thirty-hundredweight truck. And then at the end firewood would be gathered, bedding and mosquito nets set up, and in no time a meal would be served. One rule always observed was a halt just before sunset for the evening prayer. In a station things were a little easier for them, and normally their hours of work, although long, were regular. But I never knew a Sudanese cook who was put out on being told at perhaps an hour's notice that there would be six or seven for lunch or dinner. Somewhere hens or cutlets would be procured and caramel custard or sweet omelettes made, and a first-class meal would be ready the moment it was called for. They worked seven days a week and they made our lives infinitely easier and freer than perhaps we appreciated at the time. When we went on leave they did likewise, or alternatively took a temporary job and thus drew two salaries at the same time.

With very few exceptions they were scrupulously honest. Before I married I never carried any money with me. From time to time I used to give my butler a lump sum and if I happened to need any cash he gave me what I wanted and kept an account. From the same sum he would deduct whatever was required to keep his side of the house going. The cook worked under a similar system. I suppose that a small percentage of cash and stores may have leaked away but could one possibly be surprised at that or complain about it? The only exception I remember to all this was the case of a District Commissioner's cook who lost a series of scullions. It was the normal practice for one's cook to engage, on his own responsibility, a small boy known by the French word *marmiton*. As a rule these were lads from the Southern Sudan who had drifted away from their villages for one reason or another and, in exchange for their keep and a few shillings a week, would do the menial jobs of the kitchen. Many after a due apprenticeship became skilled cooks. In this particular case the cook came to report at intervals of every two or three months that the *marmiton* had run away. 'Well', the District Commissioner would say, 'I suppose you'd better look out for another lad.' The cook would agree and another boy would be found. He too after an interval would be discovered to have made off without giving notice and without any apparent reason. Within less than a year four boys had thus disappeared. It seemed odd. The District Commissioner made discreet enquiries and the truth emerged. The cook had been selling the boys to nomads from the North. The days of slave raiding had passed, but if a boy could be picked up quietly and without the likelihood of his parents coming to know of it, well, some of the Northern tribes found it difficult to accept the fact that there was anything wrong in a form of domestic slavery that was in general benevolent, and which at that time still existed over the greater part of the Arab world where so-called slaves often achieved places of great responsibility and influence in their masters' households.

On my first appointment to Talodi in 1933 I procured as assistant butler a lad of about sixteen from a nearby village. He was a Nuba in origin, but had been converted to Islam and taken the name Ibrahim. His father's name was Koko. Ibrahim Koko grew up in my household and although I left him behind when I went to Palestine in 1938, he came back to me, still as an assistant butler, when I returned to the Sudan with Silvia at the end of the war. He saw our children arrive one by one over the years and it grieved him that all three were girls. He was himself married, but childless. When we went to Cairo in

1949, Ibrahim came with us, promoted to head butler; he had left his wife behind and sent her back to his village in the Nuba mountains. We had been in Cairo just short of a year when Ibrahim got a letter telling him, as he informed us with delight, that his wife had had a son. It seemed a very close-run thing. By 1952 we were back in Khartoum and Ibrahim's wife and the little boy were installed in our domestic quarters. And then one day, when the little fellow was two and a half or so, he fell and cut his head on the spike of an iron railing. The child was unconscious and bleeding severely. Ibrahim was in an agony of apprehension. Silvia was alone in the house. She bundled Ibrahim and the boy into the car and drove to the hospital. There was a Sudanese doctor on duty but no nurse or anaesthetist. It was a surgical case. Would she be prepared, the doctor asked, to give the anaesthetic; it was a simple matter, and he would show her what to do. She had never been in an operating theatre before except as a patient, but she willingly, if apprehensively, accepted the challenge. She was a little late for the lunch party we were giving that day, but it was a small price indeed for the years of service Ibrahim had given us.

While political and constitutional developments in Khartoum made little direct impact on our day-to-day work in Western Kordofan, they were beginning to create an awareness, as much among our tribal leaders as among merchants and townsmen, that a new era was beginning. During my first year in Nahud, despite Egyptian protests and a boycott by the *Ashigga* party, the Ordinance had been passed setting up a Legislative Assembly with virtually full legislative powers, and an Executive Council. The *Umma* party welcomed it and we held our elections towards the end of 1948 without any local trouble, although there were disturbances in Khartoum and other towns where the *Ashigga* were strongly represented. At the same time an important development was the formation a few months later of a *Khatmi* break-away group which called itself *Al Jabha* (the National Front). This new party represented those of Sayyed Ali Al Mirghani's followers who, increasingly disenchanted with the extreme pro-Egyptian views of the *Ashigga* and of Ismail El Azhari in particular, sought a relationship with Egypt in which Egyptian influence would be less dominant. The party had Sayyed Ali's approval.

Meanwhile a review of the existing system of local government in both urban and tribal areas had recommended the introduction of elections of all Council members by secret ballot in place of the traditional methods that had long been practised in rural areas. It was a step on the road to theoretical democracy that satisfied a Westernised minority and disturbed a conventionally minded majority.

Early in 1949 Silvia and the family left Nahud for El Obeid and Amanda was born there at the end of March, the first British girl to make her initial appearance in Kordofan. Knowing that our elder child Peta was a girl, the Sudanese hospital orderlies had been particularly concerned on my behalf that this time it would, God willing, be a boy. 'If it's a son,' they said to me brightly, 'you will slaughter a bull.' I willingly agreed. 'And if it is a girl,' they added most soberly 'we will have to make do with a goat.' 'How comes it,' the Ruler of Kuwait said to me some years later, 'that you have only succeeded in siring three girls? You look fit and strong enough. It must be,' he continued after a pause, 'that your microbes are weak.' At least he appreciated that the fault was mine and not Silvia's. But when Amanda was a fortnight old she developed gastro-enteritis. News of this reached me in Nahud one evening. I drove through the night to El Obeid. She was in hospital, unconscious and attached to a saline drip. Silvia was in bed with chicken pox. A padre happened to be in El Obeid and as Amanda was not expected to live, he came and christened her, while a little group of nursing sisters stood around her cot in tears. Miraculously Amanda recovered and as soon as she and Silvia were fit enough to travel, the family went off for a spell of leave in Cyprus.

It was a lonely summer and, political and constitutional problems apart, it was a bad one in Western Kordofan. Rain fell widely in late May and early June, but although it continued steadily in the far south, the north and centre of the District missed the July rains which were essential if the crops were to survive. All the early sowings died and the continuing drought prevented the use of such limited seed grain as remained. The wells dried out and many people were forced to abandon their villages and move south to camp in areas where water was available. The Sheikh of the Hamar, Munim Mansur, and I did a prolonged tour and satisfied ourselves that much of the Hamar tribal area would be close to starvation by the early winter unless relief was found. We arranged to move in supplies of grain from the railhead at El Obeid and the worst of the danger was averted. We had trouble too of a different sort in a group of hills at the eastern end of the District where there were a number of small pagan Nuba villages. Here tribal authority was weak and a party of young men who had been found guilty by their Chiefs of cattle theft went on the rampage and burnt down the Court House. The trouble spread. I had to pay three visits to the hills, and finally ask for a platoon of the Sudan Defence Force to do a 'flag march' in the area before the affair was satisfactorily settled without force.

I was recovering from an attack of dysentery when I was told that at the end of the year I would be transferred to the Sudan Agency in Cairo as deputy to E.C. Haselden.* This was exciting news. Western Kordofan had provided immense interest and a vast variety of problems, but I looked forward to an involvement in all that was now happening in Egypt, and to the complexities of Anglo-Egyptian-Sudanese relations.

The Sudan had no diplomatic service and no overseas representation, but it maintained both in London and in Cairo an Agency which was in effect a liaison office, designed to keep the Government in Khartoum in touch with the Co-domini on consular, commercial, cultural and other routine matters. Political affairs were handled through the Foreign Affairs departments of the two Governments direct to the Governor-General. But the Sudan Agent in Cairo was in a position to observe all that passed between the Governments of Egypt and the Sudan. A move to Cairo would mean that Silvia and the children would be able to enjoy a more comfortable life, and that our periods of annual separation would be reduced from about four months to nearer two. We had been in Kordofan well over four years.

I left Nahud some months later, spent a short autumn leave with Silvia and the children in Kyrenia on the north coast of Cyprus, and took up the Cairo job in December. Moving from the Sudan to Egypt involved the usual irritating but at the same time comical acceptance of the shadow rather than the substance of Egyptian laws and regulations. For one thing all our bedding had to be fumigated. If we had been travelling in the opposite direction there might have been some point in it. As it was, a Sudanese doctor friend in the Central Hospital in Khartoum went through the motions of dealing with our blankets and mattresses and gave us the necessary certificates. Our grey African parrot was condemned to three months quarantine at Aswan, but his extensive repertoire, including Police parade orders which he had got word-perfect in Nahud, a fund of Arabic oaths learnt from the stable lads, together with a prolonged fit of coughing and throat clearing ending with a monumental expectoration, so touched the humour and melted the hearts of the frontier officials that in true paradoxical Egyptian style they released him after twenty-four hours, and sent him up to Cairo in a *wagon-lit* compartment in charge of the guard. Our furniture travelled by lorry from Nahud to Khartoum, by train to Wadi Halfa, by barge to Aswan and again by train to Cairo, and was in poor shape when it arrived, but we got it patched up, and settled in to a very new sort of life.

* E.C. Haselden, CMG, *b.* 1903. Sudan Political Service 1926–53.

Egypt at the beginning of 1950 was drawing to the end of an era. The age of the great Pashas and the sovereignty of the effete and obese Farouk were shortly to be swept away by the young Colonels. But for the moment it provided a scene of extraordinary colour, variety and confusion.

9
EGYPT
(1949–1951)

Since 1931 I had passed through Egypt many times, spending a few days in Cairo or Alexandria or Port Said; and during one leave before the war I had gone off to the Western Desert for a fortnight and visited the Oasis of Siwa. Both before and during the war I had travelled extensively in Sinai. But that was the limit of my experience. In the next two years I was to learn rather more about this country in which the gulf between the lives of the rich and the poor was wider than I have ever seen elsewhere.

Of all the nationalities I had known and with whom I had worked there were none, it soon seemed to me, more paradoxical than the Egyptians, or who combined so many good qualities with so many shortcomings. For centuries they had been subjected to plagues, epidemics, droughts, floods and famines. Small wonder that these constant afflictions had affected their physique and their mentality. At the crossways of the land and sea routes linking Europe with Africa and Asia, Egypt had been invaded and fought over for centuries. The victors had ruled the country and left behind their blood and their cultures. The Arab invasion had given Egypt the permanent legacy of Islam and its language. Both nature and history had combined to make the Egyptians an unusually complex people: unpredictable, tortuous and full of contradictions. Curiously remote from realities, they appeared to possess an ability to believe passionately what they knew emphatically to be untrue. Deserts separated them from their neighbours to the east, west and south. North of them was the sea but they were not a seafaring people. In consequence their mental horizons were often as obscured by mirages as were the horizons of their own deserts. Egyptians could be kindly and at the same time extraordinary callous; they could show gentleness at one moment and unthinking cruelty the next; they could switch suddenly from stoicism to emotionalism, from pride to self-denigration, from arrogance to obsequiousness. Their sense of humour could turn in a flash from malevolence to penetrating self-criticism. But despite the harsh and appalling conditions in which so many of them lived in villages or in slums, they preserved a vast capacity for the ridiculous and a disarming ability to laugh at and discredit themselves. There was a good deal of the Irish about them.

In a regimental Mess I once sat listening to a stirring patriotic song rendered by a blonde and full-bosomed contralto, calling on Egyptians to sacrifice themselves to the struggle against Israel and world Jewry. My host, the Colonel, turned to me at the moment when this ringing challenge reached its climax. I assumed that he was about to make some solemn comment, and that he would have tears in his eyes and a catch in his voice. But he whispered: 'You will be amused to know that this girl is a Jewess.' He turned away, his face took on a look of appropriate gravity and with his handkerchief he delicately dabbed his eyes. A friend of mine driving his car through one of the main streets of Cairo found himself surrounded by a noisy and menacing crowd. A villainous-looking fellow, wild-eyed, grubby and unshaven, pushed his face in through the window, grinned maliciously and made a threatening gesture. My acquaintance was smoking a pipe, and through some inexplicable reflex he took it out of his mouth and summoning up a courageous smile offered it to the man. The atmosphere was metamorphosed. The fellow took a puff. A cheer went up. The pipe was handed back and a way was cleared for the car to proceed. Where else in the world would one see, as I saw, at a state afternoon reception on the occasion of King Farouk's birthday and while we were all listening intently to a speech by the Prime Minister, a well-dressed man remove his tarbush, calmly fill it with cakes and sweets from a tea table and replace it on his head without a change of countenance? At the height of anti-British demonstrations in 1951 a swarm of bees settled in Qasr Al Nil in the heart of Cairo. Pedestrians fled and the traffic was held up. Unable to think of any alternative the police sought the aid of Mrs Wise, an English lady well into her sixties and living in retirement near the British Embassy with her husband, Major Wise, who many years earlier had commanded the Cairo City Police. It was remembered that Mrs Wise had once kept bees. She went to Qasr Al Nil and took the swarm; the crowds emerged from shelter and the traffic moved on. Sailing on the Nile one afternoon I was alarmed to see several corpses floating past. I returned to the boat-house and told the Egyptian in charge. 'Why, bless you sir,' he said, 'that's nothing to worry about. We always get them going past at this time of year when the University final examination results are announced. The young gentlemen who have failed take it very much to heart, especially if a number of their relations have helped to pay the fees. They find it difficult to face the family, and choose the Nile as an easier alternative.'

Egyptian Government offices, under their high pargeted ceilings and frequently lined with gilded panelling, were grubby and crowded and chaotic; the gardens of their occupants' villas were a model of order and neatness. The dignity of their Criminal Court proceedings was constantly at the mercy of lemonade and Coca-Cola sellers who wandered at will, tapping their bottles with a metal opener to attract custom. When I was returning from leave one year the passport officials at the airport had been obstructive and aggressive, but when I reached my apartment block the armed policeman on duty laid his rifle against the outside wall and insisted on carrying my two suitcases up to the flat on the seventh floor. The King was popularly despised, yet when he drove through the streets of Cairo the crowds cheered and clapped wildly. At a time when anti-British feeling was particularly acute the Egyptian Government decreed that no British firm would be permitted to tender for any work in Egypt. The representative of a well-known company of British contractors went to see a Minister. 'Pay no attention,' he was told, 'here are the forms, fill them up and send them to me.' Across the tender forms had been printed in red: 'No applications from British firms.'

Their blatant shamelessness became at times almost irresistibly endearing. I had an acquaintance in the Army, a friendly jovial Major, with whom I dined from time to time. 'You know,' he said one evening, 'I was at the siege of Falluja in Palestine. It was awful. The Israelis were relentless in their attacks. We were very hard pressed. Morale was low in some units including, I must admit, our own of which I was Second in Command. We had already had a number of desertions and after a great deal of thought I too decided to abscond. It was not an easy decision to make but after all I had my wife and five children to consider. I had fought well and done my share which was more than could be said of some of our leaders. I took the opportunity of being off duty one evening, and shortly after midnight I slipped away with the object of making my way down to Gaza. I did not think it would be too difficult to concoct some excuse that would enable me to avoid answering any awkward questions that might subsequently be asked. Having got clear of our position I made my way through olive groves and vineyards, and just before dawn I found myself beyond the area of farmlands and on the edge of the desert. Conscious that not only Israeli patrols but also ill-disposed Bedu could well be around I proceeded with great caution. I was in uniform and my first essential was to conceal my identity with some sort of civilian disguise. And then creeping down a dry wadi bed in the half light I espied a Bedouin woman. She was sitting on a rock wearing a long dark robe, her face shrouded under a veil. These two garments, if I could obtain them, were exactly what I needed. I approached the woman, who gave the impression of being of some age, with delicacy and care. To frighten her would be fatal. "Auntie", I whispered as soon as I was within earshot, "Auntie,

God's Peace be on you; I will give you ten pounds for your robe and your veil." The woman, although seemingly startled, remained seated. She made no reply but turned her head away in evident rejection. The price, it seemed, would have to be raised. "Twenty pounds", I whispered, reinforcing my urgency with a persuasive smile, "twenty pounds, here in notes." I pushed the money towards her. Again the woman moved her head, sharply this time, and as she did so the veil fell away. Imagine my discomfiture', said the Major, 'to find myself looking into the harassed face of my own Commanding Officer.'

How far were all these strange paradoxes something fundamental? Or were they perhaps a symptom of the *fin de siècle* through which Egypt was passing? Certainly things were soon to change, and with the coming of the young Colonels and the departure of the old Pashas Egypt was about to acquire a new self-confidence and a sense of purpose.

How different these people were from others I had known in the Arab world, for all that they spoke Arabic, professed Islam, and had played a leading part in the development of Arab learning, thought and art for over a thousand years. How different they were from the Sudanese. Although because of centuries of slave trading there was some Sudanese blood in most Egyptians, no two peoples could have been less alike. From the Arab invasions of the ninth and subsequent centuries the Northern Sudanese had inherited, in addition to Islam and the Arabic language, dignity, solemnity, great physical courage and the patience that comes from life in a harsh and arid land. From their African stock they had preserved vigour and a great sense of humour. The two elements had combined to create a people of robust physique and character. Apart from small scattered communities, two hundred and fifty miles of desert separated the most northerly of the Sudanese from the most southerly of the Egyptians. The Nile united the two countries geographically and to some extent economically, but the lip-service paid by politicians to the Unity of the Nile Valley overlooked and obscured the fact that the two peoples were neither basically homogeneous nor always mutually sympathetic. This, for over fifty years, had been one of the principal sources of friction between Egypt and Britain. The Sudan Agency in Cairo provided a ringside view of this conflict of attitudes.

The Sudan Agent was E.C. Haselden. When I arrived in Cairo in December 1949 as his deputy, he had already held the appointment for almost five years. He had served in the Eastern and Western Sudan and in Khartoum; he was a first-class Arabist and spoke French fluently. Long experienced in the problems of Egypt and the ways of Egyptians, the Sudan Government could have had no better envoy. And he provided me with invaluable guidance on how to approach Egyptian politicians and civil servants and foreign diplomats, and on all the colourful and unpredictable elements that made up the official, economic and social life of Egypt. Silvia too had a kind adviser in his witty and artistic wife Lily.

A previous Sudan Agent (1932–5), John Hamilton,* was now Political Liaison Officer between the British Ambassador in Cairo and the GOC British troops in Egypt. A bachelor, he had acquired over the course of eighteen years in the Sudan, Egypt, Lebanon and Iraq a vast acquaintance of every nationality and persuasion represented in the Arab world and beyond, and his flat in Gezira was a caravanserai where one might meet any one of them at any time. He too was my valued mentor.

The Sudan Agency was essentially though not officially a consulate, but its activities also covered a good deal of political reporting. This meant that the Sudan Agent needed not only to look to the interests of the Sudanese in Egypt, but also to cultivate the confidence of as wide a range as possible of Egyptians — particularly politicians, senior civil servants and the professional and merchant community. Furthermore he needed to keep in touch with the British and the other embassies in Cairo. Not only the Egyptian Government but others — and the Americans in particular — were appallingly ill-informed on what was happening in the Sudan. Nor, as we saw it, was the British Embassy always as knowledgeable as it might have been, or as objective as we would have wished. Egypt had no excuse for such ignorance, for there were many Egyptians in the Sudan; but other countries lacking diplomatic representatives or residents had limited means of learning. If they were sensible, which many were, they came to us for information and advice. And if the Sudan Agent and his deputy could speak French as well as Arabic so much the better. The stream of visitors at the Agency was constant and most of our written work had to be done in the afternoons and evenings. Social life was full, and if worthwhile contacts were to be made it was necessary to accept its demands.

We had found a comfortable flat in Gezira, and Ibrahim our butler and Abdelrahman Ahmed our cook came up from the Sudan to join us. They were appalled by the cold of an Egyptian winter and we had to buy them long-sleeved woollen vests and long-legged

* J.A. de C. Hamilton, CMG, MC, *b.* 1896 *d.* 1974. Joined Sudan Political Service 1921. Seconded to Egyptian Government 1935 and subsequently to British Diplomatic Service.

woollen underpants. Without the amused tolerance and tireless help of Ibrahim and Abdelrahman, we would never have been able to entertain as often and as widely as the work required. It was an exciting and busy life and we delighted in it. For recreation we sailed John Hamilton's boat, watched polo, exercised our friends' ponies from time to time, and walked.

In 1949 the governing party in Egypt was the *Wafd*, led by Nahas Pasha, which had come into existence under Zaghlul Pasha after the 1914–18 war with two principal objectives. The first of these was the complete and immediate independence of Egypt, then a Protectorate, and the second was that Egypt should have an equal share with Britain in the administration of the Sudan, which was always at the heart of the Anglo-Egyptian problem. Egypt, claiming sovereignty over it, feared that even if the independence of Egypt was achieved, a British presence in the Sudan would mean British control over her lifeline, the headwaters of the Nile. Egypt's economy was based on the cultivation of cotton, and the development of cotton-growing in the Sudan, both by irrigation and in areas where rain was sufficient, was by no means what the Egyptians wanted to see. What Egypt was interested in was that the Sudan should be the source of her basic foods. The Sudan's economic advance was a threat.

These ambitions and fears had led over the years to the fostering of a strong anti-British movement in Egypt which had culminated in the assassination in Cairo in 1924 of Sir Lee Stack, the Governor-General of the Sudan. To this incident the British Government had reacted with determination and dispatch. In the face of some armed resistance by Sudanese units in the Egyptian Army in Khartoum, all Egyptian troops and a large number of Egyptian officials were removed from the Sudan. The Sudan Defence Force was created, and posts held in the administration and other services by Egyptians were progressively taken over by Sudanese. The first positive but in fact unpremeditated step towards the Sudan's independence thus came about not by Egyptian politicians aiming to that end, but by the British Government's practical insistence that the future of the Sudan lay with the Sudanese.

The *Wafd*'s policy had boomeranged and for a while the party went into the wilderness, but not for long. By 1930 they were back in power, now with Nahas Pasha as their leader. For the next twenty years or more, and until the young Colonels took control, first under Mohammed Neguib and then under Abdel Gamal Nasir, Nahas led the *Wafd*. There were spells when the party was in opposition but its hold on the country remained powerful and Nahas remained a popular hero.

While in the Sudan things were shaping themselves with growing momentum towards greater autonomy, the problems that faced Egypt in 1949 were formidable. At the height of the 1948–9 Palestine war King Farouk had divorced his popular Egyptian wife Farida. His subsequent antics, his womanising, his gambling and his quarrels with the *Wafd* and particularly with Nahas himself had lost him what little was left of the popularity he had enjoyed a few years before. The *Wafd*, by their drifting failure to grasp the country's external and internal problems, had alienated much of the support they had previously commanded. A great cotton scandal was exposed in which the Prime Minister's wife was found to be deeply implicated. Over forty-five relatives of Nahas held senior Government posts. The Press, generally ill-informed and irresponsible, lent itself to transient battle cries that bamboozled the public and failed to bring realism into either news or comment. With a few exceptions the Civil Service, whose salaries absorbed 35 per cent of the country's budget, was idle and corrupt. Many of the King's closest associates were known to have been involved in the embezzlement of Army funds. The religious leaders were out of touch with the modern world.

The Army, after the defeat and scandals of the Palestine war, had turned with mounting sympathy to the secret aims of the 'Society of Free Officers'. Meanwhile the Army Commander, Haidar Pasha, a caricature of an old-style military leader with a swashbuckling manner and a Turkish moustache, had refused to allow the Government Auditors to examine the Army's finances. In consequence two Auditors-General resigned. When a number of Senators protested they were displaced by Royal Decree. The poor grew poorer and the rich richer. The cost of living rose and unemployment increased. In this sorry record the only encouraging signs lay in the ideals of the young officers and in the rapid emancipation of women and the extent and success of their voluntary organisations. If ever a country was ripe for revolution, it was Egypt.

As for the future of the Sudan, the exchanges lay between the Foreign Office in London, the Governor-General in Khartoum and the British Ambassador in Cairo on the one hand, and the Egyptian Government on the other. In the Agency we had no direct responsibility. The British Embassy's primary concern was to come to an agreement with the Egyptians, and the Sudan tended, perhaps understandably, to be a secondary consideration. In consequence the Ambassador did not always see eye-to-eye with the Governor-General. Few of the Embassy staff knew the Sudan, and they could not be expected to share the concern for, and loyalty to, the interests of the Sudanese that we felt in the Agency. So Kit Haselden and I did our best by frequent and informal contacts to keep them closer to the realities, as we saw them, than they might otherwise have been.

But if the British Embassy in Cairo sometimes misjudged the Sudan problem, the Americans, obsessed with out-of-date conceptions of British colonialism, seemingly found it impossible to understand what we were trying to do. In consequence they gave much misguided encouragement to Egyptian ambitions. Their prejudices were partly but not entirely removed when in 1952 they sensibly posted a representative to Khartoum.

Desperately in search of some spectacular achievement, the *Wafd* hammered away at securing the evacuation of British troops from the Canal Zone and an acknowledgement of Egypt's sovereignty over the Sudan. In consequence, by the latter part of 1950 relations between Egypt and Britain were strained nearly to breaking point and the Egyptians were threatening abrogation of the 1936 Treaty and the 1899 Condominium Agreements. There were demonstrations in Cairo and in other towns. There was already talk of a military coup and of the King's probable abdication.

Throughout this difficult period in Anglo-Egyptian relations, we pursued our business in the Sudan Agency, free of pressure or obstruction. Although we held no diplomatic status, our routine contacts with Egyptian ministries and when necessary with Egyptian ministers themselves were remarkably courteous and friendly. We were not an important factor in the Anglo-Egyptian dispute but we were a visible sign of the now detested Condominium, and the Egyptians could very easily have made life difficult for us. As part of the paradox they were often very helpful.

Discussions between Britain and Egypt continued intermittently but without any progress throughout our first year in Cairo. The old arguments were repeated, the old answers given. From time to time, like a wicked fairy in a pantomime, Ismail El Azhari appeared on the Egyptian stage, said his piece to Egyptian applause, and made his exit.

In the Sudan 1950 was a year of political uncertainty, a year in which the leaders of the two great sects and the political parties which supported them watched impotent and restless while the Co-domini quarrelled over their future and came to no conclusions. In December this growing sense of frustration came to a head in a motion tabled in the Legislative Assembly which called on the Governor-General to request the Co-domini to make a declaration granting self-government to the Sudan at an early date. Despite Egyptian objection the debate was held. On 15 December the motion was lost by a single vote, but a few days later the Assembly passed a motion requesting the Governor-General to appoint a Commission to amend the existing Legislative Assembly and Executive Council Ordinance of 1948, with a view to granting these two bodies a fuller measure of autonomy.

The Governor-General accepted this request and a Constitution Amendment Commission was set up in March 1951 with a British judge, R.C. Stanley-Baker,* as Chairman and thirteen Sudanese members representative not only of the *Umma* Party, which alone formed the Assembly, but — and this was significant — the National Front (*Al Jabha*). It will be recalled that the National Front had broken with the *Ashigga* in 1949 and stood for a form of 'Dominion status' under the Egyptian Crown. The *Ashigga* refused to co-operate. The Commission set to work in April 1951 and finally completed its task in November.

And then into the midst of these political storms the King introduced an element of grotesque romantic comedy. As a means of restoring his waning popularity, he decided to re-marry. The Crown Jeweller, who knew the King's tastes, was ordered to keep an eye open for a likely young person. A couple came to his shop in search of an engagement ring. The Jeweller persuaded them to return in two days' time and in the meanwhile informed the Palace that he believed he had found an ideal candidate. In concealment Farouk was present when the couple next came to the shop, and he fell in love with the girl on sight. She was Narriman Sadek, the daughter of an obscure official, and her fiancé was a young diplomat. She was just sixteen. Farouk ordered the cancellation of the engagement and the story swept through Cairo. Tutors in English, French and Italian were engaged and Narriman was sent abroad, with a diplomatic passport, to learn deportment. And also to learn 'democracy', so my driver told me. Be that as it may, an engagement was duly announced and the marriage was arranged for 6 May 1951.

Whatever he and the Sudanese might think of the King and these escapades, it was clearly necessary for the Governor-General to send a suitable wedding present. We were consulted by the Secretariat in Khartoum and our advice was that the present should be very large, very flamboyant and symbolic. We suggested a vast copper dinner gong, suspended by silver chains from the points of two of the largest bull elephant tusks procurable in the Sudan, with the base of the tusks set in an immense block of local ebony. The suggestion was accepted and this artifact was duly made and sent down the Nile to Aswan and thence by train to Cairo in a huge wooden case. I went to the station, collected it and brought it to the Agency where we

* R.C. Stanley-Baker, *b.* 1914. Sudan Political Service 1937–44. Barrister-at-Law 1946. Judge of the High Court 1948. Retired 1954.

unpacked it. It was enormous and fulfilled all our expectations. Each of the tusks weighed over a hundred and thirty pounds. The ebony base was eight feet long and two and a half feet wide. The diameter of the gong was over three feet, and beside it there hung a great knobkerrie with which to strike it. The whole gigantic piece required at least six men to life it. Representatives of Government departments, the Services and the *Corps Diplomatique* were invited to deliver their presents at the Abdin Palace on the Friday before the wedding. It was a memorable scene as the ministerial and diplomatic cars drove up, and as the Secretaries carried into the Palace the neat packages containing gold cigarette boxes, jewelled caskets, musical boxes, clocks and other objects of art and *vertu*. I arrived in a furniture van. Eight huge Sudanese porters, hired for the occasion, unloaded the gong and bore it into the Palace. It dwarfed everything else in size and barbaric splendour. It stole the show. For once something made in the Sudan, an independent achievement, had been accepted by the Egyptians with wholehearted approval.

By the late spring and early summer of 1951 there were increasing signs of the probability, sooner or later, of a military coup, and Egyptian civil servants and businessmen grew more and more bitter in their criticism of the regime and of politicians of all parties.

Silvia and the children had gone home in mid-May, and two months later I was able to take leave and join them. I spent a fortnight in Bisley. We got together a Sudan team and we triumphantly won all the prizes open to us: the Junior Kolapore Cup, the Junior Mackinnon Cup, the Nobel Cup and the Colonial Prize for which by special dispensation the Sudan, though not a Colony, had been allowed to shoot. Our competitors came from Africa, the West Indies, the Far East and the Falkland Islands. It was as well that neither the Egyptian nor the Sudanese press got wind of our involvement in these competitions. They would have enjoyed misrepresenting our harmless achievement.

By the time of my return in the early autumn the situation in Egypt was growing steadily worse. There were violent incidents in the Canal Zone, 'Freedom Regiments' — semi-guerilla units — were being formed, and the Government withdrew all civilian labour from the British military areas. The workers there, deprived of a source of livelihood that was worth £500,000 a month, flocked to Cairo and demonstrated outside the Prime Minister's office until they were dispersed by police baton charges. There were violent demonstrations in Cairo and Alexandria in which students played a large part and which led to many casualties and much damage to property. The police were out in force daily — and yet we went about our affairs unaffected. We went to the 'Muski' shopping area, we visited mosques and we had picnics. For two shillings the nearest policeman would see to it that we were not molested by touts or bothered by beggars.

And then, on 6 October, Nahas Pasha the Prime Minister announced to a crowded and frantically excited meeting of Parliament that the Government had abrogated both the 1899 Condominium Agreement and the 1936 Treaty. In a scene of wild enthusiasm King Farouk was proclaimed 'King of Egypt and the Sudan'. In addition a bill was introduced creating a new Constitution for the Sudan. This was a very unwise step for the Egyptians to have taken, for apart from Ismail El Azhari and his immediate supporters, there had been no consultation with the Sudanese parties. The National Front protested. Two results immediately followed from Nahas's announcement. The first was that the British Government repeated the two basic principles on which their policy towards the Sudan had always stood. These were that they could agree to no change in the status of the Sudan without consultation with the Sudanese, and that they upheld the right of the Sudanese freely to choose what their ultimate status would be. The second result was the passing of a motion in the Legislative Assembly in Khartoum deploring the Egyptian Government's attempt to impose Egyptian sovereignty on the Sudan without consulting the Sudanese people, and thanking the British Government for its support and for its refusal to use the Sudan as a bargaining counter in its attempts to reach agreement with Egypt on other matters. Although the Assembly was not a fully representative body, the motion undoubtedly reflected the views and the mood of the great majority of the Sudanese.

In Egypt the situation continued to grow more confused and chaotic. British military installations in the Canal Zone were attacked by the 'Freedom Regiments' and there were fatal casualties on both sides. Although relations between the British and the regular Egyptian armed forces remained surprisingly cordial, there was much speculation on the likelihood of a British advance on Cairo, and anti-tank obstacles were erected across the roads leading from the Canal. In Cairo the demonstrations grew in number and size and the police frequently opened fire. The extraordinary charade that Egypt and the Sudan were now one country was maintained to the extent that the meteorological bureau's weather forecasts referred to 'north-west winds blowing towards the south of the Kingdom of Egypt reaching Nubia on their way to Atbara'. Anticipating that at any moment the Egyptian Government might take possession of the Sudan Agency, we packed up all our top secret files and removed them to a place of safety.

Amid this growing confusion I was told that I would be required to return to the Sudan before the end of the year to take charge of the Political Section of the Civil Secretary's office in Khartoum. A move at this stage came as a disappointment because I enjoyed the work I was doing, and a great deal was about to take place in Egypt that I was anxious to witness. The country was on the verge of chaos; the Government was in disarray; the monarchy was tottering; the crowds were out of control; the situation on the Canal was critical; and a military *coup d'état* might come at any moment. However in the Political Section in Khartoum I would continue to be very much involved with affairs in Egypt, and the Section would certainly provide a far wider range of activities. There were other considerations too. With the situation in Egypt so uncertain Khartoum would be a safer place for the family. I would be working directly under James Robertson and I looked forward to that. Silvia and I therefore set ourselves, in the latter part of November, to pack and to say good-bye to our numerous friends of many nationalities, and, particularly sadly, to Kit and Lily Haselden.

These last few weeks provided two final examples of the corrupt and almost comically confused way in which the Egyptian Civil Service machine operated at that time. I had suspected that we might run into difficulty in getting our personal possessions out of Egypt. We had no diplomatic status to help us, but we did have a number of friends in most Government Departments. I made enquiries and learnt that I would need exit permits for almost everything, and books were a particularly sensitive item. The Customs authorities could not give an exit permit for books; that was the responsibility of the Censorship Department, so I called at the Censorship offices. Any books that I wished to take out of the country, I was told, would need first to be read by the Censor. How many did I have? 'Four or five hundred', I said. The Censorship officer smiled. 'That will naturally take a long time,' he said happily. I consulted friends who reassured me. '*Il faut être pistonné*,' they said. All I needed was a contact or two; and contacts were not all that difficult to find. My first contact was a member of the staff of the National Bank of Egypt. He undertook to introduce us to Shukri Bey, an Army officer with a cousin in the Censorship Department. I met Shukri Bey, and he was friendly and helpful. As an officer, he said, he was naturally not in a position to assist me personally or directly, but he thought — he paused — he would be able to put me in touch with a civilian in the Department who, subject to a mutually satisfactory arrangement, would be able to provide the necessary certificates. He made a telephone call and it was agreed we should meet later in the day at Groppi's restaurant. We met and to my surprise the civilian proved to be a young and very attractive Swedish woman. I ordered coffee and cakes. She was married, she said, to an Egyptian Army officer in the Censorship Department, where she too worked — as a film censor. But she could equally well censor books if necessary, and she did not think she would find it too difficult to let me have an exit permit. All I needed to do was to pack my books in boxes and have them ready at my flat where, if it suited me, she would call the following afternoon. After she had gone Shukri Bey briefed me further. A sum of money — and he quoted a surprisingly modest sum — would need to be ready in an envelope which Ibrahim our butler would hand to the lady on her arrival at the flat. In due course I briefed Ibrahim. The lady appeared punctually as arranged, she took the envelope and Ibrahim showed her into our dismantled drawing room where eight large wooden boxes containing all our library lay packed and all but nailed up. She applied a seal to each box and handed me a signed certificate. 'Remember,' she said, 'anything by T.E. Lawrence or Major Jarvis or Glubb Pasha is on the index, but I don't suppose you have any of their books.' She smiled. Ibrahim let her out and we were over that hurdle.

Then there was the matter of Silvia's jewels. The final act in the serio-comic drama of our time in Cairo came at the airport, at midnight on the eleventh of December 1951. We had been due to fly on the evening of the tenth, but heavy rain had put the runways out of commission for twenty-four hours. I had gone to a lot of trouble some weeks before to ensure that we would have no difficulty in taking Silvia's jewels with us. A number of frightened people were trying to get their valuables away to Europe, and the Customs were being particularly strict. It would certainly not do to try and smuggle them out. So I had taken the jewels to the headquarters of the Customs Department where after each item was examined, weighed, valued and recorded, I was given my permit valid for twenty-four hours before or after our planned departure date, the evening of the tenth. We drove to the airport in two cars, our Nanny, the two sleepy children, our African grey parrot in his travelling cage, the white Persian cat in a basket, and twelve pieces of hand baggage. Kit Haselden was there to see us off. Very slowly but not without courtesy our luggage was checked and opened, the export certificates for the parrot and the cat were examined, and a long time was spent in making certain that these two creatures had been correctly recorded and described.

Parrots have a curiously strong sense of occasion and timing. They will repeat certain things that they associate with certain events, sounds, times of the day and even seasons of the year. Our African grey would say 'I want my breakfast' in the mornings but never in the afternoons. She would repeat 'Happy Christmas' over and over again from late November until mid-January but never at any other time of the year. She had been taught, when her cage had been covered for the night and the edge of the cover was gently lifted, to say 'Bugger off.' In order to confirm the entry on the veterinary certificate which showed 'African grey parrot', the Customs officer lifted the edge of the cover and peered into the cage. The automatic response was loud and clear. For a moment the officer's face showed an extraordinary mixture of emotions, and then fortunately his sense of humour came uppermost. He exploded with mirth and his colleagues were doubled up with delight.

By now the plane had already been delayed for over an hour, and the other passengers had embarked. It was just after midnight. Perhaps because I wanted to show that I had been at pains to follow to the letter all the Customs export regulations, or that I felt it was wise to declare rather than remain silent, I reminded the senior Customs officer that there were of course my wife's jewels. Here was the export certificate. He examined it. He paused and looked up at the clock. 'But this, I fear, is out of date,' he said, 'it expired yesterday.' Yes, the jewels had been correctly listed but it was unfortunate, he would like to help, but as the senior officer at the airport he was compelled — as I would doubtless appreciate — to respect the absolute letter of the law. We argued. It was no good getting angry, but equally a light-hearted approach got me nowhere. The jewels, he insisted, would have to be held by the Customs authorities until I next came to Egypt when doubtless a new export certificate could be issued. The jewels were placed in a large stout envelope which was sealed and I was given a receipt. Kit Haselden undertook to do everything possible to get them released. Silvia as always was entirely calm. Inwardly I doubted whether we would ever see them again. We boarded the plane at half past one in the morning. The kaleidoscope of lights along the road to the airport and the orange glow that lay over Cairo dropped away beneath us. The plane turned south into the darkness. We had come to the end of a colourful and a very strange chapter.

10

SELF-GOVERNMENT IN THE SUDAN

(1951–1954)

Returning to Khartoum in that mid-December of 1951 after two years in Cairo, I found myself with the advantage of a useful background of Egyptan politics and personalities but with the need to re-establish friendship with leading Sudanese whom I already knew, and to get to know those I had not met hitherto. In taking over the Political Section of the Secretariat, I was fortunate in having two experienced and able assistants, Jock Duncan* and Ahmed Mekki Abdu. I had met Jock Duncan when I was in Nahud and he was serving in the Upper Nile, and earlier he had himself been an Assistant District Commissioner in Western Kordofan. He had now been in the Section for well over a year, and his acquaintance with the political leaders and his familiarity with all that was happening were of immense help. Ahmed Mekki lived in Omdurman, the political centre of the Sudan, and was a valuable link with all that went on there. We worked to James Robertson through his deputy A.C. Beaton from whom I had taken over Western Kordofan in 1947.†

One of the first notables on whom I felt bound to call was the Head of the Religious Courts, the Grand *Qadi*, Sheikh Hassan Mudathir. Despite his elevated religious office and the extent of his scholarship in Islamic law and practice, Sheikh Hassan was no pedant in outlook or manner. His welcome was warmhearted and urbane. I made my call a few days before Christmas and on Christmas Eve received from him a traditional card. On the outer cover was a beaming Santa Claus, and inside the following verse:

May Santa bring you all the best
From out his reindeer sleigh,
The dolls and toys and picture books
Your heart could wish today.

Whatever may be said about the content, the thought was charming and encouraging.

Abdulla Bey Khalil, Leader of the Legislative Assembly, was an old friend. By any standards he was a man of exceptional wisdom

* J.S.R. Duncan, CMG, MBE, *b.* 1921. Sudan Political Service 1942–56. Diplomatic Service 1956–80. Author of *The Sudan* and *The Sudan's Path to Independence 1952*.

† A.C. Beaton, CMG, *b.* 1904. Sudan Political Service 1927–54.

and integrity, and in his dark, deeply lined, rough-hewn face and sturdy figure there lay a great fund of warmth. He had retired from the Sudan Defence Force some years before with the rank of Brigadier and had turned reluctantly, but from a sense of duty, to politics. At the time of its creation in December 1948 he had accepted the leadership of the Legislative Assembly, an appointment he still held. In the coming two years and until Ismail El Azhari became Prime Minister, I was to see much of Abdulla Bey and the more I saw of him the more I admired his steadfast honesty and sincerity. After I left the Sudan we were happily to meet again in the Gulf and in Nigeria.

I also saw much of the two Sayyeds. No two men can have been less alike, and no two men can have distrusted each other with a greater depth of suspicion. Each commanded the absolute support of two million potentially fanatical followers. Sayyed Abdelrahman, the posthumous son of the Mahdi, was sixty-seven. The first twenty years of his life had been spent in obscurity in Blue Nile Province where, in due course, he made a fortune out of cotton, a fortune he was not averse from parading when it suited him. Articulate, emotional, shrewd, he was an impressive figure, tall, lean and lined. By contrast Sayyed Ali, the elder of the two by six years, was reticent and reserved and at pains to declare that he was a religious leader, uninterested in politics or position. Compared with his sectarian rival he was unusually short; this was a matter on which he was sensitive, and his shoes were made with extra high heels. He had spent his formative years in Cairo studying religion and law. Although possessed of a measure of personal charm and a gentle amiability, he lacked the dynamism of Sayyed Abdelrahman. He lived unostentatiously and invitations to his modest house in Khartoum North, across the Blue Nile, were rare. While talk with Sayyed Abdelrahman ran constantly on politics, it was frequently difficult to induce Sayyed Ali to speak of anything but the problems of the world as a whole, or at most the history, personalities and economic future of the Middle East. He was well informed, but while Sayyed Abdelrahman was eager to express his views, often with some vehemence, Sayyed Ali preferred to ask questions, keep his own counsel and take refuge in pious generalities.

Sayyed Abdelrahman had adopted a practice that had been common in Oxford when I was there, namely the invitation to breakfast. These parties were often of some grandeur. A doorkeeper welcomed you on arrival at the metal gate set in the high wall of his ornate Khartoum residence. Inside, a second doorkeeper escorted the visitor across the lawn and past the tame storks. A secretary then led the way up the steps of the verandah where the Sayyed, poised and benign, seized one's hand with a semi-royal gesture and ushered one indoors. Little time was wasted. The head butler would announce the meal and about a dozen people, most of them leading members of his family or staff, would move to the dining room, the Sayyed taking the head of the table. Grapefruit first, then porridge or, if one wished, cornflakes. The waiters changed the plates and one was offered fried Nile perch fringed and garnished with slices of small green limes. There was toast and butter at one's elbow, and tea or coffee as one preferred. Another change of plates and there would be liver with fried or scrambled eggs. Finally Cooper's Oxford marmalade, a tribute perhaps to the fact that Oxford was marginally better represented in the Political Service than the Other Place. The conversation, after a moment or two of introductory pleasantries, would turn to politics. Often it was illuminating and valuable, that is if the Sayyed was in a relaxed and expansive mood. When his spirits were low it would be a catalogue of grievances about the ingratitude of Government in the face of his own staunch and unquestionable loyalty and the inexplicable favours shown to his opponent Sayyed Ali, and charges that in the Provinces the administration was giving open assistance to all political parties except his own — the *Umma*. Whichever performance Sayyed Abdelrahman was in a mood to give, he gave it with dignity and a persuasive technique.

Hospitality with Sayyed Ali seldom went beyond morning coffee or an afternoon tea party. His style was very different.

These then were the two magnetic fields around which the political leaders in the Northern Sudan and hundreds of thousands of tribesmen moved in orbit.

At the beginning of 1952 there were eleven political parties in the Northern Sudan, and these fell into two groups. There was the 'National Front' group standing for the unity of the Nile Valley, with the *Ashigga* as the preponderant party. But the *Ashigga* was in some disarray, due to personal rivalries, and was shortly to emerge as the National Unionist Party (NUP) with Ismail El Azhari as its leader. The remaining parties numbered four, but none had a membership of any size. Their policies ran from complete fusion with Egypt to Dominion status under the Egyptian Crown, to a preliminary stage of union leading to independence. The Group was also associated with the 'Sudan Trade Union Federation' (STUF) and the 'United Group for Sudan Liberation', both of which were largely Communist-inspired.

In opposition to the 'National Front' stood the 'Independence Front' group consisting of six parties in all, four of which were of small account. But all six stood for complete independence, either immediately or at an early date. The two parties which enjoyed a substantial following were the *Umma* and the Socialist Republican Party (SRP). The Socialist Republicans, formed in December 1951, were a new and interesting development for they represented something of a swing against the narrow sectarianism of *Ansar* and *Khatmia*, of Sayyed Abdelrahman and Sayyed Ali. The party's supporters were moderates who feared Sayyed Abdelrahman's alleged ambition to become King of the Sudan as much as Farouk's recent assumption of that empty title. The party had attracted both Mahdist and *Khatmi* followers, and it was a 'country gentlemen's party' to the extent that a number of tribal leaders had given it their support. It had therefore been assumed by some to be a cunning creation of the British, the work of the Political Section of the Secretariat and of the Administration in the Provinces. Needless to say it was no such thing. There were no organised political parties representing the Southern Sudan.

We had been in Khartoum for a month when two events took place each of which was to signal a significant move forward in the Government's relations with the Sudanese and the Co-domini. The first was the publication of the report of the Constitutional Amendment Commission which, it will be remembered, had been set up some ten months before to recommend the next steps to be taken in constitutional advance to full Self-Government. Although the Commission had been condemned by both the *Ashigga* and the Egyptians, the '*Jabha*', the less extreme of the pro-Egyptian parties which had advocated Dominion status under the Egyptian Crown but with the right to secede, had joined it. The Commission had had its problems and it had broken up over the difficult subject of sovereignty, but by then it had already completed its work and its report was to form the basis of the subsequent proposed Self-Government Statute. Work on drafting the statute was to begin immediately. The second event was the Cairo riots of 26 January when the mobs came out on a blind rampage of destruction and murder, in which several of our friends lost their lives in particularly horrific circumstances. It was the end for the *Wafd*, and the beginning of the end for the monarchy. Nahas was dismissed, and over the next five months Egypt was to have four different administrations. Meanwhile General Mohammed Neguib was elected President of the Society of Free Officers Committee. The King, who correctly suspected him of disloyalty, was incensed but powerless. From now on the Free Officers were to emerge in open challenge to the Palace, and within a few months Farouk was gone. Throughout that spring and summer Egypt's involvement in her own internal problems put an end to all useful discussion with the British Government.

The Cairo riots had one curious and satisfactory result for us personally. Following the pattern of Egyptian paradox, a senior official of the Customs Department called on Kit Haselden in the Agency on the morning after the violence of January 26. Forty million pounds worth of damage had been done in Cairo, buildings which had been set on fire were still smouldering, the streets were full of stones and broken glass, and in Ismailia a battle between Egyptian and British troops had resulted in heavy Egyptian casualties. One would have imagined, as Kit had already feared, that this would signal the final disappearance of Silvia's jewels. But the Customs Official handed Kit the sealed envelope with every sign of satisfaction and withdrew. The jewels were intact. They reached Khartoum in the diplomatic bag a few days later.

The draft of the Self-Government Statute was presented to the Legislative Assembly early in April 1952. Over the course of the following weeks it was discussed in the Assembly, passed with amendments in May, and sent to the Co-domini for approval. It provided that the next Government should consist of an all-Sudanese Council of Ministers, with an all-Sudanese Parliament of a Lower House and a Senate. The Lower House would be an elected body and elections would be either direct or indirect depending on the degree of advancement of the electorate in any particular constituency. The South would be fully represented. It limited the powers of the Governor-General to certain responsibilities for the public service and the three Southern Provinces. The draft Statute met with general approval, and the more extreme pro-Egyptian Sudanese and the Egyptian Government were for the moment thrown off balance. We felt that something substantial had been achieved and we now looked to the Co-domini, and to Britain in particular, to support what had been generally accepted throughout the Sudan as a reasonable set of arrangements leading to the next stage, Self-Determination. Our only fear was that a delay in the implementation of the draft Statute would disappoint and dishearten those Sudanese who supported it, and give opportunity to the Egyptians to undermine it. In the expectation that the draft would be acceptable and that elections would be held by the end of 1952 at the latest, the life of the Legislative Assembly, which had already been extended by nearly a year, was not renewed. As things turned out the draft as it stood failed to get the agreement of the Co-domini and we had to carry on for well over a year without any representative body, and particularly without any Southern representation.

The Egyptian Army coup and the abdication of King Farouk in July, and the emergence of General Neguib as leader of the Revolutionary Council early in September, brought an entirely new and powerful factor into our affairs. General Neguib was a realist. His mother was Sudanese and he knew the Sudan. He had been at school in Khartoum and he had served as a regimental officer in the South. He hoped, as every Egyptian did, to see Egypt and the Sudan united and all British influence removed, but he knew that an attempt to impose unity would defeat its own purpose and that the Sudan could best be won by a show of sympathy with the general desire of the Sudanese to decide their eventual status. His warm personality, his realism and his Sudanese blood gave him immense advantages in the direct approach he now began to make to the Northern political parties. Having been thrown off balance, the Egyptians now regained the initiative and the General was not slow to exploit it. He invited representatives of all the Northern Sudanese political parties to Cairo in October for separate discussions, and they went. In these talks he accepted the principle of the Sudan's right to Self-Determination. All he asked in return was the prior removal of all British influences. Once the British were in retreat he was confident that he would be able to influence developments so that a close constitutional link with Egypt could be guaranteed. In addition to reassuring those who went to Cairo, he sent his own representatives to the Sudan. Here the variety and the type of inducements they were able to make secured him further support.

The American Embassy in Cairo had at last come to realise that a permanent listening post in the Sudan would give it a more authentic appreciation of what was happening there. In October 1952 it sent a liaison officer to Khartoum. He arrived with many pre-conceived ideas, particularly about the South, but he toured the country and as the months passed we felt that at last the Americans were learning. Alas, no sooner had he come to trust us than he was replaced, and we had to start the process all over again with his successor. It was notable that the French liaison officers who were in Khartoum from 1952 onwards, first Baron Louis de Cabrol and then Count Victor de Lesseps, saw the situation that was developing clearly and almost by instinct. France was an imperial power and understood the difficulties in getting rid of imperial responsibilities. As an embryo British mission we had as Trade Commissioner first Derek Riches* and later his successor Philip Adams.† Neither could have been more helpful.

Following General Neguib's contacts with the Northern politicians, Anglo-Egyptian discussion on the draft Self-Government Statute got under way in the late autumn of 1952. The Egyptians

* Sir Derek Riches, KCMG, *b.* 1912. Later British Ambassador to Libya, the Congo and Lebanon.

† Sir Philip Adams, KCMG, *b.* 1915. Later British Ambassador to Jordan and to Egypt.

called for two far-reaching amendments. These were the Sudanisation — before Self-Determination and within a period of three years — of the complete Administrative Service, the Police and the Sudan Defence Force, together with other appointments; and a further limitation of the Governor-General's powers, particularly the safeguards covering the three Southern Provinces which had been provided for in the draft. We saw great danger in these proposed changes and argued forcibly against them with our Sudanese friends and in our telegrams to London and Cairo. Few Northerners were acquainted with the South and Southern feelings, and the fault was not altogether theirs. We now urged the Northern parties to send a joint delegation to discuss these fresh proposals with Southern leaders. They were not prepared to do so. The Egyptians made these changes a breaking point. In spite of their deep distrust of Egyptian ambitions, the Independence Front was prepared to pay almost any price for an acknowledgement of the Sudan's right to independence; so in January 1953 all the Northern parties signed agreements in Khartoum accepting the Egyptian amendments.

During October and November 1952, the outcome of the talks between the Northern Sudanese political representatives and General Neguib was still under discussion by the Co-Domini. Major Salah Salim, who had been one of the leaders of the July coup, arrived in Khartoum as the General's liaison officer with the Northern parties. Like many of his countrymen he possessed considerable charm and was eminently plausible. He was young and like King Farouk he wore on all occasions dark sun-glasses. He was to achieve much publicity as a result of being photographed dancing with Southern tribesmen dressed only in his underpants. In the British Press he became well known as the 'Dancing Major'.

I met him shortly after his arrival in the Sudan and in a long and surprisingly frank private talk he made it perfectly clear that he had little sympathy for the — as he saw it — dangerous conception of Sudanese independence. He was ready to pay lip-service to the principle of Self-Determination, but only as a step towards the unity of the Sudan with Egypt. He believed — as every Egyptian had believed for fifty years or more — that Britain had no business to be involved in the Sudan's constitutional and political development. The Nile, which was essential to the security and economic life of Egypt, linked the two countries in a natural bond. The Sudan, as both the Egyptians and the British themselves were agreed, was still a backward and undeveloped country, and it would be a generation before the Sudan would be sufficiently advanced and united to manage even its own internal affairs unaided. The

Governor-General, Sir Hubert Huddlestone, had said as much publicly only a few years before. Surely therefore, this persuasive and articulate young man argued, it should be the Egyptians — linked by geography, blood, religion, language and the interests of mutual security with the majority of the people of the Sudan — who should provide the brotherly guidance of which the Sudanese still stood in need. This was the view which Egyptians of the eras of both King Farouk and General Neguib had impressed on the British and American Ambassadors in Cairo with such singular success. It was, of course, one side of the picture only, and it conceded nothing to the rights of two and a half million Southerners. I met Major Salim several times thereafter. Our attitudes were poles apart and I never trusted him an inch. Nor did I believe that in the end he would succeed with the Sudanese; he was too smooth, too sinuous and too pleased with himself.

The Independents having given their agreement, despite the misgivings of men like Abdulla Bey Khalil, the ground was cut from beneath our feet and those of the British Government; we were left without room for manoeuvre and the Anglo-Egyptian Agreement followed on 12 February 1953.

'The Egyptian Government', the Agreement began, 'and the Government of the United Kingdom of Great Britain and Northern Ireland firmly believing in the right of the Sudanese people to Self-Determination and the effective exercise thereof at the proper time and with the necessary safeguards have agreed as follows.' There were then fifteen Articles and three Annexes providing for a Governor-General's Advisory Commission, an Electoral Commission and a Sudanisation Committee. All three represented, for the moment, a major triumph for the Egyptians, who had little doubt that when the time came they would have so manipulated things that the Sudan would opt for a form of union with Egypt. They were determined to do everything possible to ensure that it should be so.

Those of us expatriates who had the future and the welfare of the Sudan at heart were dismayed — not least because it seemed to us that the Independence parties had in a sense betrayed themselves in accepting an Egyptian solution on the future of the Sudan that would put the steady development of their country at risk. The Southerners, who formed a third of the whole population of the country, had not been consulted by any of the political parties. The Governors of the three Southern Provinces had talked to and warned the Northern politicians, and their warnings had been ignored. The price that the Northern Sudanese were now ready to pay, and particularly in regard to the South, seemed to us a recipe for disaster. Events were to prove the magnitude of the disaster when in August 1955 Southern units of the Sudan Defence Force mutinied and a civil war began that was to last for nearly a generation and to cost thousands of lives.

During the years before the First World War the two main problems of the Southern Provinces had been the pacification of the country and the establishment of a sound administration. It took time, for the South remained for many years suspicious of any administration linked to Khartoum. But by the 1920s these two objectives had been achieved. The confidence of the tribesman whose history had taught him — with justification — to fear Northern influence was won by a group of administrators whose service was largely confined to the South. Until the early 1930s it was the practice — rightly — to keep officers for long periods in the South where continuity of service and a knowledge of the local languages and conditions could be counted on to ensure trust and co-operation. Southern loyalties became very strong, and members of the administration with many years of Southern service found it difficult to reconcile their local loyalties and their protective feelings towards a backward people with the concept of a united Sudan in which, without special safeguards of some kind, Northern influence would inevitably be overwhelming. It must be remembered too that the North was Muslim and the South principally pagan, and that Christian Missions operating in the South provided much of the educational and some of the medical services.

It is arguable that at an early stage the South should have been severed from the North. There was little in history, and nothing in culture, language, religion or tradition to justify the maintenance of frontiers that had come about merely as a result of the scramble for Africa. Had the Sudan been a colony and not an Anglo-Egyptian Condominium, the splitting off of the South in the early years might have been feasible, although the three Southern Provinces, primitive and landlocked, would never have constituted a viable independent territory. In 1924 when Lord Allenby presented the British ultimatum to the Egyptian Government, following the assassination in Cairo of Sir Lee Stack, it might perhaps have been possible to include a demand for a separate identity for the South. Thereafter, with the growth of a sense of nationality among the politically conscious Sudanese, any such policy would scarcely have been practical. But in failing at an earlier stage to unite the two parts of the country more effectively, our record lies open to criticism not least in the view of Northern Sudanese. What we could have done, and what we failed to do, was to post more Northern administrative officers and other Northern civil servants to the Southern Provinces before the Second World War. There is no reason to suppose that they would not have gained the confidence of the Southern tribesmen and learnt their languages, and worked with them as successfully as their British colleagues did. In the sphere of education, association between the two halves of the country could have been a great deal closer. It remained far apart. Excessive paternalism, perhaps bred by memories of the slave trade, tended to live on for too long in the South, and in the last analysis defeated its own ends.

The problem of constitutional development in the South came to the fore soon after the end of the Second World War. It became an issue of importance when plans were being made for the establishment of a Legislative Assembly. Should the Assembly include Southern representatives or should the South be provided with its own forum and perhaps federate with the North? A conference was held in Juba in 1947, attended by Northern and Southern leaders, as a result of which it was decided that Southern representation should be included in the proposed Legislative Assembly. Thereafter the lot of the South was to be an integral part of the whole Sudan, but this did not alter the fact that much in the way of history, culture and religion separated the two, and that the South was still backward and undeveloped relative to the North. Such was the background to the Southern problem and to the need for the Governor-General's special responsibility for the South, which the Sudanese themselves had written into the draft of the Self-Government Statute, and which all the Northern parties, under Egyptian persuasion, allowed to be removed. The sudden arrival in the South in 1953 and 1954 of great numbers of Egyptians and Northern politicians with extravagant promises perplexed the Southerners and strained the fabric of an administration which depended for its stability on a respect for tribal traditions and loyalties, and the authority of the existing Government. These were the factors that led to the mutiny and all that followed. The responsibility for the tragedy of the South rests on the Government of the Anglo-Egyptian Sudan, the Egyptian Government, the Northern politicians prior to 1 March 1954 and the Government of the Sudan thereafter.

We were dismayed that although the British Government had always upheld the principle that the Sudan's status would not be changed except after consultation with the Sudanese through constitutional channels, a position which the Foreign Secretary had reinforced only a few years before, it had, as a result of the Northern politicians' acquiescence in General Neguib's offer, found itself unable to do other than accept a *fait accompli*. An agreement had been reached without any consultation through constitutional channels. By withholding agreement to the draft Self-Government statute, the Co-domini had effectively prevented the holding of elections in 1952, and this had put us in a straitjacket. There was nothing we could now do apart from accepting and trying not to appear disapproving or embittered to our Sudanese friends and colleagues. It fell to me, feeling little enthusiasm for my task, to draft the speech, with its tribute to General Neguib and its welcome for the Agreement, that the Governor-General made in front of the Secretariat and in the shadow of the equestrian statue of Kitchener, on the morning of February 14. The crowds rejoiced, but for those of us who believed that we could see a little beyond this gathering of fifty thousand enthusiastic townsmen to the lives of the millions whose day-to-day welfare had for long been our concern, it was not a happy event. That night the Governor-General gave a reception at the Palace. The band of the York and Lancashire Regiment, which formed a part of the garrison of Khartoum, beat retreat with impeccable precision on the floodlit lawn under the palms which stretched their smooth white trunks regally into the night. It was a moving occasion which gave us back a moment of pride.

Two months later James Robertson retired and left. He had carried with outstanding ability an immensely heavy burden during a time of great difficulty. A.C. Beaton became Civil Secretary and I left the Political Section and moved in as his Deputy. Bill Luce came up from his Governorship of Blue Nile Province to take over the appointment of Adviser to the Governor-General on Constitutional and External Affairs with John Kenrick as his assistant.*

In this time of pressure and long hours there was little opportunity for recreation, but I occasionally got an afternoon's polo at Omdurman, or a sail on the Blue Nile, or a dawn sand-grouse shoot. Silvia was a leading member of the Khartoum Amateur Dramatic Society and regularly took a part in their productions. Once a fortnight, in a group under the direction of Jock Duncan, we would spend an hour or two enjoying and exercising ourselves in Scottish country dancing, to the music of a gramophone on the lawn.

Much of our work was now with the three bodies which, under the terms of the February Agreement, were to be set up as part of the processes that would eventually lead to Self-Determination — the Electoral Commission, the Governor-General's Advisory Commission and the Sudanisation Committee. All three were to have foreign chairmen and members in addition to Sudanese representation. The foremost concern of some of these distinguished guests was for their housing. They had been used to standards much grander than we were able to provide unless we were to turn out

* J.W. Kenrick, OBE, *b.* 1913. Joined Sudan Political Service 1936. Sudan Defence Force 1941–4. Retired 1955.

existing occupants. They were put out too by the heat and the insect life of Khartoum, and particularly by the sanitary arrangements that consisted of a nightly collection of buckets and their removal by open camel carts to pits in the desert. They felt that money, which could only sparingly be found for schools and dispensaries and roads in the Provinces, would have been better spent in providing the capital of the Sudan with water-borne sanitation. The camel carts did, it is true, sometimes momentarily interrupt one's evenings in the garden. But the bucketmen, many of them from the Nuba Mountains, were particularly humorous and courteous. When Silvia arrived in Khartoum as a bride the word got around, and for the first fortnight of our temporary stay the fresh bucket, which we found in position each morning, was decorated with a sprig of bougainvillia blossom. One evening when Arthur Charles' mother was sitting alone on the lawn in the semi-darkness the bucketman, out of respect for a lady of her years, stopped as he made his way along the pathway from the back quarters, deftly adjusted the balance of the bucket on his head, and made her a polite bow. But it was not long before the new Government found the money to support a plan, made some years earlier, to enable the better parts of Khartoum to dispense with the cart, the buckets and the shadowy figure slowly leading his camel by the light of a hurricane lantern.

The Electoral Commission was the first to come into operation. It assembled early in April 1953. Its Chairman was Mr Sukumar Sen, an Indian, and his Commission consisted of one American member, one British, one Egyptian and three Sudanese. They reviewed the Electoral Law and after making a number of not unreasonable changes set themselves to supervise the elections. The arrangements for these were confined to the Sudanese members of the Administration, and took place over a period of five weeks in November and December. Considering the propaganda put out by Cairo and the inducements offered to the voters by the large number of Egyptians who flocked into the Sudan for this purpose, it is a tribute to the Sudanese throughout the country that order prevailed. Mr Sen, with whom I worked happily, was well satisfied with the help we had given him.

The National Unionists secured fifty-one out of the ninety-seven seats in the Lower House and twenty-one out of the thirty elected seats in the Senate. The *Umma*, who had been over-confident, were horrified. There can be little doubt that Egyptian propaganda had played a significant part. Egyptian money, distributed not only to individuals but also to religious, educational and other institutions, had played perhaps a bigger part, but the *Umma* had been unwisely blatant in their pre-election propaganda. Memories of the Mahdia were still alive and there still existed a genuine fear over much of the country of what might happen if the Mahdists came to power. Britain was leaving, and Egypt provided a lifeline to be used if necessary and discarded if no longer required.

Parliament was opened on January 1954. The opening was informal and was solely for the purpose of electing a Prime Minister and a Speaker. The Prime Minister elected was Ismail El Azhari. On the 9th he announced his Cabinet; seven of his Northern colleagues were given portfolios. He himself took the Ministry of Interior. Three Southerners became Ministers without portfolio.

Although I had heard of El Azhari as leader first of the Graduates' Congress and later of the extreme pro-Egyptian *Ashigga*, and although we had met briefly on several occasions, it was not until he became Prime Minister and Minister of the Interior that we were brought into close and often daily contact. His comfortable figure, benevolent appearance and gold-rimmed glasses masked a character of single-minded ambition, political astuteness and shrewd opportunism. His expressed aim — he said so in 1951 — was to become President of the Sudan, and he achieved it in 1964. For the first two or three months A.C. Beaton was Permanent Secretary to the Ministry of the Interior, but as his deputy and designated successor I came, as the weeks passed, into increasingly close contact with our Minister. However much I had disliked and distrusted his policies, however often he seemed to me and to many others unscrupulous and irresponsible, my only course was to try and win his confidence and if possible a measure of his friendship, and in so doing attempt to exercise some influence. The first few weeks were not easy, particularly the days leading to the tragic events of 1 March.

That day had been chosen for the formal opening of Parliament, and the Government had decided at very short notice to invite a number of foreign representatives and to make it an occasion of considerable splendour. Against all the advice which we gave him, Azhari took two fatal decisions. The first was to invite General Neguib and the second was to declare 1 March a public holiday. The *Ansar*, bitter and incredulous over their defeat in the elections, eagerly took the opportunity and mustered in order to display their hostility to growing Egyptian influence. They flocked into Khartoum. The public holiday brought on to the streets thousands of others, *Ansar* and *Khatmia*, who would otherwise have remained at work. At the airport, where Neguib's plane was due to arrive at eight in the morning, twenty thousand tribesmen, most of them *Ansar*, were massed before first light. In the area of the Palace and the Secretariat, thousands of *Khatmia* were gathered. When I reached my office shortly before eight the whole of the grass square between the Secretariat and the Blue Nile was seething with a wildly excited crowd. With great difficulty the Governor-General succeeded in escorting Neguib from the airport into the Palace where, together with Mr Selwyn Lloyd, the British Foreign Secretary, they became virtually besieged, *Khatmia* on one side, *Ansar* on the other. The outcome was inevitable. The fighting began soon after eleven. Azhari and his Ministers had betaken themselves to his first-floor office next to mine, and we watched helpless while the fury which they had unleashed erupted on the lawns thirty yards away. We watched while rival groups hacked and stabbed at each other, as the ground became covered with the dead, and as the wounded dragged themselves away. We watched while Hugh McGuigan, the British Commandant of the Khartoum Police, who only three days before had sat with us in the Prime Minister's office and stressed the potential dangers, led a party of his men in an attempt to restore order. We watched while he and his Sudanese assistant and more than a dozen of their men, armed only with batons and shields, were cut to pieces. The Sudan Defence Force was called in, and when it opened fire the crowds fled. When the fighting was over thousands of slippers, turbans, spears and clubs, the abandoned litter of the conflict, lay scattered in front of the Secretariat and around the Palace walls.

At a moment when it seemed as if the Secretariat might be attacked I phoned Silvia. I have little doubt that had the *Ansar* realised that the Cabinet was assembled on the first floor and the guard consisted of a Sudanese corporal and four men, both would have been overwhelmed. I told Silvia to keep indoors, and to post Ibrahim at the garden gate. Ibrahim was a Mahdist, our area of Khartoum was Mahdist, and I had no great fear for their immediate safety unless the Sudan Defence Force failed to restore order. It succeeded and the rival hosts dispersed, the Mahdists surging past our house, frenzied and chanting, while Ibrahim stood at the gate.

Between the main entrance of the Palace and the river front the crowd had gathered ten or twelve deep and for five hours milled and surged, shouting slogans and brandishing swords and spears. Facing them, their backs to the closed doors, stood the Palace sentries, half a dozen young British soldiers. They remained quite still, making no move against the crowd, and the crowd did not molest them.

The formal opening of Parliament was postponed and a State of Emergency proclaimed. A disgruntled and puzzled General Neguib flew back to Cairo at dawn on 2 March and the other distinguished foreign guests also took their departure.

To Azhari's credit he made no attempt to blame the tragedy and the humiliations of 1 March on his British advisers. Nor did the

Government take any action against the *Umma* party or the *Ansar*. There was talk of arresting Sayyed Seddik, Sayyed Abdelrahman's son, Abdulla Bey Khalil and other *Ansar* and *Umma* leaders, but wisely the suggestions were set aside. The situation in the Western Sudan, the homeland of Mahdism, was full of possible danger and we withdrew all British women and children from the Blue Nile and the Western Provinces. Disillusioned by the events of 1 March, faced by the menace of their aftermath and even the possibility of civil war, Azhari began to look at things with greater realism. He was still under constant pressure from the more extreme and irresponsible of his supporters, he was constantly surrounded by Egyptians, and he still saw problems in terms of immediate political advantage. Nonetheless there were occasions in the months that followed when he responded to patient explanation and good humour. I now saw him daily, often for an hour or more, and I think he gradually began to realise that I was doing my best to be helpful. I certainly went out of my way to show him all the respect due to a Prime Minister, but I was also outspoken whenever he proposed to do something I thought was wrong or knew to be illegal. The Governor-General too treated him with particular courtesy and consideration, and the effect began to show. He became at least more friendly.

Yet, although we had a tolerable working relationship throughout a difficult year, and each of us went through the motions of expressing mutual confidence and respect, Ismail El Azhari was one of the very few Sudanese I ever met who seemed to me to fall short in the two qualities that were almost a national characteristic: warmth and generosity. A year after nearly all the British had left the Sudan, he made a speech to mark the achievement of Independence. 'Colonisation', he declared, 'sat heavily upon the land for fifty-seven years, tyrannising over its population, destroying its peculiarities, and spreading hatred and separation between the people in order to ensure a long period of occupation.' It was not a felicitous speech. It was just thirty-three years since he had graduated from the Gordon Memorial College, an establishment financed by private subscriptions raised in England.

Despite their initial success in negotiating the Agreement and in the victory of the Unionists in the elections, the Egyptians failed to bring about the ultimate conclusion they had so confidently expected. The means they employed to strengthen their hold so antagonised the Independents that from the middle of 1954 onwards there was a very real danger of conflict. Their activities also brought about a gradual but steady change of heart among many Unionists. The Governor-General's Advisory Commission, designed to counteract all exercise of his personal influence, particularly in the South, failed in the long run to have the effect the Egyptians had hoped of it. While the Pakistani Chairman, Mian Ziauddin, brought no great weight to the Commission, the crude irresponsibility of the Egyptian member Hussein Zulfikar Sabri and the Southern member Siricio Iro was outweighed by the patience and tact of the Governor-General supported by the experience and urbanity of the British member Sir Laurence Grafftey-Smith.* The intrigues of both the Egyptian and the Southerner eventually antagonised the previously pro-Egyptian Sudanese member Dardiri Mohammed Osman. He became an Independent.

During the spring of 1954 much of my time was taken up with the Sudanisation Committee as established under Article 8 of the Agreement. The Committee's duties were to 'complete the Sudanisation of the Administration, the Police and the Sudan Defence Force and any other Government post that may affect the freedom of the Sudanese at the time of Self-Determiniation'. With the help of Robin Young,† who was in charge of Personnel in the Secretariat, I prepared a plan of ordered withdrawal whereby Sudanese would take over in the Provinces and in the Ministry of the Interior, starting with the more junior posts and moving upward to District Commissioner, Deputy Governor and finally Governor. Rather more than a hundred administrative officers would be leaving and it was a matter of numbers and timing. I timed the exercise so that it would be completed within the required three years. Three years would give a minimum period for Sudanese administrators to gain experience of work in posts which, in the normal course of promotion, they would probably not have reached for another seven or even ten years. This applied particularly to the South where the number of experienced Sudanese administrators was fewer than in the North. We already had three Sudanese Deputy Governors in the North, and a number of Sudanese were in charge of Districts. We also had a number of *Mamurs* ready for promotion. But we had to find over a hundred additional Sudanese administrative officers from somewhere, and they had to be first-class men. Time was needed to recruit and train them and to give them experience in the field. We had already in 1952 created an embryo Sudanese Diplomatic Service and in doing so we had creamed off some of the best of our Sudanese administrators. Rapid constitutional change, uncertainty and a measure of unrest in the South and in the western Mahdist Provinces were laying an

* Sir Laurence Grafftey-Smith, KCMG, KBE, *b.* 1892. Diplomatic Service 1914–51. High Commissioner in Pakistan 1947–51. Author of *Hands to Play*.

† R.G.C. Young, OBE. Sudan Political Service 1949–55. He went on to a distinguished career in Aden and Oman. His father, F.T.C. Young, had been a member of the Political Service from 1910 to 1936.

additional burden on the administration. All this sound, logical and practical sense made no impact on the majority of the Sudanisation Committee. Three years, in the Committee's opinion, was a ludicrously long time. The Prime Minister's first thought was that two years ought to be enough. The Committee then declared that eighteen months would do. The pro-Egyptian press argued that a fortnight would be ample. In the event we were manoeuvred into completing the operation in nine months. Step by step with the Sudanisation of the Administration, the Police and the Sudan Defence Force, the Committee applied itself to other posts that unaccountably appeared to them to affect the freedom of the Sudanese in exercising their right to Self-Determination. In consequence British officials whose posts had not been Sudanised elected to resign, and the functioning of the whole Civil Service was seriously affected.

The Governor-General's Palace, with its white arched colonnades, deep shaded verandahs and green-shuttered windows, looked out across the Blue Nile. No other viceregal residence radiated quite the same sense of stability and poise or generated a stronger atmosphere of imperial history. From a lesser building on the same site Turkish and Egyptian Pashas and Beys had ruled the Sudan throughout most of the nineteenth century. Here General Gordon had died and here, in 1954, a British Governor-General gave his annual Palace Ball for the last time. Up the curving white marble stairway that rose from the river entrance and past the wall displays of Dervish weapons taken at Omdurman the guests moved to meet Sir Robert and Lady Howe, the women in long dresses and elbow-length white gloves and the men in mess kit or tails, wearing the stars and neck collars of their Orders and the minatures of their medals. The lawns and the Imperial palms were floodlit. The Palace servants, under the command of old Daud who as a boy had seen Gordon, moved among the guests with immense dignity. A British regimental band played quick or slow fox-trots and waltzes. Few of the Sudanese guests danced but they were nonetheless an essential part of this scene in the imperial tradition which was about to fade into history. The independent Sudan, however much it would be built on British foundations, would never wish to preserve a custom so essentially alien. At one o'clock in the morning the British and Egyptian National Anthems brought the occasion to an end.

It is difficult to assess what the Prime Minister's thoughts were at this stage. He was under constant pressure from his pro-Egyptian supporters and his Egyptian friends, all of whom were expressing fears of what the administration might possibly be hatching in the South, or even with the *Ansar* in the Western Provinces. But I think that by the middle of 1954 he had come to realise that the British were not intriguing against him and that the Egyptians, elated by their apparent success, were increasingly antagonising many of their previous supporters. General Abdel Gamal Nasir had become Prime Minister, with General Neguib as President, and the latter's position grew progressively more hazardous throughout the autumn. Major Salah Salim was touring the Sudan assiduously, and directing his activities particularly to the South. It cannot have escaped Azhari's notice that the Major was cultivating Southern contacts more on behalf of Egyptian interests than in the interest of a united Sudan. There was no question of Major Salim working to preserve the free and neutral atmosphere requisite for Self-Determination.

It has been rightly said that the Sudanese understood the British a great deal better than the British were ever able to understand the Sudanese. There was much in Sudanese thinking which the British, despite the honesty of their intentions, frequently misunderstood and misjudged. In the early days this did not greatly matter; their own unambiguous position as benevolent guardians was enough for the practical purposes for which they had come temporarily to the Sudan. As time passed and the Sudanese became more aware of what was happening in the rest of the world it began to matter much more. We failed to realise how quickly time was passing and how quickly the Sudanese were adapting themselves to the modern world and to the influence of developments outside the Sudan, particularly in Egypt. We looked down on the Egyptians because we considered them unreliable, effete and corrupt, and knew that generally the Sudanese thought likewise. But we did not appreciate early enough that, despite its shortcomings, Egypt was bound to take a leading part in influencing the political thinking of the Sudanese leaders. They spoke the same language in more senses than one. We thought of Ismail El Azhari primarily as an ambitious self-seeker, but whether he was or not, he reflected the basic thinking of a great many politically-conscious Sudanese. We made the mistake of judging the Sudanese, whom we liked and admired, much as we judged ourselves. When we discovered that their way of thinking differed widely from our own we were surprised.

The Egyptians, as so often in the past, overplayed their hand, and if any one man can be said to have undermined the Egyptian case for the Unity of the Nile Valley it was the man who helped to deprive King Farouk of his throne and his assumed Sudan title — Major Salah Salim. He too misjudged the Sudanese. The single event which put an end to any chance of union between the two countries was the ousting and subsequent house arrest of General Neguib by Colonel Nasir in November 1954. Finally, and ironically, the one man whom the Egyptians believed could be trusted to contrive the unity of the Sudan with Egypt — Ismail El Azhari — astutely saw where the Sudan's proper interest lay and outmanoeuvred them.

Despite all that had been disappointing and disheartening in the terms of the Agreement and its implementation, the many friendships that existed between the vast majority of Sudanese and British remained unimpaired throughout this time of change. In private conversations and in larger gatherings Sudanese of all levels and persuasions spoke with sincerity, sometimes perhaps with a shade of embarrassment, of the achievements of the past and the uncertainties of the future. The goodwill was genuine enough. Only among the more extreme pro-Egyptian politicians was one conscious of a brash and triumphant coldness.

By the end of November all but a handful of senior members of the Political Service had left. Officers of the Sudan Defence Force and Police and a number from other Departments had already gone. I was about to hand over to Mohammed Esh Shaigi whom I had known for over fifteen years and greatly liked. Of a regime that had lasted for fifty-five years there remained in Khartoum the Governor-General, Bill Luce, his Adviser Jock Duncan who had succeeded John Kenrick, and an ADC. Very few senior British officials continued to serve after the end of 1954 but among them was John Carmichael.* At the time of Self-Government he had become the Permanent Under Secretary in the Ministry of Finance, having previously been Financial Secretary. He now became Financial and Economic Adviser, and continued to serve as such until his retirement in 1959. What else remained? It is hard to say. In 1930 Odette Keun, a Dutch freelance journalist born in Constantinople, published a monograph entitled *A Foreigner looks at the British Sudan*. The last paragraph of her short but perceptive treatise, which was banned in Egypt, ran as follows:

> Nobody can guess what will become of the Sudan. But whatever else vanishes, realities remain indelibly written in the collective consciousness of mankind, and neither triumph nor defeat, past nor future can erase their marks. The realities here are that while the English governed the Sudan they released slaves, and suppressed slavery; they increased prosperity, gave education, protected the weak and the outraged, defended and taught strength and courage to those who were else the predestined victims of Chiefs and priests; fought disease and postponed death. So long as our species endures, these things will enter into the composition of its spirit and form part of its heritage. There is ultimately no other significance to human endeavour and no other reward.

* Sir John Carmichael, KBE, *b.* 1910. Joined the Sudan Civil Service 1935.

This was one side of the picture certainly. But was there another? There were friendly and thoughtful Sudanese who believed that once the British departed — admirable as they admitted our administration to be — the sectarian problem of *Ansar* and *Khatmia* would settle itself. The Sudan, they were convinced, would preserve her independence against Egyptian ambitions, and at the same time succeed in maintaining friendly relations with her northern neighbour. They suggested that even the South would cease to be a problem. They did not in so many words anticipate Ismail El Azhari's bitter accusation that we had spread hatred and separation between people in order to ensure a long period of occupation, but perhaps the germ of the thought was there.

I do not think that as the time for our departure came, we felt resentful that the Sudanese had finally decided to do without our help and advice; that, anyway, had always been the ultimate aim. What disturbed us was that they appeared to have secured the way to independence through the good offices of Egypt, which we distrusted, and had done so by surrendering reservations in the Constitution which we believed were essential if the country was to remain as stable as it had been in the past. Perhaps we erred in trying to maintain for too long the levels of efficiency and integrity which marked our own administration. This was understandable enough, since independence always comes sooner than the guardian considers prudent. We wanted more time to be sure that there would be no serious falling off in the standards we had set. We fell into the same error in other places as events beyond our control forced us into the surrender of our imperial power and responsibilities. Consequently when the handover came, in the Sudan and elsewhere, our successors had been denied some of the experience and training they might have had if wider authority had been given to them sooner. But time was short. It always is. Nevertheless the faults were not all on one side. Many years later a wise and experienced Sudanese, himself a politician, declared that in 1954 he and his political colleagues failed to realise that their duty was to be the servants and not the masters of the people, and that the people failed to understand that self-government meant self-discipline.

In the years following the Sudan's declaration of independence in December 1955 there were civilian governments and military governments, coups and counter-coups. There was trouble with Egypt, there was conflict with the Mahdists and there were seventeen years of war in the South. The Sudan took its chance. Today she is independent, on the face of it united, and in close and friendly association with Egypt. Of all the countries of Africa and the Middle East she is apparently as stable as any. She represents a political and cultural link between Africa and the Arab world. Much of what we worked for has endured, including a large measure of friendship and mutual respect. For our part there can only be pride in a contribution which we know to have been good.

Ismail El Azhari had courteously suggested that I should be the last of the Administration to leave, and equally courteously arranged for us all to travel to Port Sudan in a private railway saloon. Cressida had been born in January 1954 and on 14 December that year we left Khartoum; Silvia, the three children, Anne Wardle our Nanny, and — once again peering suspiciously through the bars of his travelling cage — our grey African parrot. At Port Sudan the courtesies were preserved to the end. I was given a Police Guard of Honour before embarking, and the Sudanese Commissioner saw me away in his official launch. As the ship drew out into the Red Sea I watched the Condominium flags flying over the roof of his office just as they had been when I arrived in 1931. A year later they would be replaced by the horizontally striped yellow and blue flag of the independent Sudan.

11
KUWAIT
(1955–1957)

At the end of 1954, when I left the Sudan under the terms of the Anglo-Egyptian Agreement of the previous year, I had served for twenty-three years in various parts of the Arab world. I was forty-five, had a wife and three small children, and had no job. I had earned a pension of around six hundred pounds a year and the sum of seven thousand pounds in compensation for loss of career. We had no house in England and no other assets apart from two or three thousand pounds in investments. We went to Brighton and settled in to three rooms in an hotel on the sea front. It was January and very cold.

As a first step towards finding a job I went to London and lunched with 'John Willie' Robertson. 'Don't be in too much of a hurry,' he said, 'the Colonial Office seems to be interested in you.' This, as far as it went, was reassuring but I kept in touch with Geoffrey Hawkesworth who was in charge of an organisation designed to help in finding employment for those of us who had left the Sudan as the result of the political settlement. All that he could offer was the management of a soda-water factory in Northern Nigeria at £3,000 a year. I felt that somehow I ought to be able to do better than that. A fortnight later I was invited to call at the Foreign Office where I was seen by Harold Caccia, the deputy Permament Under Secretary.* He offered me the appointment of Political Agent Kuwait. It was flattering to feel that I was in the way of being sought after by both the Diplomatic and the Colonial Service, but to choose between a firm offer and something unspecified, and about which I was unable to discover anything, was not easy. It was only much later that I found out that the Colonial Office interest referred to by Robertson lay in the Chief Secretaryship of Aden. Harold Caccia and John Henniker-Major, the Foreign Office Chief Clerk responsible for personnel and postings,† were both persuasive. Kuwait would mean the rank of Minister, a salary and allowances of £6,600, a contract for three years renewable possibly for ten, annual leave of

* Lord Caccia of Abernant, GCMG, GCVO, *b.* 1905. British Ambassador in Washington 1956–61. Head of the Diplomatic Service 1964–65.

† Sir John Henniker-Major, KCMG, CVO, MC, *b.* 1916. Assistant Under Secretary Foreign Office 1967–8. Director-General British Council 1968–72.

forty-two days, and other minor inducements. But the appointment carried no pension provision. With somewhat limited generosity I would be entitled to a grant of a week's salary for every year of service if I completed seven years in this tropical post. For all the romantic ideas about Kuwait I had had on my visit there in 1938 my interest was tempered by the thought that it was hardly the place for small children. There would have to be long periods of separation every year. But the same consideration would apply equally to any offer the Colonial Office might have in mind. I thought it unlikely that they were considering me for an appointment outside the Arab and certainly the tropical world. Harold Caccia was sympathetic and he gave me a fortnight to think it over. Silvia and I discussed it and decided to go off to Austria and ski. With this crossroads in our lives to be negotiated, it seemed a good way of coming to a balanced decision. Silvia had skied a great deal before the war. I had never done so. Forty-five was old to begin but not too old. We had always wanted the children to learn to ski while they were young, and they now did so, and in due course all became enthusiastic skiers. It was the same with riding. If nothing else we have given all three girls a lasting love of these two activities.

As our fortnight of grace drew to an end and nothing further emerged from the Colonial Office, we accepted the offer of Kuwait. As on previous occasions when we were faced with a posting which would inevitably involve some hardship for her and considerable disruption in our family life, Silvia never hesitated in advocating acceptance of whatever fortune might bring. As it turned out our decision was the right one.

As a preparation for Kuwait it was agreed that I should serve for two months in the Foreign Office starting in April. This would enable me not only to learn something of Diplomatic Service methods and procedures and to study the history of our relations with Kuwait and our current policies, but also to meet people inside and outside Government concerned with our relations with this small but important state.

Tucked into the north-western corner of the Persian (or, as it is now often called, the 'Arabian') Gulf is the Bay of Kuwait, a natural harbourage of great strategic importance. On its southern shore stands the modern city of Kuwait, and fifty miles to the north across the desert is the Iraq frontier. Eastwards, over the sea, lies Iran. To the south and west stretch the deserts of Saudi Arabia. Roughly astride the same parallel of latitude as Cairo, Florida and Delhi, the Emirate of Kuwait enjoys a cool winter of four months, and for the rest of the year suffers an unbroken spell of appalling heat. Here, as a fifteenth-century Persian poet aptly put it, 'the panting sinner receives a foretaste of his doom to come.'

Recent archaeology has revealed traces of Stone Age settlements on the mainland of Kuwait and of commercial links dating back five thousand years between Failaka island at the mouth of the bay and India. The island has also yielded evidence of Greek commercial activity in the second century BC. But neither the town nor the surrounding coastlands has a history of any significance. In the middle of the eighteenth century the ancestors of the present Ruling family, the Subah, drawn from the Utubi section of the Anaiza of Central Arabia, established on the southern shore of the bay a trading settlement and built a small fort — a *Kut* or, in the diminutive, *Kuwait*. Kuwait prospered and rapidly grew to be the principal commercial centre for the transit of goods between India, Muscat, Baghdad and Arabia, while its seamen soon gained a reputation for being the finest in the Gulf. The astute business sense of the people of Kuwait and the shrewd political judgment of the Ruling family owe their origins to two centuries of trading, and to their skilful outmanoeuvering of the political and territorial ambitions of Persia, Egypt, Arabia, Turkey, Germany and Russia. All coveted Kuwait's commercial and strategic importance, but Kuwait remained independent. And then there was Britain, whose trading relations with the Emirate date from the late eighteenth century when the East India Company moved the southern terminus of its eastern overland route to Kuwait from Basra. For a hundred years commercial contacts between the representatives of the two communities, British and Kuwaiti, remained harmonious.

In 1891 the Emir of Nejd, Abdel Rahman Ibn Saud, and his son Abdel Aziz, driven from their dominions by the Ruler of the Shammar, took refuge in Kuwait. There they remained until 1900 when the son set off with a small raiding party and not only recovered his father's possessions but in due course established himself as King of Saudi Arabia. In spite of occasional differences the friendship between the two Ruling families has been close and cordial ever since.

In the closing years of the nineteenth century Turkey, her empire already in decline, laid claim to sovereignty over Kuwait on the grounds that it formed a part of Turkish-dominated Iraq. Although British influence had already been established further down the Persian Gulf, there appeared no reason to oppose the Turkish claim despite the Ruler Sheikh Mubarak Subah's call to the British Government for protection. He was given no encouragement until it became apparent that Russia also had ambitions in Kuwait, namely the establishment of a port, a coaling station and a railway terminus for a line to the Mediterranean. This moved the British Government to act. On 21 January 1899, the British Resident in the Persian Gulf arrived in Kuwait and two days later an 'exclusive engagement' was entered into with Sheikh Mubarak, great-grandfather of the present Ruler, similar to an agreement that had been made with the Sultan of Muscat a few years earlier. The engagement bound the Sheikh never to cede any of his territory to a third party nor to receive the representative of any foreign power. In exchange he was accorded British protection. Within a year Germany, with her own Berlin-Baghdad railway project in mind, also endeavoured to secure a concession for a terminus in Kuwait. Sheikh Mubarak stood by his agreement, and the generous offers made by the Germans were rejected. But for the Ruler's loyalty to the engagement, Britain's diplomatic, strategic and commercial position in the Gulf over the succeeding half-century would have been very different. A year later Britain in her turn was able to manifest her loyalty to the engagement by supporting the Sheikh in his rejection of a German-inspired Turkish ultimatum. When a Turkish warship carrying troops steamed into the bay she found a British naval vessel already there. The Turkish commander prudently withdrew. In 1904 the first Political Agent was appointed to Kuwait and took up residence in the town. He was Colonel S.G. Knox. Three years later an area of land was leased to Britain by the Sheikh for use as a naval base and coaling station. Britain had secured an imperial asset of immediate and subsequently of even greater value.

During the First World War Sheikh Mubarak stood loyal to the Allies, and in return the independence of his Emirate under British protection was recognised. In 1919, when King Abdel Aziz ordered an attack on Kuwait and again in 1929–30 when a revolt of Saudi tribesmen led to an invasion of Kuwait's territory, Britain fulfilled her responsibility by providing armed protection. In 1961 she was to do so again for the last time in the face of a threat from Iraq.

In the early summer of 1938 I spent part of my leave from the Sudan in the Gulf, Iraq and Palestine. I had taken passage in a small coastal vessel from Port Sudan to Basra which had visited Aden and passed up the coast of the Hadramut and Oman, through the Straits of Hormuz to Bahrain and thence to Bushire. We had then crossed the Gulf to Kuwait. The sight of Kuwait in the early evening light stirred me unaccountably; it struck me as one of the most exciting-looking places I had ever seen in the Arab world. The waterfront was crowded with dhows. Beyond stood the town, grey and white with a few small minarets rising above the skyline. Kuwait lay huddled within its crenellated walls that encircled the town on its landward side and ran down to the water's edge. Beyond stretched the desert. This was the sort of place I wanted to explore. Basra and Baghdad and Jerusalem, the objects of my journey, were romantic enough, but this drew me far more. I knew no one in Kuwait and had no visa. The ship's Captain was unable to help or to offer advice, but he made no objection to my attempting to land. I hailed a boat and clambered down the ship's side on a rope ladder. My canvas holdall was lowered to me and we made for the harbour. Here I was met by a white-robed Customs officer and an armed Beduin gendarme. Had I a visa? No. Had I the British Political Agent's permission to land? No, but he was a friend (I had no idea even of his name) and would welcome me once I had spoken or written to him. 'Maybe', the officer answered, 'but it is now too late in the day to get in touch with him and until tomorrow you cannot be permitted to leave the harbour.' There was the Customs shed and a wooden bench on which I could sleep. My custodians were resolute but not at all unfriendly; I was offered tea and coffee. In the morning I would be permitted to send the Political Agent a message. Spreading my great-coat and making a pillow of a spare shirt I settled down and slept. My note next morning to the Political Agent brought an invitation to call, and with a small boy carrying my holdall I was released from the Customs area and made my way through the heat and movement of the waterfront to the Agency. The port area smelt of fish and ropes, and spices and roasting coffee, and above all there was the pungent throaty scent of shark oil. The Agency faced the sea — a long bow-shaped building, with arches over the ground- and first-floor verandahs; it housed both the offices and the residence of the Political Agent. A few thorn trees grew in the dusty compound where the Union Jack flew. A hundred yards away stood the watchtowers and battlements of the Ruler of Kuwait's Palace.

The Political Agent was Captain Gerald de Gaury. He had been a regular soldier in the 1914–18 war. He had served in the Iraq administration and held diplomatic posts in Iran; he knew King Ibn Saud, and was a good Arabist. He was also elegant and urbane. He received me with kindness, and for nearly a week I stayed in Kuwait as his guest. Under his guidance I wandered through the markets and around the fourteen-foot mud walls, built within two months in 1919 by a levée of the entire population as a defence against a Saudi invasion. The gates, guarded by Bedouin watchmen, were barred at sunset and opened at dawn. De Gaury drove me out into the desert. I visited the harbour whence every year three hundred dhows sailed to the pearling grounds down the coast. In the evenings we drank coffee with the merchants or played backgammon in the cool of de Gaury's upper verandah. I then left Kuwait to spend a month in Iraq and Palestine. Such was my first introduction to Kuwait, and never could

I have imagined that thirteen years later I would myself become Political Agent and for a while a minor figure in this rich Arabian tapestry.

In 1934 a joint British-American enterprise consisting of the Anglo Persian Oil Company and the American Gulf Oil Corporation had discovered the presence of oil in the vicinity of Kuwait, and the Ruler had granted a concession. The two companies thereupon agreed a fifty-fifty partnership and jointly established the Kuwait Oil Company. At the time of my visit, oil had been found in some quantity thirty miles south of the town and fifteen miles inland. Although the war held up exports until 1946, Kuwait in 1938 stood on the threshold of acquiring immense wealth.

To return to 1955, I had worked in both Cairo and Khartoum with members of the Diplomatic Service, and because our views on the future of the Sudan and in particular its relations with Egypt had differed widely, I had come to regard most of them as being a shade too smooth in manner, over-cautious in approach, and sometimes insulated from realities. This judgement I was soon to revise. Once I was working with them, I quickly came to appreciate their abilities less subjectively. These men possessed a range of qualities and a style which, though sometimes dissimilar in emphasis from those that had characterised the Sudan Political Service, came in the aggregate to approach very closely to what we judged to be our own 'mystique'. The Diplomatic and Sudan Services had many similarities. They were recruited mainly from the public schools and universities and broadly they represented the pick of the product of Oxford and Cambridge. In selecting candidates for the Diplomatic Service much emphasis was placed on academic distinction. The Sudan Service had looked rather more to active habits and evidence of leadership and enterprise. Perhaps it was a little less polished and a little less conventional. While the Diplomatic Service, by its very nature of employment in different parts of the world, though generally in a comfortable environment, developed characteristics of flexibility and objectivity, the Sudan Service called rather more for individuality and initiative. The Diplomatic Service officer worked as a member of a team while his Sudan counterpart had worked in greater isolation, shouldering responsibilities of a wider range earlier in his career than the young diplomat. But basically the individual qualifications demanded in both services were the same. They were perception, judgement, patience, trustworthiness and loyalty.

The Agency in Kuwait and other similar posts in the Gulf had in the past always been administered from India and staffed by members of the Indian Political Service. When India became independent in 1947 this arrangement ended, and responsibility for the Gulf was taken over by the Foreign Office, although a number of ex-members of the Indian Political Service continued to serve there. The Diplomatic Service had few men at that time with the necessary language qualifications and training for service in the Gulf. These were posts which called for Arabists, and for the sort of experience which many members of the Sudan Political Service had come to acquire. For ten years or more after 1955 most of the posts up and down the Gulf therefore came to be held by ex-members of the Sudan Political with temporary or permanent appointments in the Diplomatic Service.

I found little difficulty in adjusting myself to working with men who viewed problems and personalities in much the same way as I had learnt to do, and who held the same sort of values. I was a little older than most of the Agency staff but the fact that I had come from another service to take charge of a diplomatic post was accepted with generosity by these regular members of the Service. Of the four Secretaries who at different times worked with me in the Kuwait Chancery all have remained warm friends, and all later attained Ambassadorial rank.*

Silvia and I had already come to that stage in our family life which is unavoidable in an overseas service once the children begin to grow up, and which so many of our friends shared with us. For half the year the family is split between home and abroad. In setting out for Kuwait we decided to leave the children in England but once we were established there Silvia would return and come back to Kuwait in the autumn with the two younger ones. Peta, now at boarding school, would join us for the Christmas and subsequent holidays. We travelled rather excitingly by train through Yugoslavia to Athens, flew to Beirut, spent a week among the pinewoods of Lebanon, flew to Bahrain to meet the Political Resident Bernard Burrows, responsible for the whole area of the Gulf,† and finally to Kuwait. It was May and desperately humid and hot.

Kuwait in 1955 was a very different place from the uncomplicated Arab town of 70,000 inhabitants, with its coral or mud-brick houses and narrow sandy streets, that I had known in 1938. The walls still stood but only a year later they were to be bulldozed into dust. Parts of the old town and market, with all their colour and movement

* They were D.A. Logan now Sir Donald Logan; A.A. Acland now Sir Antony Acland; A.K. Rothnie now Sir Alan Rothnie; and J.C. Moberly. In addition there was the Economic Councillor N.M.P. Reilly, CMG, a man of unbounded vitality and enthusiasm.

† Sir Bernard Burrows, GCMG, *b.* 1910. Deputy Under Secretary Foreign Office 1958–62. Permanent British Representative North Atlantic Council 1966–70.

along the sheltered lanes, were steadily being replaced by supermarkets and asphalt streets. The population, reinforced by many Palestinian refugees and other immigrants, had more than trebled in under twenty years. Concrete blocks of offices, shops and flats now looked down on an endless procession of air-conditioned and ceaselessly hooting cars. Pepsi-Cola, Kitty-Cola, Sinalco, Ford, Cadillac, Sanyo and other hideous advertisements jostled for attention along every street. At night the neon lights took over. Outside the town, cement works, a fresh water distillation plant and a dozen other signs of prosperity — mostly the product of British engineering interests — rose where for centuries goats had grazed on the desert scrub. In the bay a score or more of freighters were anchored, waiting to unload their cargoes into lighters — this would continue until the modern harbour was completed. All but a few of the dhows had gone, and the three hundred pearling vessels had been reduced to a dozen. But at the edge of the town close by the shore, within the walls and alongside the Ruler's Palace, stood the same Agency building, with offices on the ground floor and residence above. The Union Jack flew from its tall flagpole in the compound. Very dimly the ghost of Lord Curzon, who visited Kuwait in 1903, lingered on among the framed photographs of my predecessors which lined the corridor between the entrance hall and the Chancery.* Everywhere there brooded the relentless heat.

Twenty miles to the south of Kuwait lay Ahmadi, white and shining, the sprawling administrative and technical centre of the oilfields. It was a neat and tidy place of straight lines and newly planted trees, geared for efficiency, and to provide for the wellbeing and recreation of a community of half a dozen nationalities. On every side plumes of dark smoke were visible by day, and by night the red flares burning off surplus gas.

For Britain and, to a slightly smaller extent, for the United States, the privileged relationship they had acquired with Kuwait gave them great economic and strategic benefits. The Kuwait Oil Company, which in 1955 was producing nearly fifty million tons of crude oil a year, was a joint Anglo-American enterprise, now fifty per cent British Petroleum and fifty per cent Gulf. All the senior staff were either British or American. A big oil company is more than a commercial enterprise. It is inescapably concerned with the social,

* One of them on retirement had been appointed to the Queen's Bodyguard for Scotland and had been photographed in his full regalia of feathered bonnet and so on, and armed with bow and quiver. I was once showing an Arab notable this gallery, which included a number of his earlier acquaintances, when he stopped astonished at the sight of this bowman. 'Good God', he said, 'I never realised there were Policital Agents in Kuwait before the time of firearms.'

political and economic progress of the country in which it operates. The senior staff of the Kuwait Oil Company, and the General Manager Leland Jordan* in particular, were as well aware of their responsibilities in these spheres as they were of their technical problems. Thus the Kuwait Oil Company and the state worked harmoniously together. The Company's chief adviser on local and particularly Bedouin affairs was Harold Dickson, who had served for many years in India, Iraq and the Gulf and before the war had been Political Agent Kuwait. I too had reason to be grateful for his advice, for his knowledge of the older generation in Kuwait was unrivalled.†

In Kuwait a Development Board, responsible under the chairmanship of Sheikh Fahad, one of the Ruler's brothers, for submitting major projects to the Government, was mainly British in composition. The Board operated a Plan which had been drawn up three years before under a cost-plus system whereby five British contracting firms each took a Kuwaiti partner with whom they shared a fifteen per cent profit; however not only did the cost-plus system prove more expensive than the Kuwait Government had foreseen, but Kuwait had begun to grow increasingly resentful of the privileged position of the 'Big Five'. The Government's finances and its investment policies were watched over by British advisers. Although the Sheikh ruled his state through a 'Superior Council' consisting of his own family, he and they were heavily dependent on their British advisers and technicians.

The 1899 treaty relationship between Kuwait and Britain meant that the Ruler's overseas representation and his foreign policy were, at least officially, controlled by Britain. Apart from the United States Consul and a semi-official Saudi Government agent, there was no foreign diplomatic representation in Kuwait. All contacts between the Ruler and other governments were made through the Political Agent, or were supposed to be. At Bahrain a British naval base ensured control of the Gulf by ships of the Royal Navy and the American Navy. Kuwait was a prize that Iraq or Iran or Egypt would happily have seized had they been presented with the chance. In 1961 Iraq in fact attempted an invasion and Kuwait called for and was immediately provided with a British military reinforcement.

Before I left London it had been impressed upon me that the maintenance of our political and economic position in Kuwait was of national importance. The policy was that while the complete

* This warm-hearted Texan was awarded an honorary KBE in 1958.

† Colonel H.R.P. Dickson, CIE. His widow, Dame Violet Dickson, DBE, has remained in Kuwait to this day.

independence of Kuwait should be our ultimate goal, our immediate aim should be to ensure, in co-operation with the Ruling family, political and economic stability of such a character as would preserve and be in harmony with vital British interests. By discussion and persuasion and by his personal influence, it would be the Political Agent's task to ensure the achievement of these aims.

As I began to gather my first impressions I came increasingly to doubt how far the full implementation of this policy was realistic in a world where all foreign control, however inconspicious or disguised or beneficent, was becoming increasingly resented. But whatever changes in policy and procedure might have to come with time — and I foresaw that they would come rapidly — my first duty was to cultivate the confidence and, I hoped, the friendship of the Ruler and the leading members of his family who internally held Kuwait under powerful but generally benevolent control. I had not previously met any of them.

On the early morning of the day after my arrival I made my first call on the Ruler. In the coming two and a half years I was to visit him regularly once and sometimes twice a week. The procedure was always the same. I would drive across to Dasman Palace, return the salute of the quarter-guard and climb the stairs to the first floor. There, on the verandah leading from his office, the Ruler would be waiting. We would shake hands and move indoors. He was always punctual. After a cup of coffee we would begin our business which would be conducted exclusively in Arabic. His secretary Ashraf Lutfi and my own, Ismail Kaddo, would nearly always be present. Once back in my office, Ismail and I would make our record of what had passed.

His Highness Sheikh Abdulla As Salim As Subah had succeeded his cousin Ahmed, who had ruled for the previous thirty years, in 1950. Sheikh Abdulla was in his early sixties. In appearance he was a little below average height, fair-skinned, somewhat round of feature and with a grey moustache and short beard which he kept confined to his chin. His hands were fleshy and unadorned except for a plain silver ring on the fourth finger of his right hand. He had the smallest nails I have ever seen on any man. His dress was simple and plain. In manner he was quietly dignified, and deliberate both in movement and in speech. Although on rare occasions he enjoyed a joke and a little leg-pulling, I never saw him go beyond a smile or indeed show any emotion, either elation, disappointment or anger. His appearance and manner reflected his character and the Fabian style in which he administered the State and conducted his affairs. Shrewd and cautious, he preferred to postpone decisions on difficult problems, not out of lethargy or in the hope that the problems would go away, but in the belief that more harm than good is often done by making swift decisions and taking immediate action. He strongly subscribed to the Arab proverb that haste comes from the Devil and unhindered deliberation from the Merciful One.

The sudden acquisition of stupendous wealth by a community whose fathers had been sailors, pearl divers, fishermen or small merchants, combined with a great influx of European technicians, Palestinian refugees and other foreigners, had created problems of great complexity. To handle these the character of Sheikh Abdulla was admirably suited. Not only was he prudent but in the style of his personal life he set a shining example of modesty, abstemiousness and piety. While avoiding display whenever possible, he was punctilious in those of his official duties that called for ceremony and generous hospitaliy. He was approachable to all and sat daily in his Council. Kuwait was fortunate to have him at the head of her affairs at that time of pressure and adjustment.

There was a particularly endearing quality in Sheikh Abdulla's simplicity. He was a heavy cigarette smoker and one might well have expected him, one of the richest men in the world, to possess at least a silver cigarette case. Not so. He carried his cigarettes in an old battered gun-metal case of a type sold many years ago in small tobacconists' shops. The elastic band designed to keep the cigarettes in place had long since disintegrated. I was fascinated whenever he took a cigarette from this article, which was as unadorned as himself. Sometimes when I called on him he would sit, not on one of the two small sofas with which his office was furnished, but in his swivel desk chair, and he would do so cross-legged as if in the desert, and gently rock himself to and fro. He spoke once of how his office needed paintng. 'You know what Public Works Departments are,' he said, 'I have been waiting for months for someone to get the thing done.' One morning when we were talking a mouse came confidently out of a corner and made its way along the wall. 'A guest', he said, 'she is welcome.' One could not help being charmed by this sort of gentle modesty.

I came away from that first half-hour meeting with a warmth of feeling towards Sheikh Abdulla, and a comforting conviction that we would be able to work in harmony. Although there were to be times when I felt that he was over-cautious and slow to take advantage of opportunities, there were just as many occasions when I came later to realise that he had been wise in rejecting my advice, or the advice that I had been obliged to give him on instructions from the Foreign Office. Like all his countrymen he was gifted with the ability to drive a hard bargain and there were times, as I was to discover, when he could be stubborn and obstinate in pressing his own interests. But I was also to learn of the generous side to his character which would respond on occasion, and graciously, to a personal appeal.

Second in the line of precedence stood the formidable and zestful figure of Sheikh Abdulla Al Mubarak, the Ruler's uncle and a son of the 'Great' Mubarak Subah by a slave mother. Tall and heavily built, ebullient, moody, morose, impetuous and unpredictable, he was firmly attached to the British Connection, but his frequently remorseless and often severely suppressive use of the security forces, of which he was Commander-in-Chief, made him at times a disconcerting ally. As the Ruler's deputy, who acted whenever the Ruler himself was away, he was not a man with whom one wished to quarrel, but we had our differences from time to time. He was a difficult man but I had reason to be grateful to him at the time of Suez when he stood stalwartly loyal and gave me a measure of support without which our position in Kuwait might well have become untenable. The number of his palaces, the wealth he had accumulated and his occasional indiscretions in the cabarets of Beirut and Paris caused his nephew the Ruler frequent embarrassment. But he could be warm-hearted and generous.

All Government Departments in Kuwait were under the direct and day-to-day control of members of the ruling family. The Police were commanded by the Ruler's brother and eventual successor Sheikh Subah As Salim As Subah. Another brother, the dynamic and highly intelligent Sheikh Fahad, was in charge of Public Works and the Municipality, in addition to his duties as Chairman of the Development Board. Education and the Courts, except for those categories of non-Arabs over which the Political Agency had jurisdiction, were controlled by Sheikh Jabir Al Abdulla, one of the Ruler's cousins. Sheikh Jabir Al Ahmed, the present Ruler of Kuwait, was responsible for the security of the oilfields.

Although my relations with the Ruler were uniformly friendly they were exclusively on an official rather than a close personal level. It was his brother Sheikh Subah As Salim to whom, of all the Ruling family, I came closest. He lacked the depth and character of some of his near relations but his friendly and uncomplicated nature made him an agreeable and amusing acquaintance. I could ring him up at any time and invite myself to tea. We ranged widely in our talk and shared a similar sense of humour. We went hawking together and he, his son Salim then aged sixteen or seventeen, and I would go for rides in the afternoons. Perhaps the family had deliberately deputed him to form, for their own purposes, an 'intelligence' link with the Political Agent. I hope not, for I felt a warmth towards him which it seemed to me that he returned. Sheikh Abdulla died in 1961 and

Sheikh Subah succeeded to the Emirate. By then I had left Kuwait. But although I called on him several times later, his new dignity prevented me from ever recapturing even a fraction of the old intimacy. Kuwait changed a good deal in its attitudes as its wealth grew more and more astronomical — a universal human failing.

The Subah family was a close-knit but flexible unit. Over the years they had married into most of the leading commercial families and their contacts and their influence were consequently widespread. There was no Legislative Assembly or popular representation. Such active opposition to the regime as existed was confined to a small group of Western-educated young men, and because of the close watch kept by the Security Forces on their activities they acted with caution. Furthermore Kuwait's riches were rapidly becoming widely distributed. There were no poor, and most Kuwaitis were too busy making money to concern themselves over whether they were democratically governed or not. For the moment at least Kuwait was a good deal more stable than might be supposed. In 1955 there were some — including visiting British politicians — who, looking at Kuwait from the outside, believed that the Subah system of administration was outdated and no longer fitted to deal with the complications of newly-acquired wealth combined with a growth of internal political awareness and external pressure. They thought therefore that the time had come for us unobtrusively to change our allegiance and to give latent support to the emerging small group of progressives. My own view was that the Ruling family was sufficiently in touch and sufficiently astute to be able to handle their internal problems effectively, and that for us to court the opposition, however discreetly, would be neither honourable nor wise. Today, nearly three decades later, the Subahs are still ruling their state peacefully and effectively, and have shown as much flexibility as has been necessary to satisfy the majority of their people. With a population now well over a million and a quarter, of whom considerably less than half are of Kuwaiti origin, this has been no small achievement. Kuwait has been long used to balancing claims and counterclaims.

In 1955 the whole of the Arab world — Kuwait being no exception — was overshadowed by the figure of Abdel Gamal Nasir. In every barber's shop, at street corners, and in private houses brightly coloured portraits of the Egyptian President beamed confidence and avuncular goodwill. The expansion of education in Kuwait — ten thousand boys and five thousand girls — had created a vast demand for school teachers of both sexes. A large number of Palestinian educationalists had already been recruited, but only

Egypt could meet the ever-increasing need and she did so enthusiastically. The schools rapidly became powerful centres of pro-Egyptian propaganda. Every coffee shop had its radio constantly tuned to Cairo. In spheres other than education a number of Palestinians had come to hold important state appointments. The Kuwaitis trusted them, and without their experience and skills the Government would have found it difficult to function effectively. With few exceptions they were the best educated and the most intelligent of Kuwait's expatriate employees. They had less cause for self-confidence than the Egyptians and in consequence they remained discreet and circumspect. But for all the material advantages they enjoyed and the responsibilities they held, they remained essentially Palestinians living in the firm and constant hope of one day regaining their right to their national homeland. All this put strain on Kuwait's hitherto staunch adherence to its links with Britain.

The enthusiasm with which in the early 1950s British consultants and contractors had been accepted had begun to evaporate. British firms had done good work in Kuwait but they had enjoyed a virtual monopoly for five years or more and they could scarcely expect the monopoly to last. Some of them felt that it was the Political Agent's job to see that it did. Our favoured position in other spheres too was coming under scrutiny and sometimes criticism. Kuwait used overprinted British stamps; the existing Civil Air Agreement gave Britain exclusive rights to operate aerodromes; Cable and Wireless provided all telephone services and telecommunications. The British Bank of the Middle East operated most of the banking, although a Kuwait National Bank had been opened in 1952. There were other examples of the monopolistic nature of our relations with Kuwait. It was clear that these things could not go on unchallenged for much longer, and that if we were to maintain the more essential of these interests we would have to be ready to relinquish the less vital. And the greater flexibility we were able to show, the easier we would make things for the Ruler whose position between Arab nationalism on one side and his traditional friendship with Britain on the other was unenviably complicated. The pressure was to mount and culminate during the hazardous months that led up to and followed the Suez affair.

One of Kuwait's major problems was water, and in the past fresh water had had to be imported by sailing dhows from Iraq. A distillation plant, powered by waste natural gas, had therefore been one of the State's first projects and by 1955 it was producing, from sea water, over a million gallons a day. But the demand for water grew, and with it the idea that the problem could be solved by bringing water from the Shatt Al Arab in Iraq by means of a 32-inch pipeline.

This would ultimately give Kuwait up to a hundred million gallons a day to be used not only for domestic purposes but also on ambitious desert irrigation projects. The *quid pro quo* demanded by the Iraqis was apparently of a modest nature — port facilities at Umm Qasr in Kuwait territory. On the face of it the idea appeared to be an admirable one, and the British Government liked it because it was felt that an agreement of this sort would draw Kuwait closer to the Baghdad Pact. Iraq in 1955 was friendly to the West. The way the Ruler reacted to the Shatt Al Arab proposal gave me my first insight into his basic good sense.

From the turn of the century Iraq had represented a threat to Kuwait's independence but the Foreign Office felt that this was an out-of-date conception. I was instructed shortly after my arrival to press the Ruler into acceptance of the Shatt Al Arab project. He hesitated and then, typically when he was under pressure, decided to take a short holiday abroad. He went to Shtura in Lebanon, where he had a small summer residence, agreeing to discuss the problem later. There was nothing further that I could immediately do, but I felt that in order to learn more of what the Shatt Al Arab scheme would mean in a wider context and in practical terms, it would be useful for me to go to Baghdad to meet our Ambassador Sir Michael Wright and some of the Iraqi ministers. I could then visit the Ruler in Lebanon when I would be in a better position to act as an advocate of the project. In Baghdad, where in addition to the Embassy staff I met Abdel Jubbar El Shalaby, Director of the Development Board, and Yousef Geilani, Permanent Head of the Foreign Ministry, I was surprised to find it generally believed that I had only to tell the Ruler of the Foreign Office's wishes and he would automatically accept them. The more I heard of the plan the more I wondered whether, attractive as the project might appear on the surface, especially as seen from Baghdad, the Kuwaitis would ever accept a scheme which would enable Iraq effectively to control the source of their main water supply. I flew on to Beirut and drove up to Shtura. It was August and even here in the Bekaa it was hot. For two days the Ruler, supported by two of his Palestinian advisers, and I talked of the scheme. We sat together on a swinging canvas divan in his garden, and walked through his newly-planted orange grove. But once again Sheikh Abdulla was not to be persuaded to take any immediate decision. I made no progress on the problem, but felt that I had come a good deal closer to this quiet, astute and courteous man who surprised me by holding my hand as we walked through the main street of Shtura.

Throughout my time in Kuwait discussion on the Shatt Al Arab scheme was regularly revived. Eventually the Ruler made his views clear. 'The Foreign Office seems curiously blind', he said to me one day some months later. 'How do they know what is going to happen in Iraq? Have they forgotten that in 1941 the Iraqis besieged the British Embassy? Perhaps they will do so again one day. Do they want me to put my head into a noose by giving Iraq control over Kuwait's water supplies? The Regent and Nuri Es Said [the Prime Minister] are friendly to Britain and to me, but one day they will be replaced by others.' Within little more than a year of the Ruler making this observation the King, the Regent and Nuri were assassinated and the British Embassy was burnt to the ground. Three years later Iraqi troops invaded Kuwait territory and the Ruler called on Britain for military aid. In 1964 an agreement between Iraq and Kuwait, allowing the latter to draw water from the Shatt Al Arab, was eventually signed. But the project has still not been implemented.

Naval visits and indeed a considerable number of formal occasions of a similar sort were very much a feature of service in Kuwait. They were a legacy from the past. The Royal Navy and the United States Navy and sometimes the Pakistan and Indian Navies were regular callers, and the formalities were elaborate and time-consuming. Unless it was a case of the Commander of the East India Station who was an Admiral, I outranked my visitors; this meant that they called on me first and I then returned their call. And because Naval vessels were obliged to lie off in the bay, I had to go out by launch. The launch would stand two hundred yards off the ship while the gun salute was fired, and one carefully counted the shots to be sure to come down from the salute at the right moment. Then one went aboard and made one's call.

Sometimes the Ruler was involved in such formalities, and then I was obliged to accompany whoever was due to call on him. There were calls to be made on the Ruler, his family and notable Kuwaitis at the main Muslim festivals and on their return from visits abroad, and to offer condolences in cases of family bereavement. And these were answered by their calling on the Political Agent at the New Year and on the Queen's birthday. Silvia paid regular calls on the wives of the leading Sheikhs. The procedure was coffee and sweets, ten minutes of polite conversation, a whiff of incense and then departure. For all these occasions I had an impressive dark blue winter uniform with a cocked hat and a summer uniform of white drill with a Wolseley helmet, topped with a brass spike. Although this ceremonial — the gun salutes, the uniforms, the decorations, the formal courtesies and exchange of compliments, — seemed at times something of an unnecessary rigmarole, it did fulfill a certain purpose. These things provided a background of mutual respect and courtesy as among people of differing cultures; and they came naturally and traditionally to Arabs. Nearly all this ceremonial has disappeared in recent years due, I believe, to a kind of self-consciousness. It is a pity.

Among many visitors of different nationalities there came from time to time British members of the House of Commons, both Conservative and Labour, and I confess with some sadness that, with one or two exceptions, few made a particularly favourable impression on the Ruling family, and such interest and sympathy as they showed towards Kuwait and its problems seemed to us marginal. The Imperial Defence College representatives left behind them a much better impression. So too did Field-Marshal Lord Alexander of Tunis, perhaps the most impressive of all our visitors, then recently retired from the post of Minister of Defence. I took this famous soldier to call on the Ruler. He appeared to combine modesty and confidence, humility and dignity, simplicity and greatness, and this, together with his good looks and impeccable appearance, created a particular magnetism. When he said to the Ruler in answer to a question during our interview, 'Yes, I had the honour of driving His Majesty's enemies out of North Africa', there was no bombast about it. As someone once said of him, he possessed the Roman virtues tempered by Greek grace.

Bernard Burrows was a regular visitor. As Political Resident Persian Gulf he held overall responsibility to the Foreign Office for all the Gulf States, and although I communicated with London on routine matters and sent my despatches direct, I had a responsibility to him in affairs of major importance. He was a career diplomat, and I quickly came both to like him and to admire the remarkable speed and perception he brought to bear on all our problems.

Entertaining and being entertained was an inescapable feature of life and equally had its value, although it too was often a time-consuming exercise. Whenever a distinguished personage came to Kuwait, it would fall to the Political Agent to introduce the visitor, if of sufficient importance, to the Ruler. By tacit agreement this did not apply to visiting Arabs, although when Anwar Sadat came to Kuwait he showed marked courtesy in calling on me. Distinguished visitors would be honoured by the Ruler and sometimes other members of his family with a lunch or a dinner. We would sit down fifty or seventy or even a hundred. There would be a whole sheep to every dozen or so guests; a whole bustard to every five, and to every guest his own individual chicken. There would be rice and salads and bowls of sour milk. It was the custom to serve only two courses; the main dish and then a sweet, usually a simple custard. The Ruler's dinner-table provided a splendid array of cutlery, but he preferred that his guests, if accustomed to do so, should eat in the traditional manner using their right hand, and frequently he would pass a message down the table to that effect. Bitter coffee and mint tea preceded the dinner, and sweet tea and more bitter coffee followed it. And a whiff of incense or a sprinkle of scent came after the coffee. Fortunately these meals seldom lasted more than an hour and a half at the most. Twenty minutes for conversation before eating, half an hour for the meal, and half an hour afterwards was the practice.

During the month of Ramadan it was customary to ask if one might break the fast with various members of the Ruling family, and the request would be welcomed. This meant arriving a short while before sunset, waiting for the Ramadan gun and for one's host and guests to pray, before drinking a glass of water. This meal, which had already been set out, was eaten sitting cross-legged on the floor and was of a gargantuan size. There was often sufficient for five separate sittings: the host and his principal guests first, then guests of lesser standing; thirdly the various armed bodyguards, soldiers and police; and fourthly the servants, cooks and scullions. What then remained was removed and taken out for the women and children.

Our hospitality in the Agency was less imposing, but even so we entertained a good number of people in the course of the year. In 1956 for instance we had over two thousand to drinks, more than four hundred to lunch, seven hundred to dinner and nearly one thousand to other forms of hospitality. Our allowance for all this, amounting to £3,700, was not over-generous, and when the Foreign Office inspectors came to examine us in 1957 I was able to give them figures which showed that it was costing me £500 a year over and above my pay and allowances to do this side of my job effectively as I saw it. They were unmoved. Entertaining Kuwaiti notables involved difficulties when we thought that their wives might wish to be included in the invitation. The Ruler felt strongly about Arab ladies keeping to a strict standard of purdah, and so long as they were in Kuwait they did so and wore the black cloak and veil when out of their houses. But most of them, and the younger ones in particular, made frequent trips to Europe and the moment the plane carrying them to London or Paris was airborne, off came the veils and the dark mantles. There were thousands of girls in school who had no intention, once their studies were completed, of keeping to this particular tradition, and their Egyptian and Palestinian teachers discreetly supported them. So before inviting a married couple it was necessary to ask the husband whether his wife would wish to come. Usually the answer was 'Yes', but only on condition that any other guests were close family friends. Thus we were able to have Kuwaiti ladies to dinner from time to time, although they never appeared when we in our turn dined in their houses. With the Palestinians it was quite different. Their ladies were fully emancipated and were a most valuable addition to any occasion. We were seeing the beginning of vast changes in everything, but the changes in social life and the status of women came last of all.

In the nineteenth century the Ruling family and well-to-do Kuwaitis always owned a number of purchased slaves of African origin. By the time I came to Kuwait slaves were no longer bought and sold, but in a number of households there were domestic servants, watchmen and attendants born of slave parents and attached to their masters' households by ties of interest and loyalty. Many of them held positions of responsibility and trust. They were free to leave if they wished but few did. Most of the Ruling family's personal bodyguard were heavily-armed slaves, and a proud arrogant lot they were liable to be when their masters' prestige was at stake. On a hawking trip I asked one of Sheikh Subah Al Salim's slaves from what part of Africa his grandfather had come, and with studied superiority he replied, 'It isn't a question of my grandfather. My family have been slaves in His Highness's household for a great many generations.'

Occasionally a slave from beyond the borders of Kuwait, usually from Saudi Arabia, would abscond and fearing pursuit seek sanctuary in the Political Agency. Provided we were sure of his *bona fides* we would give him a manumission paper, a document in both English and Arabic declaring in the name of the British Government that the man or woman was a free person. At the head of this Certificate of Freedom was a coloured representation of crossed Union Jacks. But how deeply the slave's owner, had he recaptured his quarry, would have been impressed by this slender documentary relic of our imperial past is hard to say. I issued perhaps a dozen or so freedom papers during my time as Political Agent.

During this period I also married a dozen or so European couples, a duty that fell under the Foreign Marriages Act. By a clause of the Act the windows of my office in which the event took place had to be opened to ensure that the rites which we were exercising were in no way clandestine. There was little that could be considered sentimental or romantic about these occasions, for the greater part of the brief ceremony consisted of the recitation on my part of a solemn warning to the couple that any false statement would certainly land them in deep trouble with the law. Silvia and I did our best to compensate for these rather doleful formalities, which sometimes visibly upset the bride, by giving a small champagne party for the couple and their friends as soon as the legalisms were over.

Silvia and I seldom dined alone and if we had two free evenings a week and could get to bed before midnight we considered ourselves lucky. With all these social ties we needed some sort of physical recreation, and we found it in various ways. There was a small swimming pool and a cement tennis court in the Agency compound; we sailed once a week; there was a beach cottage where we went with parties of the Agency staff for picnics on our Friday holiday; and I rode whenever I could. And one evening a week we went Scottish dancing in the British Council. This organisation, under the able direction of John Muir, did an immense amount of valuable work.

The Agency possessed an ancient motor-launch, and this enabled me to visit the islands belonging to Kuwait and also the Neutral Zone, an area of desert and sea coast jointly owned by Kuwait and Saudi Arabia. Of the islands only Failaka was permanently inhabited; the rest — that is to say Bubiyan, Maskan, Auha, Arabi, Umm Al Maradim, Farsi, Kubr, Qaru and others — were only occupied from time to time by fishermen. But Qaru and Kubr and Farsi were occasionally visited by the Iranian Navy in support of Iran's claim to ownership; and Saudi Arabia also claimed Farsi. The Iranians would leave a plaque on the island as evidence of its belonging to them, which in due course would be removed by the Royal Navy. It seemed to me that as Political Agent, with a certain responsibility for the Ruler's foreign relations and overseas possession, I too ought to visit these islands from time to time, and whenever I did so I took with me a member of his entourage. None of the islands was of any size or rose more than a few feet above the sea; they were inhabited by thousands of sea birds and around their shores was a great abundance of fish. These short occasional expeditions of two or three days into the waters of the Gulf provided a welcome contrast to the routine of life in Kuwait.

Throughout 1955 and on into 1956 Egyptian influence was continuing to grow throughout the Arab world, and inevitably it manifested itself in Kuwait. Nasir's mission to unite the Arab world and restore Arab pride and achievement met with a wide and ready response. The West became, after Israel, the butt of the incessant outpouring of Egyptian propaganda, and the fact that Kuwait's traditional attachment to the British connection was under threat became increasingly clear. I had been in the habit of calling, generally in the cool of the evening, at the '*mejlis*' of merchant friends for half an hour's gossip. But as the flow of Egyptian propaganda mounted, I could see that my visits were causing my hosts increasing embarrassment. Not until the spring of 1957 was I able to renew these agreeable contacts. Meanwhile events were bearing us on towards the affair of Suez, than which none of the many problems that arose during our time in Kuwait posed greater difficulties. Not only did it cause us great anxiety at the time but its impact on the Arab world and its damaging effects on Anglo-Arab relations were to be felt long after. It will be as well therefore to recall the main events that led to the crisis.

In the early 1950s the Anglo-American position in the Middle East was still comparatively secure. The Russians had so far made little impact. Against the threat of worldwide Soviet expansion NATO covered Europe, and in 1954 SEATO held the Far East. Between the two lay a gap, the Middle East, which the West had hoped as early as 1950 to bridge by the establishment of a Middle East Defence Organisation. But Egypt, wary of what appeared to be an attempt to revive imperial ambitions, would have none of it. Within this perilous gap — the danger aggravated by deep divisions in the Arab world — there stood two rival states: Iraq, under the premiership of the friendly Nuri Es Said and in alliance with the Turks, and Egypt, under a potentially hostile Nasir. Britain opted for Nuri and in April 1955 joined, with Turkey and Iraq, what thereupon became known as the Baghdad Pact, shortly to be joined by Pakistan and Iran.

To the Soviets these alliances presented the threat of encirclement, and to Nasir and his ally Syria a clear manifestation of Britain's determination to split Arab unity. Events thereafter moved with alarming speed. Within less than a month of Britain's adherence to the Baghdad Pact Nasir, present at the first Afro-Asian Conference at Bandung, made the initial approaches which led before the end of September to Egypt's arms deal with Czechoslovakia. The deal radically transformed the situation in the Middle East. The Western arms monopoly was broken and the Arab world was no longer a Western preserve. Syria also put in a bid for Czech arms, and Jordan refused to join the Baghdad Pact. By the end of the year it was clear that not only had Nasir become the idol of the great mass of the Arab people, but that he was turning increasingly towards the Eastern bloc. The structure of Western defence policy in the Middle East had been undermined. 1955 was an unhappy year for Britain's prestige in the Arab World, our friends were perplexed and discomforted and our enemies looked to the future with satisfaction. The year 1956 was to prove even more disastrous.

On 1 March 1956 pressure from various directions, including perhaps Egypt, induced the young King Hussein to dismiss Glubb. Meanwhile Egypt, having pledged her cotton exports in payment for Czech arms, was in urgent need of finance to start work on the Aswan High Dam. The only easily available sources of aid of the magnitude required were the United States, Britain and the World Bank. Negotiations were opened but Nasir's increasing involvement with the Soviets during the first half of 1956 swung American opinion away from approval of the vast sum required, and in July the loan offer was suddenly withdrawn. Nasir forthwith nationalised the Suez Canal, and overnight the Egyptians successfully seized all the installations.

Britain and France, more than any other maritime nation, each had its own particular stake in the Canal. Britain was the principal user and had been the physical guardian of the Canal since the previous century. De Lesseps, a Frenchman, had engineered the creation of the Canal, and its management had always been under French control. For both Britain and France, therefore, historical pride as well as material interests were involved. For Egypt, for Nasir personally and to a less extent for the whole of the Arab world, the Canal was a symbol of out-of-date and declining imperial domination.

Egypt's seizure of the Canal met with warm Soviet approval. The Egyptians gambled, rightly as events proved, that Britain and France would take no immediate military action and that the longer they delayed the stronger the Egyptian case would become in the eyes of the world at large.

Throughout August and September we were alert to the possibility of military action being taken by Britain and France against Egypt, and in that event to the likely consequences for our relations with Kuwait. First there was Britain's call-up of reservists on 2 August, then the assembling of ships in the Mediterranean and finally the steady flow of warlike statements by British and French political leaders. The 'Voice of the Arabs' broadcasts from Cairo made full use of all this, linking our belligerent activities with Israeli influence. A plan for international control of the Canal, as agreed by the twenty-two-nation Conference in London in August, offered us hope of a peaceful settlement, but the subsequent rejection of the Menzies mission to Cairo brought the possibility of a conflict nearer. At a meeting I had with the Ruler on 22 September he spoke of his increasing anxiety, and he was much relieved when three days later I was able to tell him that a planned visit by the Duke of Edinburgh in the Royal Yacht had been cancelled. A few days later in a less pessimistic mood he went off to his Lebanese villa for a holiday, and the administration of the state was taken over by Sheikh Adbulla Al Mubarak, with whom I kept in close touch. He was no admirer of Nasir, whom he saw as a threat to the Subah regime and Kuwait's independence. I kept in constant contact too with the Oil Company, and during the early part of October we drew up plans for the protection of the American and European communities in Kuwait and Ahmadi.

The exact nature of what followed, against the background of the

October Hungarian uprising and its suppression by the Russians, may never come entirely to light. The agreements reached between the British Premier and Foreign Secretary and their French counterparts, and such collusion as there may have been with Israel, were, one may assume, arrived at without the participation of officials, so it is unlikely that written evidence on all that passed will ever emerge. It is difficult to be entirely convinced of the complete truth of Mr Selwyn Lloyd's statement to the House of Commons on 31 October 1956 that, with regard to Israel, 'there was no prior agreement between us'; or of Sir Anthony Eden's declaration to the House on 20 December that 'there was no foreknowledge that Israel would attack Egypt'. In all our anxieties and in all our calculations we never envisaged the participation of Israel in a combined Anglo-French operation, and never were we given the slightest hint from London that such a course was even remotely contemplated. Yet as early as August the French and the Israelis were contemplating a joint invasion, and on 14 October the plan for Israeli participation was being discussed at Chequers and subsequently in Paris. We were told nothing of this confused and ill-advised intrigue.

While open hostility to an Anglo-French invasion of Egypt was fully expected and as far as possible prepared for, it came as a surprise that the first manifestation of Kuwait's anti-Western resentment showed itself on 28 October in the form of a public protest against French action in Algeria. Government offices, schools and shops were closed for twenty-four hours. On 29 October Israel attacked Egypt, and the following day an Anglo-French twelve-hour ultimatum was issued to both sides ordering them to withdraw ten miles from the Canal. At dusk on the 31st Britain and France launched their air attack. To many it was a repetition of Pearl Harbour. Thereafter for five days, while an Anglo-French convoy steamed slowly across the Mediterranean, the RAF continued to bomb targets in Egypt. Not surprisingly every Arab believed that we had conspired with and now taken the side of Israel.

So much for the background. It remains to say something of the Ruler's attitude, of popular reaction in Kuwait, and how far this affected us in the Political Agency. On the afternoon of 29 October I went to the airport to welcome the Ruler back from Lebanon. I had no reason to believe that we were on the eve of a major crisis. Between nine and eleven-thirty the following evening a series of immediate cypher telegrams reached us reporting the Anglo-French ultimatum and instructing me to inform the Ruler. This was not the first intimation we had had. A BBC news broadcast had reached us half an hour earlier. It was an odd way of doing things. Alan Rothnie, Head of Chancery, and I worked on and discussed these signals with growing astonishment and disquiet until well after midnight. I then rang the Ruler's secretary Ashraf Lufti and arranged to see the Ruler at eight o'clock the following morning. When I called on him Sheikh Abdulla was cold, disturbed and glum. But he showed no sign of open unfriendliness. He assured me that although reaction in Kuwait would certainly be hostile, he would see to the maintenance of public order. During that afternoon of Wednesday, 31 October, I discussed the situation with the United States Consul Bill Brewer, with whom I was on close and friendly terms, and the same evening I called a meeting of our local Defence Committee. We had eight hundred British, other Europeans and Americans living in various localities in Kuwait and its suburbs, and nearly two thousand in Ahmadi. It might be necessary to concentrate and even to evacuate these people should public order break down.

At the time of our arrival in Kuwait we had instituted a weekly '*jour*' on Wednesdays which extended an open invitation to anyone who cared to call and have a drink between six and eight in the evening. It had proved a success in that it enabled us to meet and entertain in a modest way a great number of people of all nationalities whom we could not otherwise have invited to more formal occasions. As a rule at least thirty guests came. On this evening of Wednesday, 31 October, we were faced again with a number of long cypher telegrams and Alan Rothnie and I were unable to leave the office. Just before the '*jour*' was due to begin, Silvia met Alan outside his office. 'Is there anything you want me to do?' she asked. 'Yes', he said, 'the Political Agent and I will be busy till late, so you will have to look after the "*jour*". You will need to reassure people. Wear your most attractive dress and put on your most confident smile.' She did so. I slipped upstairs from my office to a very full drawing room for a few minutes during the evening. Silvia's calm relaxed appearance was spreading confidence to more than forty anxious people. Already Kuwait was full of rumours, and anti-British banners and pamphlets were appearing in the streets. Early next morning I saw the Ruler again. 'Listen,' he said, 'this is a very worrying situation. In the coming week I may be under pressure to do what I wish to avoid. I am therefore taking my launch and going to Failaka. No one will be able to contact me. Sheikh Abdulla Al Mubarak and his Security Forces will see to it that there is no disorder. Keep in touch with him but otherwise do whatever work you need to do in your office and avoid anything that could provoke further trouble. Warn the Europeans and the Americans to do likewise.' It was excellent advice in circumstances in which no one knew what was happening or likely to happen.

I went to see Sheikh Abdulla Al Mubarak that evening. He was in battledress, wearing yellow elastic sided boots and black and white striped socks. 'I cannot understand', he growled, 'what has come over the British Government, but don't worry. My father was a friend of the British and so am I. I will see that none of your people is molested but they must be careful and discreet. I have forbidden', he added, 'all demonstrations as well as a meeting designed to plan a general strike.' I told him that I had already warned all Europeans and Americans to avoid being seen in the town, and that we had divided Kuwait into five areas and appointed a warden from among the residents in each area to take charge and to review the situation with me in the Agency twice a day. He agreed with this plan and arranged to strengthen the Agency guard. 'If you are obliged to drive about the town you must not use your official car,' he said, 'I will lend you a car and a driver.' He was full of robust reassurance and I left him more confident than I had felt earlier in the day.

During the next week a number of anti-British demonstrations were broken up by the Security Forces, but gangs roamed the streets chanting anti-British slogans. The shops refused to serve European customers or sell British goods. Throughout the town and across the main roads leading to the Agency great banners were strung identifying Britain with Israel and calling for revenge and the death of all traitors. A demonstration which gathered outside the walls surrounding the Agency was dispersed under the leadership of one of the younger Sheikhs. With the help of the General Manager of the Kuwait Oil Company, Leland Jordan, with whom I was in constant touch, a wireless set was established in a house in each of our five areas of the town and linked with a set in the Agency. Each warden came on the air to us just after dawn and at sunset. I held a security meeting every morning with Senior members of the Agency staff. We drew up an evacuation plan involving several embarkation points from which barges would remove Europeans and Americans in the event of a severe breakdown of law and order. A Royal Navy cruiser remained hull down below the horizon. Her presence was reported by fishermen and the fact that she was there but invisible had a stabilising influence. Bill Brewer and I met daily. Despite the dismay with which we learnt in the Agency of United States naval activities prior to our troop landings and the pronouncements of the Secretary of State, John Foster Dulles, Bill Brewer came to our daily security meetings at my invitation, and our relations were never anything but close and harmonious.

On 5 November information came to me shortly before midnight that explosives were on their way to Kuwait destined for the sabotage of the oil installations. I went off and gave the news to Sheikh Abdulla Mubarak. Once again he was in his colourful uniform, virile and ebullient, and surrounded by a group of officers and friends. Heavily armed they gave the impression of a set of Bashibazooks. The following morning Sheikh Subah al Salim came to tell me that large numbers of his senior police officers and NCOs had resigned in protest againt Britain's action against Egypt. Some of my own senior staff spoke of resignation, a course I begged them to put out of their minds. So long as anything could be saved from the wreck brought about by our own Government we would need everyone's help, and nothing would be gained from resignation however high-minded our motives and however consuming our indignation.

Meanwhile British and French parachute forces had landed at Port Said at dawn on 5 November, and after a Naval bombardment, seaborne forces landed on the sixth and in the course of the day made their way southwards down the Canal, now blocked with sunken ships. The operation ended, much to our relief, at midnight on the 6/7th.

At my daily meetings with Sheikh Abdulla Al Mubarak he remained friendly and confident but he did not conceal the loss of prestige Britain had suffered. I kept in close contact too with Sheikh Jabir Al Ahmed, Governor of Ahmadi, but here my reception was much less warm. With the arrival of a United Nations contingent in the Canal Zone on the 21st, the immediate tension began to ease but the atmosphere remained cold and suspicious. I felt that nearly everything that my predecessors had achieved over the past fifty years in a place which had so long been traditionally pro-British, and the little that I had done in the past fifteen months by way of maintaining and fostering confidence and friendship, had all evaporated.

By the end of November the situation had begun to improve. The Ruler was back from Failaka and it was typical of his generous nature and, I like to think, an indication of personal regard that on his return, despite everything that had happened, he sent me two boxes of dates. It was now possible to move about the town freely and to use my own car again, but everywhere I found an atmosphere such as had never existed before. Bernard Burrows had planned to come to Kuwait to assess the situation with the Ruler and me, but Sheikh Abdulla advised us against it. I therefore flew to Bahrain and spent two days there discussing with the Political Resident, the Admiral East India Station and the RAF Commander-in-Chief British Forces Arabian Peninsula how far, if things again deteriorated, the security of the oilfields could be ensured. As I saw it, this could only be through co-operation with the Kuwait Government. Any attempt to seize the oilfields, as some were in favour of doing, would defeat its own object. But as an emergency measure we arranged that the Oil Company would lay out an airstrip south of Ahmadi which it was hoped would not come to the notice of the Kuwait authorities. They were aware of its existence within forty-eight hours.

At no time during these unhappy weeks was I ever molested or even threatened, but one Sunday afternoon I was warned, as Silvia and I left the Agency for evensong at the American Mission church, that two young men had been enquiring where I usually sat during the Service. On hot evenings the church windows were kept open. I did not take the warning very seriously but from time to time I could not help keeping an eye on the Mission compound and the wall beyond.

I had warned both Sheikh Abdulla Al Mubarak and Sheikh Jabir Al Ahmed several times that I believed that an attempt would be made to sabotage the oilfields. On the night of 11 December I was woken by my bedroom phone at three-thirty. It was Leland Jordan speaking from Ahmadi. He told me that explosives had been placed and fired over eight wellheads. Five had gone off without any harm being done, but three wells had been damaged with a loss of three thousand barrels of oil a day and one was on fire. There had also been some damage to a submarine cable and a gas pipeline. The well burnt for several days and the Kuwait Oil Company's effort to extinguish it failed. They therefore called in that celebrated world expert in putting out oil fires, 'Red' Adair. He flew in from the United States with his team of experts, set up his equipment and got to work. Within a few hours the fire was out. In the days following I had several discussions with both the Ruler and Sheikh Jabir Al Ahmed on who had been responsible for the sabotage and on the progress of police inquiries. Nothing emerged, and I came increasingly to believe that the Ruler and his advisers had connived at what had been done if indeed they did not themselves engineer it. Throughout the crisis Kuwait had remained steady — too steady for those who saw in the Suez affair an opportunity to cause the maximum harm to British interests — and had therefore felt it necessary to show the rest of the Arab world that it did not lag behind others in actively indicating loyalty to the cause of Arab unity. It was not difficult to sympathise, and I could only admire the traditional skill with which the Ruler's family had handled the situation.

The fire at Ahmadi was not the only manifestation of pyrotechnics that winter. On the morning of 30 December Ghulam Reza, our Iranian major-domo, woke me earlier than usual in a state of great agitation. In opening up the drawing room soon after dawn he had been horrified to find that an attempt had been made to set the place on fire. It was easy enough to conclude what had happened and what had been intended. Someone had entered our residence, which comprised the whole first floor of the Agency, thrown paraffin over the Christmas tree, the curtains, the sofa and the easy chairs, put a match to the tree and presumably withdrawn before making sure that the room was properly alight. The tree had burnt itself out, scorching the wall and the nearby curtains. By what seemed like a miracle the fire had failed to spread to the furniture. Most of the residence was built of wood. A single wooden staircase leading up the centre of the building from the ground floor stood between our sleeping quarters and the two rooms occupied by the three children and their Nanny. Had the fire taken a hold, not only would Silvia and I have been unable to reach the children, but there would have been no means of getting out of the building except through the upper windows. There was no fire-escape. It was an unpleasant thought. How had the intruder got in and who was he? It was not, it seemed, a very determined or professional effort. The Ruling family expressed horror and the police arrested our kitchen boy, an Iranian. But their enquiries led nowhere. Was it perhaps more of a gesture, done possibly with the connivance of someone in authority and deliberately bungled like the half-hearted sabotage of the oilwells a fortnight or so earlier? I am more than inclined to think that this was what happened, rather than a serious attempt to cremate us all.

The end of 1956 was sombre and depressing, but the oil still flowed, no member of the foreign community in Kuwait had been seriously harried or molested, and my own relations with the Ruler and his family had remained harmonious though at times somewhat frigid. I have no doubt that it had been the policy of the Ruler and the older and more conservative members of his family to avoid serious incidents however incomprehensible our Suez escapade appeared to be. With his characteristic shrewdness, he operated from behind the façade of Sheikh Abdulla Al Mubarak and the Army. Sheikh Abdulla Al Mubarak proved a staunch friend and without his support and that of his Bedouin Security Forces in keeping Kuwait steady, our position could well have become impossible. But his unpredictable and volatile nature and the current of violence in his character made him an uncomfortable friend. In relying on him, as in the crisis we were bound to do, we became firmly identified with the least popular member of the Ruling family. The embers of our imperial past were becoming cold. We had drawn heavily on the capital of goodwill accumulated in the past.

The Suez affair was more a symptom than a cause of Britain's declining influence in the world and in the Arab world in particular. The conception that Nasir and all that he represented could be toppled by military action and that thereafter all would be well was a dismal misjudgement. In the short term the effects on Britain's standing were not far short of disastrous. But looked at in a longer perspective 'Suez' only speeded up a phase in the progress of Arab nationalism and its relations with the West that would have happened in any event. It was the way that events had been allowed to shape themselves that was so damaging. Our prestige and credibility were never to be the same again. And yet no other power and no other influence fully inherited the position Britain had formerly held; neither Nasir himself, nor the United States nor the Soviets became the sole beneficiary of our discomfiture.

Whereas in the early summer of 1955, when I first arrived in Kuwait, it had seemed to me evident that we would very soon have to divest ourselves of many of the responsibilities and privileges bequeathed to us by our early association with the State, and indeed we had already begun to do so, the events of 1956 so eroded our relationship as to make all this a matter of urgency. The next year, 1957, saw an agreed surrender of several of our positions. The first concerned the exercise of criminal and civil justice. The courts in which justice was administered in Kuwait operated under two separate systems. There were the Ruler's courts and the court of the Political Agent. Broadly, the Ruler's courts dealt with Muslim Arabs, Kuwaiti or otherwise, and exercised the *Sharia*. Criminal cases occurring in Kuwait town were dealt with by Sheikh Subah As Salim and those occurring outside the town by Sheikh Abdulla Al Mubarak. An Egyptian *Qadi* presided over the religious courts responsible for cases concerning personal law: inheritance, marriage, divorce and the like. Commercial cases were generally dealt with by a panel of merchants but if the problem was particularly complicated an *ad hoc* court would be convened. The Political Agent's court, established under an Order-in-Council and administering justice under laws made under Orders-in-Council, held jurisdiction over all Europeans, Americans, Christians and certain other non-Arabs. By the early 1950s the British Government's view was that there should be only one set of courts, namely those of the Ruler exercising justice under written codes. This was regarded as a long-term policy, but policies of this sort usually come to reality much faster than anticipated.

We were fortunate in having as Registrar of our court Ahmed Hijazi, a young Palestinian who was a member of the English Bar and a man of singular ability. In his absence cases were taken by the Political Agent, and many years' experience as a magistrate in the Sudan made this a familiar and not unwelcome task for me. For regular members of the Diplomatic Service untrained in this field, the trial of a case in the rare event of both Ahmed and myself being absent could be a puzzling exercise. Not surprisingly it was the Ruler's firm wish to extend his jurisdiction by steadily widening the categories of person subject to his courts. It was our aim to persuade him, as a prior condition, to introduce modern Codes of law and procedure and to reserve the use of the *Sharia* to cases involving personal law. Although this was a step that the Ruler hesitated to undertake, we were able before I left Kuwait to make some concession towards widening his jurisdiction and to enlist support among some members of the Ruling family in favour of introducing a Penal Code and Code of Criminal Procedure. Two years after I left Kuwait the *Sharia* was augmented by a law that established courts, regulated the judicial system and adopted legal codes. Within a short time thereafter all judicial authority over foreigners was surrendered, and the Political Agent's court had ceased to exist.

From time to time I was instructed by the Foreign Office to raise with the Ruler the question of a Constitution. It was rightly believed that in the circumstances of the time the regime could not long expect to resist the setting up of some form of representative body. I discussed the idea with the Ruler a number of times, but although he doubtless saw that a development of this sort was bound to come, his own nature was such that he had little inclination to set in motion a fundamental change that he saw as being certain to challenge the position of the Ruling family. In consequence he resisted all the arguments I was able to muster by declaring that at a suitable time he would consider the whole problem with the nine members of his family who formed Kuwait's 'Superior Council'. Inevitably pressure in Kuwait mounted, and four years after I left a Constituent Assembly was elected, and two years later Kuwait had an elected fifty-member National Assembly.

Over passports and visas too our jurisdiction embraced areas where the Kuwait Government would sooner or later have to take charge. Our Consular office in the Agency issued six thousand visas a year on behalf of the Ruler to Kuwaitis wishing to travel outside the Arab world, and a Kuwaiti, although entitled to hold a Kuwait passport, could also if he preferred claim a British passport as a British-protected person. Much of this was rapidly becoming anomalous in view of Kuwait's material and social progress. Then there were the postal, telecommunication and telephone systems. The British GPO managed the Kuwait postal services and as late as 1952 it had been surprisingly suggested that the Ruler would be unlikely to want his own stamps or postal services. Five years later he wanted both very much, and during 1956/7 the Agency was involved in securing an agreement between the GPO — not without some resistance on their part — and the Kuwait Government whereby the latter secured control of its stamp and postal services. The first Kuwait stamps, bearing Sheikh Abdulla's portrait, were issued early in 1958.* Likewise telephone and telecommunications, hitherto operated by Cable and Wireless, were soon to become the Kuwait Government's responsibility.

A Civil Air Agreement, signed in 1950, had given Britain exclusive rights for ten years to operate airfields and facilities, and to grant on the Ruler's behalf privileges to aircraft of other nationalities. Here was another source of some irritation, and throughout 1956 and 1957 we were involved in a complete revision of the Agreement. These and comparable activities occupied much of my time in the latter part of 1956 and the first half of 1957. Gradually and by agreement we were divesting ourselves of services and monopolies which Kuwait wanted and which were of little importance to the British Government. The surrender of rights, responsibilities and privileges which caused growing irritation at a time when Kuwait was rapidly taking her proper place in the world had not come too soon. But our basic agreement with Kuwait was to continue until 1961 when it was formally abrogated by a friendly exchange of letters.

Despite all that had happened we held our traditional New Year reception on the first of January 1957. It came as a heartening surprise that over two hundred Kuwaitis, led by the Ruler and others of his family, attended during the course of the morning.

In May 1957 our staunch but at times embarrassing friend Sheikh Abdulla Al Mubarak brought Kuwait momentarily into the world news with a typical example of the ruthless side of his character. The Al Malika were a well-known family of Saudi origin who had moved into and occupied several buildings in the suburbs of Kuwait to which it appeared they had no legal right. The matter went to court, the case went against them and they were ordered not only to vacate the premises but to leave the country. They refused, barricaded and armed themselves — not far short of a hundred men, women and children — in the largest of the buildings, and prepared for a siege. As Commander of the Security Forces, Sheikh Abdullah Al Mubarak was called on to remove the Al Malika, and he did so with typical vigour. He sealed off the area in which the disputed property lay with troops and delivered an ultimatum, which the Al Malika rejected. Armoured cars, 25-pounders, mortars and automatic weapons were thereupon brought to bear on the rebels. Silvia and a number of our friends happened to be sailing that afternoon in

* A detailed history of the postal service in Kuwait from 1775 to 1959 by Mr Neil Donaldson appeared in *Gibbons Stamp Monthly* for January, March, April and May 1968.

the Bay of Kuwait, and were alarmed when a number of two-pounder shells fired from the armoured cars began falling into the sea around them. Prudently they put their boats about and made for the shore. I was in my office and was equally surprised at suddenly hearing the sound of heavy firing. The battle was short but it left a dozen of the Al Malika dead and over thirty wounded. The rest were captured. Much of the surrounding property was damaged. For twenty-four hours the airport was closed and business in Kuwait came to a standstill. The fate of the surviving Al Malika was for a while unenviable. Sheikh Abdulla Al Mubarak was never a man to be trifled with.

It was little more than a month after this event that a confidential cypher telegram arrived from the Foreign Office, which began: 'Following strictly private and personal for Bell'. The cypher staff had therefore stopped decyphering and the telegram was brought to me to work on. I had never had a signal like this and I set myself to unravel it with some apprehension. The further I proceeded the more incredulous I became. The telegram enquired whether I wished to be considered among others for appointment as Governor of Northern Nigeria and, if I were interested, invited me to fly to London as soon as possible. I had no hesitation in accepting this utterly unforeseen offer. Silvia was in Switzerland with the children, and I had no means of telling her of what seemed, if all went well, to be a remarkable development in our lives. But I had little doubt that she would be pleased. She had never been greatly enamoured of Kuwait and had said that the only time she really enjoyed being there was the period of the Suez crisis, when she felt that her presence was perhaps of some value. It was, and not only to me.

So I flew to London. At the Colonial Office I met for the first time the Secretary of State, Alan Lennox-Boyd,* and he asked me whether the idea of Northern Nigeria interested me. I said it did. A Nigerian Constitutional Conference was in session at Lancaster House. Self-Government for the three Regions and eventual independence were under discussion. He asked me about Kuwait and Silvia and the family. He then offered me a large brandy, had one himself and the interview came to an end. Did this mean I was to be offered the appointment? In some perplexity I went off and called on Jock Macpherson, the Permanent Under Secretary, whom I had last seen as Chief Secretary in Jerusalem during the war. He said that the Colonial Office had already tried to get hold of me for Aden, but Selwyn Lloyd had refused to release me. He said nothing positive about Northern Nigeria but he asked me to remain in the Colonial

* 1st Viscount Boyd of Merton, CH, *b.* 1904, *d.* 1983.

Office for the rest of the afternoon as he thought the Secretary of State might like to see me again. When eventually I called on Alan Lennox-Boyd a second time he made the offer positive, subject only to the Queen's consent. I would need to be in Nigeria in October, and the appointment was to be for five years. The Constitutional Conference had brought to London James Robertson, now Governor-General, and the retiring Governor of Northern Nigeria Sir Brian Sharwood-Smith, both of whom I met that evening. I rejoiced in the prospect of working with 'John Willie' again.

There followed a day of further meetings in London. I phoned Silvia in Switzerland and told my mother. It was perfect June weather. The parks were full of people sitting in the sun. On my flight back to Kuwait, which I now planned to leave in August, I spent a day with Silvia at Rossinière near Château d'Oex. I went on and spent a day in Baghdad. Sir Michael Wright, our Ambassador, had invited Ali Mumtaz, Minister of Foreign Affairs, General Sami Fattah, Minister of the Interior, and Abdel Hamid Khadim, Minister of Education, to talk once again about Iraq-Kuwait relations, the Shatt Al Arab scheme and frontier demarcation. It was agreed that the Minister of Foreign Affairs would meet the Ruler. This was a notable advance in recognising that in some areas at least Kuwait had now reached a point in which direct discussion with another government was to be encouraged. A year earlier the official view had been far less flexible. The idea of such a meeting had in fact been firmly over-ruled when I suggested it.

When some weeks later I told the Ruler that I would shortly be leaving Kuwait he characteristically gave no indication of his feelings. But whatever he may have thought about me personally — and I believe he liked me well enough — he must have been vexed that my term of service was being cut short at a time when I was just beginning, after a little more than two years, to understand something of Kuwait and its problems. By mid-August I was back in England with the prospect of two months or more before being required to take up my new appointment.

During the five years of my Governorship of Northern Nigeria I saw the introduction of Self-Government in 1959 and the achievement of Independence for the Federation of Nigeria a year later. These constitutional developments left me, for the last two years of my service, without power but with perhaps a small measure of influence. I was in an unusual position: a British Governor serving as such in an independent ex-colonial territory. Of the events that led to this unusual assignment I hope to write in due course.

Thereafter fortune gave me a number of temporary appointments: in the Arabian Gulf, in the Federation of South Arabia, in Oman and in the Gilbert and Ellice Islands. The last of these was followed by the offer of the post of Secretary-General of the South Pacific Commission. I accepted it and spent the years 1966–9 in the French island of New Caledonia. Other short-term appointments came thereafter which brought me back to the Arab world. They took me to the last remote corners of the Arabian Peninsula and for the last time into the company of tribesmen whose view of life was still largely untouched by the influences of the West. Here the last rays of the twilight of empire still lingered faintly. The good fortune which had always accompanied me continued to do so.

INDEX